The Great Mental Models:
Economics and Art

The Great Mental Models

Economics and Art

SHANE PARRISH
and Rhiannon Beaubien

Cornerstone Press

5 7 9 10 8 6 4

Cornerstone Press
One Embassy Gardens
8 Viaduct Gardens
London SW11 7BW

Cornerstone Press is part of the Penguin Random House group of companies
whose addresses can be found at global.penguinrandomhouse.com.

First published in the US by Portfolio, an imprint of
Penguin Random House LLC, New York, in 2024
First published in the UK by Cornerstone Press in 2024

www.penguin.co.uk

A CIP catalogue record for this book is available from the British Library.

ISBN 9781529945720

Book design by Daniel Lagin

Printed and bound in Great Britain by Clays Ltd, Elcograf S.p.A.

The authorised representative in the EEA is Penguin Random House Ireland,
Morrison Chambers, 32 Nassau Street, Dublin D02 YH68

www.greenpenguin.co.uk

Penguin Random House is committed to a
sustainable future for our business, our readers
and our planet. This book is made from Forest
Stewardship Council® certified paper.

Contents

ART

Introduction

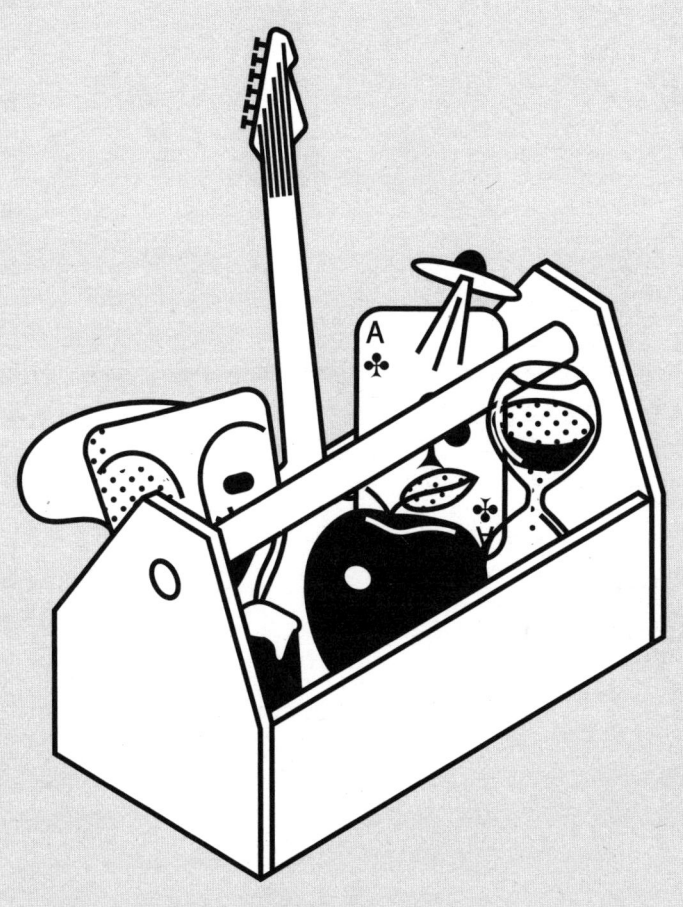

W e learn so much from the world if we are willing to take the time to let it teach us. Each discipline we study contains fundamentals that provide insight into many of the common challenges we face. These fundamentals make up *Farnam Street*'s latticework of mental models, a way of approaching new ideas, situations, problems, and challenges with a toolkit of valuable knowledge.

Volume 1 of *The Great Mental Models* introduced nine general thinking concepts to start building a framework of timeless knowledge. Time and again, those models have proven indispensable in both solving problems and preventing them in the first place.

Volume 2 continued the journey, exploring fundamental ideas from physics, chemistry, and biology. Truths about the physical world, from the forces that allow us to manipulate energy to the behaviors that drive the actions of all organisms, are constants that can guide our decisions so that our actions are aligned with how the world works.

Volume 3 considered the core ideas of systems thinking and mathematics. Although these subjects can appear impermeable, as soon as we start taking them apart, we quickly see that they are easily accessible. Not only that, they describe many of the behaviors and interactions that govern our lives.

Volume 4 covers economics and art, exploring the relationship between two disciplines often hidden in plain sight, influencing all our behavior, the world we live in, and the meaning we find.

About This Volume

This volume explores some of the core mental models from economics and art—a fitting pair.

Economics is as much art as it is science. While the core models we have selected from this discipline remain timeless principles, they are not unchanging laws of nature. Much of our individual economic behavior is based on the stories we tell ourselves and the ones culture tells us.

> Price is what you pay; value is what you get.
>
> —BEN GRAHAM[1]

It seems obvious to study economic models when tackling life's challenges, especially when it comes to our work and business lives. So much of the modern world hangs in the economic balance, affecting job mobility, wages, social safety nets, and entrepreneurial success. And that's not even considering the massive economic wheels of governments at all levels, from local to national, which also affect our lives over the short and long term.

Art offers something more elusive—meaning. What is life other than a story, with plot and characters? There is a reason the language we use with ourselves, after something happens, is that we are "turning the page" or "starting a new chapter."

However, we're not here to educate you with ten hot tips for negotiating a raise or six ways to write a good plot. Instead, we're going to cover foundational models. We'll show you how they apply in their core discipline and how you can use them to better understand the world we live in.

> Once you know the key principles and basic facts [about economics], you can make some robust judgments without knowing the technical details.
>
> —HA-JOON CHANG[2]

Take something as fundamental as supply and demand, something many of us have heard about for most of our lives. High supply of and low demand for an item means prices are likely to become or remain low; the reverse is true for high demand, low supply— prices for that item are likely to skyrocket. In this volume, we look at examples, including sex work and car sales, to show how these economic concepts shape behavior.

In the economics section, we'll cover such bedrock ideas as debt, monopolies, and trade-offs as mental models for confronting everyday issues in our lives. Each chapter discusses the concept at hand, then offers a case study or two illustrating how the concept has played out in history. These economic models can spark creative solutions to common problems, giving you the advantage even in situations where not one cent is in play.

> The purpose of art is washing the dust of our daily life off our souls.
>
> —PABLO PICASSO[3]

As with previous volumes in this series, each chapter in this book explores an idea—say, the concept in its original discipline. Then, we'll show you how it can apply in other ways. Some of the models are metaphors, others have a more literal application.

When looking at historical examples through the lens of a model, it's important to remember we are not attempting to demonstrate causation. We are telling a story to illustrate a point. We are not saying, for example, that what happened in a particular moment in history happened because a particular historical figure used the described model to guide their decisions. Instead, we are showing how you might understand that bit of history differently when you use a particular model as a lens, or giving you a different perspective on why a particular person's decisions led to the outcomes they did. In so doing, we hope you will gain inspiration for applying the same model to nonintuitive situations in your own life.

Finally, note that all these models, as with those covered in the previous books, are value neutral. They can be used for good or evil, as defined in whatever era you are in. They might work well in one situation but not in another. We try to balance use of the models with noting some of their limitations, so that you have ideas about when you might want to take an alternate approach.

Together, we will learn the differences in how to apply each model through the stories we have chosen to explain them. Each example is crafted to give you insight into where the model can apply. You can take the elements of each story as a signpost directing you to find similar situations in your life where the lens of a particular model will be most useful.

> What is art? I feel that if we see art as something isolated, something holy and separate from everything, that means it's not life. Art must be a part of life. Art has to belong to everybody.
>
> —MARINA ABRAMOVIĆ[4]

All models are wrong, but some are useful. The ones in this book aren't perfect, but they can be useful. Think of them as a mental toolbox: you won't use every tool for every job, but with practice, you'll learn which one works best in each situation. Just like a hammer is for nails and a wrench is for bolts, different mental models solve different problems. Collect them, experiment with them, and figure out what each one is good for.

About the Series

For those new to the series, *The Great Mental Models* is designed to give you the education you were never taught in school. We want to give you both knowledge from the core disciplines and a framework for using it in everyday life.

One of our goals for the series is to provide you with a set of tools built on timeless knowledge that you can use, again and again, to spot opportunities others miss, avoid problems before they happen, and live a better life.

The Great Mental Models is a guide to dozens of mental models, spread across four volumes, that define and explore the foundational concepts from a variety of disciplines. We then take each concept out of its original discipline and show how you can apply it in less obvious situations. We encourage you to dive into new ideas to augment your knowledge toolbox and also to leverage what you already know by applying it in new ways to gain a different perspective on the challenges you face.

A mental model is simply a representation of how something works. We use models to retain knowledge and simplify how we understand the world. We can't relearn everything every day, so we construct models to help us chunk patterns and navigate our world more efficiently.

Farnam Street's mental models are reliable principles that you can see at work in the world time and again. Using them means synthesizing across disciplines and not being afraid to apply knowledge from different areas far outside the domain they usually cover.

Not every model applies to all situations. Part of building a latticework of mental models is educating yourself regarding which situations are best addressed by which models. This takes some work, and you're likely to make some mistakes. It's important to constantly reflect on your use of models. If something didn't work, you need to try to discover why. Over time, by reflecting on your use of individual models, you will learn which models will best help you tackle which situations. Knowing why a model works will help you know when to use it again.

Let's dive in.

ECONOMICS

The first rule of compounding:
Never interrupt it unnecessarily.

–CHARLIE MUNGER[1]

Scarcity

When resources are finite.

It sometimes feels as if we have temporarily solved the problem of scarcity and replaced it with the problem of excess.

—MATT HAIG[1]

conomics, as a field, exists because of a fundamental problem we face as individuals, groups, and a species: how to allocate scarce resources to meet limitless needs. All resources are scarce, meaning there is a finite amount available.

Scarcity is like having one pizza for a hundred people at a party. You don't have enough for everyone who wants it. In economics, scarcity means a limited supply of things people want or need, such as money, time, or raw materials. One way to look at the development of human societies over time is as a process of overcoming different kinds of scarcity. Technology enables us to increase our access to scarce resources or to decrease our requirements for them.

Scarcity forces creativity and invention. When we run up against limits, we find ways to increase supply of or reduce demand for resources. While eliminating scarcity is unlikely, technology helps us make resources go further.

Where there is scarcity of something, its price goes up. For a resource to have economic value, it must be both scarce and desirable. If something is scarce, but no one wants or needs it, then it has no or low value. If something is desirable but not scarce, its value is also low or nonexistent. A resource can be valuable purely by dint of being scarce—for example, if owning it serves as a signal of wealth.

Perceptions of scarcity impact our ability to make decisions. Not only does scarcity trigger our biological instinct for self-preservation, it often results in making trade-offs. We become fenced in by perceived limits, whether they reflect actual limits or not.

Experiencing temporary scarcity of something essential can impact our actions for a long time after. For example, someone who grows up in poverty and then, later in life, makes a lot of money may continue to fear running out of money or may retain frugal habits that are no longer needed. The Great Depression is an example of this; many people who grew up during the Depression maintained the same resource-preserving behaviors well after it ended.

> Looking back at how our time or money was spent during moments of scarcity, we are bound to be disappointed. Immediate scarcity looms large, and important things unrelated to it will be neglected. When we experience scarcity again and again, these omissions can add up.
>
> —SENDHIL MULLAINATHAN AND ELDAR SHAFIR[2]

When we lack what we need, we are often forced to make complex, even constant, calculations, which is mentally taxing and leaves less attention for other things.[3]

Scarcity may be harmful to us when it comes to the requirements of living, like food, but that doesn't mean abundance is always good news for our thinking. The kind of abundance many people in wealthy countries experience is something altogether new in human history. Food, for example, has never been more abundant in wealthy countries. Yes, we need to eat, but we don't need to eat a lot of refined sugar. When a resource that has been scarce for much of human history becomes abundant to the point where we can access more than we need or have the capacity to use, we may struggle to stop consuming it.

When one resource becomes more abundant, something else tends to become the bottleneck restricting how much we can consume. Making a lot of money, say, can come at the expense of not having enough time to spend it. We may need to moderate our use of one resource to allow us to realize the benefit of another.

Sometimes, making something more abundant (whether in reality or perception) can go both ways in terms of affecting how much of it people consume. Usually, the more abundant something desirable is, the more of it we consume. Think rice in Asia, bread in Italy, coconuts in Costa Rica—the abundance of something brings its price down. However, if we expect something desirable to be in short supply, we may behave in detrimental ways. The possibility of a short supply of a resource can trigger the urge to hoard as much of it as possible for ourselves, as we saw with the hoarding of basics like toilet paper during the early days of the COVID pandemic.

Scarcity can also perpetuate itself. When access to a resource has previously been severely limited, leading to high economic value, it creates strong incentives to maintain its scarcity, even if the resource actually becomes abundant. Take diamonds: for centuries, their supply was tightly controlled, making them expensive. Now we can grow flawless diamonds in labs, but the industry still works hard to preserve the perception of scarcity. They're not selling diamonds; they're selling the story.

Scarcity is the business model of the luxury sector. Luxury brands take advantage of one particular aspect of psychology: the fact that the more scarce something is, the more we want it. Hermès can make more Birkin bags but chooses not to. Fewer than 100,000 Birkins are made every year, and the process of buying one is famously difficult—it involves either waiting for months or having a purchase history with Hermès. This controlled scarcity is key to the high prices of the luxury sector.

Scarcity as a model is very useful as a tool for second-order thinking. If I get more or less of something, what is the result? More money? Great! What will I spend it on? How will my life be different when I've made those choices? For example, money seems to be the most sought-after resource, since it's key to obtaining many others. Yet lottery winners often end up richer (at least temporarily) but not much happier, having walked into new problems: loss of privacy, risk of exploitation, being valued for your money and not your character, and struggling to balance a huge new responsibility in a way your family and friends see as fair.

In our personal lives, scarcity can be a great motivator. When we think about reducing scarcity, maybe we think about learning new skills to increase our income. Maybe we think about changing jobs to earn a higher salary or decrease our commute. In both cases, we are aiming to give ourselves more of a resource, either money or time, and therefore to reduce the scarcity of those elements in our lives.

When considering how to reduce scarcity, it's equally important to consider what effects that reduction in scarcity might have. As in the example of lottery winners, we need to do a little second-order thinking and say, "Now that I have more money or time, what am I going to do with it?" It's just as important to think, "If I do those things, then how does my life change?"

Many seem to think that having a three-million-dollar net worth or a salary of five hundred thousand dollars would solve most of their problems. They are often surprised to find out that due to lifestyle creep (increasing your living standard to match a higher salary), many people with high salaries spend most of what they make and feel the same financial pressures as the rest of us. Whatever economic rung of the ladder you're on, that cohort has its own financial cues, expectations, and mores. It's about acknowledging that changes in one part of a system will often generate changes in another part.

Reducing the Scarcity of Information

To help us understand just how far-reaching the consequences of reducing scarcity can be, let's look at the abundance of information created by the printing press. Exploring moments in history like this is not the same as evaluating the control we have over our individual choices, and the changes wrought by the printing press were almost entirely out of the realm of being predictable by its inventor. But the printing press is an excellent example of how changing scarcity can have rippling consequences in areas you might not initially consider.

Before it, manuscripts were hand copied by scribes. Manuscripts were also often written on parchment, and these two factors go a long way toward explaining why there was comparatively little written material around. Parchment, made from animal skins, takes longer to produce than paper, and hand copying is time-consuming. Even if sufficient scribes could be hired to produce a manuscript in a few days, we can easily imagine how many copies a printing press could produce in the same amount of time.

Information, before the printing press, was scarce. This scarcity meant that it required work for scribes to find manuscripts to copy. Christopher de Hamel explains that "the keeping, borrowing, begging, or hiring of exemplars [books to copy] was an important preliminary to the business of writing a medieval book."[4]

Further, hand copying inevitably introduced errors. Although many manuscripts display evidence of review, in that they contain corrections, it is a certainty that not all errors were caught. A scribe was lucky to have one text to copy; having two of the same, for comparison, would have been an inconceivable luxury. Because of the reality that hand copying risked perpetuating earlier errors while also introducing new errors, older texts often were more accurate. The scarcity of manuscripts also meant there was no way of knowing if more, better, or more useful information was out there. There was no index of all known works, no compendium of knowledge.

People did not learn from manuscripts in the way we learn from books today. Manuscripts were not shared widely and thus were not considered a learning tool for the average person. Knowledge was shared verbally and directly. To learn how to do something, you had to be taught by someone who already knew. Most information was passed along orally, and on a need-to-know basis.

The printing press caused a radical change in the availability of written information and its preservation and future utility. "After the advent of printing," Elizabeth Eisenstein explains in her seminal work on the subject, "the transmission of written information became more efficient."[5] Scribes no longer had to wander in search of texts; copies of manuscripts were widely available. People no longer had to learn solely by being taught in person.

These initial changes caused widespread ripples of change throughout Western European society. It's impossible to cover all of them here, but let's look at a few.

First, different theories and ideas could be compared and considered together for the first time. "Different texts," Eisenstein explains, "which had been previously dispersed and scattered were also being brought closer together for individual readers."[6] Can you imagine the power of having so many ideas in one's library? In scribal culture, you would have been lucky to have one book on mathematics. After the printing press, you could have multiple texts on a single subject, allowing for a more complete picture of the state of knowledge in a subject.

The reduction in scarcity of information quickened the pace of developing new information. Putting different texts together highlighted inconsistencies and contradictions and inspired investigation and resolution. "An enriched reading matter also encouraged the development of new intellectual combinations and permutations.... And then, later on, the creation of entirely new systems of thought"[7] were added to the pool of available information, Eisenstein notes.

Second, new types of written products emerged. There was "the job-printing that accompanied book-printing. It lent itself to commercial advertising, official propaganda, seditious agitation, and bureaucratic red tape as no scribal procedure ever had."[8] This point is about the creation of structures that go with the creation of new products. More information meant new possibilities for communicating and using that information, which in turn created new categories of information.

Take propaganda. By definition, propaganda involves wide distribution. It is targeted at the masses. Whether it's leaflets, radio broadcasts, or internet memes, propaganda can exist only if there is technology to replicate it in sufficient volume to reach large numbers of people. Propaganda couldn't exist in scribal culture; there wasn't enough potential for reproduction and dissemination. The printing press allowed for a new type of written product, propaganda, that in turn supported the creation of organizations that could use it.

Being able to trace the effects of the printing press on areas such as business possibilities, organizational development, and social structures shows us how widespread the impact of decreasing the scarcity of information was.

Third, books offered educational independence. "There is simply no equivalent in scribal culture for the 'avalanche' of 'how-to' books which poured off the new presses, explaining by 'easy steps' just how to master diverse skills, ranging from playing a musical instrument to keeping accounts."[9] In *The Printing Press as an Agent of Change*, Eisenstein recounts many examples of how the availability of educational books undermined the guild system and changed the nature of apprenticeship.

More information meant that students did not necessarily require teachers. This in turn put pressure on teachers to contribute something more to education than could be provided in books. It also meant that people could shop around to find lessons that interested them versus relying on what was available in their town. People could develop skills that didn't exist in their area, thereby increasing the availability of a wide spectrum of services.

Competition, therefore, also increased. Before books, if the local blacksmith didn't want to take you on as an apprentice, you would likely be stuck unless you could move to another village. After books, assuming you were literate, there was at least the possibility of teaching yourself the basics (especially because the use of images also increased with the printing press) so that you could start your own blacksmith shop.

Fourth, more people could participate in creating information. "Sixteenth-century editors and publishers . . . did not merely store data passively in compendia," Eisenstein writes. "They created vast networks of correspondents, solicited criticism of each edition, sometimes publicly promising to mention the names of readers who sent in new information or who spotted the errors which would be weeded out."[10] This was an early form of crowdsourcing. Books were not the same as manuscripts; they were not something that was merely copied. They were analyzed, challenged, and developed. The printing press created the notion of an edition, the idea that a text would be updated as new information became available. Increased engagement with the printed word created a feedback loop that worked to further reduce the scarcity of information. "After printing, large-scale data collection did become subject to new forms of feedback which had not been possible in the age of scribes."[11]

Finally, underpinning all of these changes was the way preservation changed. Eisenstein writes, "Of all the new features introduced by the duplicative powers of print, preservation is probably the most important." The printing press transformed the nature of preservation of written text, changing texts from something you tucked away for safekeeping to something you shared widely. Now, you preserved something by printing it on paper, many times, and sending it out into the world. "The notion that valuable data could be preserved best by being made public, rather than by being kept secret, ran counter to tradition . . . and was central both to early modern science and to Enlightenment thought."[12]

Although we can imagine increased public information had all sorts of effects, one tangible outcome was the reduction of inefficiency. Knowledge being less scarce means it's more accessible. Therefore, less effort needs to be directed at preservation: "Successive generations could build on the work left by sixteenth-century polymaths instead of trying to retrieve scattered fragments of it."[13]

Printing meant that knowledge could be recorded in many places and be made accessible for future retrieval.

When Johannes Gutenberg constructed his movable-type printing press, he could not have foreseen all the changes the invention would ignite. Not all reductions in scarcity will have the same impact. However, the more fundamental the scarcity being reduced, the higher the likelihood of widespread impact. This is the lesson for our lives. Time and money tend to be our two most fundamental resources, although there can be others. When you reduce the scarcity of a core resource in your life, the effects are likely to be significant. It is thus worth some effort to identify such reductions as they occur and plan for managing those changes as best you can. Abundance has its own consequences.

> A wealth of information creates a poverty of attention and a need to allocate that attention efficiently among the overabundance of information sources that might consume it.
>
> —HERBERT A. SIMON[14]

Conclusion

Scarcity shapes our choices and drives our actions. When something is scarce, it suddenly becomes valuable. We want it more because there is less. It's the principle that underlies everything from the price of gold to the thrill of the hunt.

Scarcity isn't just about material things. It applies to time, opportunities, and ideas. It's why we're drawn to the exclusive, the limited-edition, the one of a kind.

In economics, scarcity is a foundational principle. There are infinite wants and desires but limited resources. We can't have everything, so we must choose. Scarcity guides those choices.

Some businesses operate with a scarcity mentality, removing shock absorbers and operating lean, with just enough resources to produce the day's goods. This model is prone to disruption with the slightest hiccup and signals to employees that they're in a culture of scarcity, triggering our biological instinct toward self-preservation. We subconsciously hoard things of value to gain an individual advantage.

Scarcity can work to your advantage. Imagine you've got a rare combination of qualities: you're honest, hardworking, and smart. People like that are scarce, and the world tends to reward them disproportionately. It's not just about being good at one thing; it's about having a mix of traits.

The key to navigating scarcity is understanding its power, recognizing when it's driving our choices, and asking if those choices align with our true values and goals. Sometimes, scarcity creates real value. But sometimes, it's just a mirage, a trick of the mind.

Supply and Demand

Scarcity drives price.

We need each other to do things that we can't do for ourselves. If we are intimately connected with each other, we just give things to each other; if we don't know each other we find another way to handle it. If you think about it, each according to his or her abilities and each according to his or her needs is sort of the same thing as supply and demand.

—DAVID GRAEBER[1]

S upply and demand describes how people manage the allocation of scarce resources by setting prices. If lots of people want something that's rare, like the latest gaming console, the price goes up; if something's plentiful and not many want it, like old smartphone cases, the price drops.

The dance between supply and demand sets the rhythm for market prices. When demand outstrips supply, prices rise until the number of people who want something drops, decreasing demand. When supply outstrips demand, prices fall until more people want something, reducing excess supply.

Supply and demand are actively stable; the two are never really at an equilibrium. The relationship between them is dynamic, always changing.

The basic supply-and-demand curves are predicated on the assumption that no one agent can influence price—everyone, firm and individual alike, must work with the price as dictated by the market. But in reality, both supply and demand can be manipulated. Some firms are large enough, in terms of their market share, that they can affect supply. Thus, the total supply of something is not necessarily equal to the *available* supply; firms can create artificial scarcity to increase the perceived value of their product. A great example of this is luxury goods. Limiting the supply of a good so it can be sold at high prices can lead to greater overall income than selling a greater volume at whatever price the market agrees upon.

Demand can also be manipulated. In *The Origin of Wealth*, Eric D. Beinhocker writes, "On the demand side, our preferences determine the relative attractiveness of products and services competing for our attention"[2]—and those preferences can be easily influenced. Marketing can convince individuals to want something, or more of something, that they previously had little desire for. Marketing can also create demand for new ways to meet unfulfilled wants. Josh Kaufman notes in *The Personal MBA* that "the essence of effective marketing is discovering what people already want, then presenting your offer in a way that intersects with that pre-existing desire."[3]

Often, supply and demand are discussed in terms of one commodity, like shoes or pizza, but the reality is we have a variety of choices when it comes to supplying our demands. These choices create change and instability in markets; it's part of how new businesses rise to challenge incumbents. Even though we may have a preference for orange juice over apple juice, our demand for orange juice can be filled by many different orange juice producers. On top of that, there are many ways to satisfy our thirst with substitutions like water.

How supply and demand intersect in a world of choice was first explored by economists Joan Robinson and Edward Chamberlin, who wrote about "imperfect competition." Marketing and advertising play a role in imperfect competition by convincing us to choose one brand of boot over another. The danger of a boot monopoly forming as the result of a successful marketing campaign is limited by the other boot manufacturers, who market their own products to slightly different audiences. Thus, there are enough players in the field that new boot sellers could enter the market.

This reality of choice makes supply and demand nuanced. Although the demand for boots may stay static for a while, the fluctuating demand for different styles and brands creates movement and change in the boot market.

Rarely can we demand that which we don't know is possible. To twist the old quote, no one was clamoring for cars at the end of the nineteenth century; they were interested in faster horses. According to economist Joel Mokyr, most new technology throughout history was invented "if not randomly then in a highly unpredictable fashion."[4] Demand was thus probably not a major factor in what people invented or improved.

We tend to not demand things that require no energy for their production. As economist Eric Beinhocker explains, "On the supply side, things with low entropy have value. By definition, things with low entropy are scarce and require energy, materials, and information for their creation." Entropy, as a reminder from volume 2, is a measure of disorder—the more ways things can be arranged, the higher the entropy. In the land of products, we see immediately that to supply something requires energy. The energy of nature, of individuals, and of machines are required to produce everything we buy; we would never value something that can exist without energy inputs of some sort. Of course, we tend to overvalue the results of human and machine labor, and undervalue the incredible energy required to grow a tree or an elephant or maintain an ecosystem.

We often think of supply as fixed, believing that there is only so much to go around. But increased demand often leads to a larger supply pool: for example, of votes, doctors, and university degrees.

The complexities of supply and demand highlight the impossibility of a central control of all economic production. Our consumption would have to be confined to a small handful of goods, and trying to plan in a way that met supply and demand would limit, if not eliminate, innovation.

The model of supply and demand speaks to how complementary interests and competing interests intersect. In a traditional supply-and-demand graph, both the consumer and the firm have a complementary interest: one wants to buy, and the other wants to sell. But they also have a competing interest: one wants to pay the lowest possible price, the other wants to receive the highest possible price. The result is an economic win-win. The complexities of the model also illustrate how the win-win is vulnerable to interference.

Never Underestimate the Power of Demand

Where there is demand, there is often supply. If there is a market for something—meaning people willing to pay—some enterprising person will try to serve it.

It happens occasionally that people demand something that the larger society deems unacceptable to supply—think illegal drugs, jeans and other Western products in Eastern Europe under communist regimes, medical treatments banned in one country but available in another—so laws are created to try to prevent the transaction from taking place. A major challenge in these situations is that laws can only effectively target the supply side; they can try to stop certain goods or services from being sold in the marketplace. It is much harder to regulate the demand side, because ultimately, it's impossible to legislate that someone no longer want something. Often, in situations where only the supply side can be regulated, underground markets are created. Demand still exists, and people operating outside the legalized market provide products to meet it.

Throughout the centuries, there are many ways governments have tried to regulate the supply of sex work (and, less often, the demand for it). Looking at the history of prostitution laws through this model demonstrates the challenges of regulation and the power of want. Social attitudes toward sex work have changed across time and place, but in most cases, attempts to make the industry conform to prevailing social standards have focused almost exclusively on the supply side. Historically, where sex work has not been banned outright, regulation has involved confining sex workers to specific locations, specifying dress codes for them, and/or requiring mandatory health checks. These regulations target the people, mostly women, providing the sexual services.

For example, in medieval London, historian Kate Lister writes, "prostitution was not illegal . . . but it was very heavily regulated, and the tactics deployed to control it were stigma and zoning." Laws were passed requiring "harlots" to dress a certain way so they wouldn't be mistaken for ladies, and brothels were mandated to be outside city walls, except for one central street, Cock Lane. "The extensive regulations governing life in the stews were intended to control the sex trade, rather than stamp it out,"[5] but control always meant supply-side regulation.

This type of regulation—stigma and zoning—has been (and still is) practiced in many countries. In seventeenth-century Japan, sex workers were divided into three categories based on the services they offered and confined to specific walled areas in a city. In eighteenth- and nineteenth-century France, sex work was meant to be confined to state-supervised brothels, and a program of public hygiene was instituted whereby women suspected of prostitution were detained and treated for venereal disease. Of course, as Kate Lister explains in her book *Harlots, Whores and Hackabouts*, "This approach did very little to help the women selling sex as no one was screening their clients."[6] Focusing on the supply side without having similar measures on the demand side meant that venereal disease continued to spread.

There have also been times in history when an outright ban on sex work was implemented. "In 1259, the authorities of Bologna passed a statute that banished all sex workers from the city. Any woman caught selling sex was to have her nose cut off." In China, after the rise of the Communist Party in 1949, sex work was made illegal, and the floating brothels that had served an international clientele were abolished. Sex workers were arrested and forcibly retrained.[7]

Still, in all of these places, sex work did not disappear. In the case of China, "the communists were successful in forcing sex work underground, which only resulted in fewer rights for those selling sex."[8] Sex work did not disappear, because the demand for it didn't go away. In the case of Italy, "by the mid-fourteenth century, Italy's enthusiasm to eradicate sex for sale had been replaced with a grudging realization that this was just not going to work. Faced with the futility of abolition, a policy of legalized, municipally regulated prostitution was introduced."[9] Italy went back to regulating the supply side with restriction and stigma.

In rare instances, countries have tried to deal with the health aspects of sex work by placing constraints on the demand side. In the late nineteenth century, the British Army "initially tried to control rates of venereal disease by mandating regular examinations of [its] men, but this proved to be very demoralizing and deeply unpopular." Similarly, during World War II, "even the American war office realized that attempting to enforce abstinence simply did not work, and instead issued all serving men with condoms and launched a safe sex campaign, largely stigmatizing 'fast women' and 'goodtime girls.'"[10] Faced with the inability to regulate demand, these militaries fell back on targeting the supply side with regulations (approved brothels) and stigma.

The majority of the time, then, attempts to regulate the sex industry have centered on the supply side. But because demand cannot be regulated, these supply-side interventions have had little to no impact on the volume of the sex trade itself. Regardless of social norms or legislative preferences, "no attempt to abolish or control either the selling or buying of sex in our collective history has worked. All that happens when either the provider or the client is criminalized is that sex work is forced underground, creating opportunities for exploitation and abuse without recourse to legal protection."[11] The reason is simply that supply is created to meet demand.

This example demonstrates how difficult regulation can be when one can tackle only one side of the supply-and-demand relationship. It also shows how powerful demand can be, as it easily creates large, robust markets outside of traditional governance structures.

Out of Thin Air

Invention is the mother of necessity.

—THORSTEIN VEBLEN[12]

Demand is not always a binary. Beyond whether you want something or not, how much of it you want forms your demand. You may prefer coffee and thus not have any demand for other caffeinated beverages. But among coffee drinkers there is a range of demand: How many cups a day? Black, or with sugar and cream? Americano? Espresso? Demand can get quite complex.

A company that can provide you with one cup of black coffee per day is not going to be as competitive as one that can provide more options and higher quantities. But if all you know is the one cup you can get at your local diner, how do you know you could live a life where you drink seven macchiatos a day? You aren't ever going to demand that. But a company that can supply those macchiatos has a lot to gain by convincing you that you should.

In the history of creating demand to encourage consumption beyond what anyone reasonably needs, the gold star goes to General Motors, which was able to shift automotive demand from a binary (car: yes or no?) to a continuous desire to have the newest car. When cars first hit the roads, it was Ford that was the industry leader. Ford developed mass production techniques that allowed the company to build more cars more cheaply, filling the binary demand for cars with the Model T. Model Ts were all the same, available in one color—black—from 1914 to 1925, and their design didn't change for years. These characteristics allowed for extremely efficient production. Car ownership had been possible for only a few decades, and Ford and the Model T filled the early demand better than anyone else.

If it wanted to stay in business, GM had to figure out a way to compete. Instead of trying to outdo Ford in fulfilling initial ownership demand, Alfred P. Sloan, president of GM, decided to target people who already owned cars. He created demand by "getting existing car owners to upgrade."[13] Convincing people to want more of what they already had led to the birth of the car model year. "The

GM president believed the company's future depended on its ability to deliver a new look for each of its lines every year," writes William Knoedelseder in his book *Fins*, "thereby enticing people to trade in last year's model for this year's new and improved version."[14]

New models are not new cars. To put a brand-new car into a production line is significantly more expensive than simply changing the visual design elements. As Knoedelseder points out, "It didn't take an automotive genius to see that restyling a car was cheaper than reengineering it."[15] For the most part, a new model of an existing car was relatively unchanged under the hood. People were essentially buying the same car; the only difference was in how it looked.

At the same time, in order for you to recognize that your neighbor has just purchased the latest Cadillac, it can't be drastically different from the one sitting in your driveway that you bought two years ago. Increasing demand for visually updated cars "would only work if the cars were styled in a way that people found alluring, changing enough to make each year's new model look distinctive, while also maintaining continuity with previous models and avoiding radical changes that might deter buyers."[16]

GM's head of design, Harley Earl, implemented a schedule of change, following the direction of Sloan to "stimulate the public's appetite for new GM models without rendering the older models unpalatable in comparison."[17] To maintain the demand for new styles rather than, say, new capabilities, "Harley developed an ingenious process for delivering gradual, carefully planned change. He introduced major styling innovations . . . in the Cadillac, then passed them down in succeeding years to the less expensive makes."[18] This way, the higher-end products always had the possibility of attainment. The more often you traded in, the more often you could increase your status. The styling updates could give the owner of a new Chevrolet more cachet than an owner of an old Cadillac.

Earl's design cycles were precise. The design teams operated on a three-year cycle: Year One—new model; Year Two—facelift and freshen up; Year Three—restyle fenders, deck, and hood. "As a result, every GM sedan, coupe, convertible, and station wagon looked new and different every year," writes Knoedelseder.[19] And every year, thousands of people lined up to trade in their old models.

What's remarkable about this story is the idea of creating demand for a new version of something that offered no real increased value. The new model years didn't work better; they didn't run faster or have better performance. They just looked different. Buying a car one model year different from your own cost you money in exchange for no benefit other than a psychological one.

In explaining the ethos of GM car designers, Earl once said, "Our big job is to hasten obsolescence. Since 1934, the average car ownership span has gone from five years to two years. When it is one year, we will have a perfect score."[20]

Sure, over time, car performance has improved. But GM helped condition people to not wait for technology to develop or functionality to fundamentally change. People trading in their new cars so often because of the availability of a different front grille or paint options meant that engineering could move much more slowly.

It's possible that GM's reliance on style to drive sales contributed to its eventual significant loss of market share. Although some in the company wanted to make drastically different cars in the wake of World War II—notably, smaller ones, like those available in Europe—GM's management stayed committed to the trends it had created: more chrome, more flash, more accessories, ubiquitous fins. The success of American Motors, and then of Volkswagen, in selling smaller cars with limited style changes thus came as a surprise to the company.

In the mid-1950s, "industry writers and critics [began] questioning the practice of annual model change."[21] It started to look less like innovation and more like manipulation. Admittedly, this is a tough line to navigate. Companies exist to make a profit; without profits, they die. But demand cannot grow forever. Buying a new car every year may be effective in terms of short-term profit, but it's inefficient in terms of resource consumption. If everyone buys a new car every year, what happens to all the used ones? And, as we now well understand, the resources needed to manufacture cars are finite. There is no world where a company can make a new car for every person on the planet every year forever. For every action, there is a reaction.

There is no doubt, however, that GM's development of the model year and its impact on the demand for cars was pivotal in terms of how products are marketed. They helped create the world of the upgrade, where the question "Does it still work?" is less important than "Does it still look good?" and "What am I signaling about my status by owning it?"

Conclusion

Supply and demand are the push and pull determining availability and price. Their dance is never-ending. A sudden shortage can send prices soaring; a new discovery can send them crashing.

But supply and demand aren't just about price; they're also about allocation. They determine who gets what, and how much of it. When supply is low and demand is high, resources flow to those who are willing and able to pay the most.

Markets react to supply and demand. When demand exceeds

supply, it encourages investment by companies to create substitutes or more supply. On the other hand, when supply exceeds demand, it discourages investment until a profitable balance is restored.

Economic cycles are driven as much by human nature as by resources. When profits are flowing, it encourages overconfidence, greed, and complacency. When profits are nowhere to be found, it encourages fear, savings, and ruthless efficiency.

As individuals, we're all part of this dance. Every choice we make as consumers and every decision we make as producers shapes the contours of supply and demand. We are the market, collectively determining what has value and what doesn't.

Next time you're at the store, or negotiating a salary, or launching a product, remember the forces at play. You're not just a passive participant but an active agent in the dance of supply and demand. Your choices matter. Make them wisely.

SUPPORTING IDEA:
Game Theory

ECONOMIC ACTIVITY IS PRIMARILY BASED ON THE DECISIONS MADE by individual actors and the ways their decisions impact other parties. Game theory is a mathematical means of modeling how different decisions made by agents lead to different outcomes, with particular focus on interactions and how they lead to benefits (payouts). The field is useful for understanding economics, but it can also be applied to other fields such as biology, military strategy, and psychology.

From a single mathematical model of a game, we can draw insights about a wide range of real-world situations wherein people seek the best possible payouts for themselves. Games aren't predictive, but they can help us see the mathematical underpinnings of our decisions, stripped of distracting detail.

Optimization

Perfecting the possible.

The most important
optimization is to
do the right thing.
A close second is to
do the thing right.

—JON BENTLEY[1]

If economics is defined as the study of how people allocate scarce resources, optimization is crucial for considering how and why we make allocation decisions. Optimization is like finding the best way to pack your luggage so that everything fits. In economics, it's about making the best use of resources, like time or money, so you get the biggest benefit or profit with the least waste. It's all about achieving the smartest balance for the best result.

Many economic theories assume that people will always seek to gain the maximum possible benefit from deploying their resources. It is a fundamental assumption to understanding economic behavior that people "do the best for themselves given how much money they have and how much things cost."[2] Of course, everyone has a different optimization formula, because everyone places different values on things. And we're never optimizing in only one dimension. We may want to make sure we get a certain value when we spend money, but not at the expense of the poor use of a portion of our time. That balance, however, is subjective: for some people, spending an hour to save a dollar is a valuable use of their time, while others would rather forgo the dollar than lose an hour in which they could pursue other activities. Companies also optimize in multiple dimensions. Yes, they tend to seek to use resources in a way that maximizes their profits, but they often also simultaneously seek to optimize factors like employee satisfaction or brand reputation.

The concept of optimization comes up in many different fields, because in all areas there is something we want to optimize. Businesses want to optimize their supply chains; coders want to optimize their algorithms. There are also many explorations of optimization in mathematics, which usually seek to describe how one can optimize in a particular situation (we covered one of them in the global and local maxima chapter of *The Great Mental Models*, volume 3). In biology, as well, we can trace through evolution how different species have optimized for their environment.

Some economists postulate that the economy, far from ever being in or even nearing equilibrium, is itself an evolutionary system.[3] For businesses to survive the evolutionary pressures the economic system places on them, they must be able to adapt. When we consider optimization using an evolutionary model, we immediately see a dynamic component: you don't reach optimal capacity, then stop. Optimization requires ongoing experimentation and adjustment. It always involves risk, because the environment isn't static and there are always new combinations to try. Optimization is not like choosing from a menu with all options defined, available, and constant. There are also temporal divisions within the concept—short-term and long-term optimization—and they often require taking different paths.

It's worth it, here, to dive deeper into the idea of optimization in biological evolution, because there are clear parallels to economic actors. If evolution would eventually produce organisms perfectly optimized to their environment, then why do species go extinct? Although there are multiple reasons for extinction of species, one is an inability to adapt when the environment changes. Say a species of insect has developed a feature that allows it to be the only one to drink the nectar of a certain flower. This strategy is so successful that the insect consumes nothing else. If that flower dies off because it can't survive the increasing global temperatures caused by climate change, then that insect species will very likely die off as well. When the environment is stable, being the only one to access a food source is great—you have no competition. But when the environment changes, that optimization becomes a liability.

Companies face an analogous conundrum. If they optimize for the current environment and are successful, they could corner a market and have great success. But when the environment inevitably changes, they may not be able to adapt, because the market for the products and capabilities they've developed has disappeared. For companies to adapt and evolve, they need to keep some options open. But keeping options open means diverting resources away from immediate needs—choosing to optimize not for the moment but instead for the ability to stay around and play the long game. As Eric D. Beinhocker explains, for businesses, there is a constant tension between "how much should be invested in executing for today versus adapting for tomorrow."[4]

When it comes to individual choice, we all have our own optimization criteria. And this changes over time. What's important to us now may not be important to us ten years from now.

Knowing that our needs and desires change can inform our evaluation of what is optimal. For example, spending a lot of money on a fancy car might be optimal today because of the associated status boost you receive, but spending more than necessary on cars may lead to a narrower range of choices when you need to move into a retirement home several years from now. So, factoring my optimal retirement into how I optimize today will inevitably lead to different choices in how I spend my resources.

Furthermore, in a novel economic situation, we cannot predict what might be optimal. We have to experiment and frequently try multiple optimization formulas. Like companies, we also have to take risks, because our environment changes. When we take the concepts behind optimization in evolution and apply them analogously to the much smaller timescales of our lives, we see that seeking the optimal contains the necessity of ongoing adjustment in reaction to environmental changes. Our optimization formulas usually change when we have kids or switch careers. We are also likely to update them in response to situations like recessions, pandemics, and wars.

Our optimization efforts involve trade-offs 100 percent of the time. We do not get everything we want. We exchange our incomes for goods and our time for experiences, and we negotiate all of these decisions within a complex web of billions of other people who are pursuing their own optimization formulas. One way to think about optimization is that, as Beinhocker writes, "human beings will seek their maximum happiness state within the constraints of their finite resources and will trade their way to get there."[5]

Because we all have different optimization formulas, it's very hard to evaluate others' choices. Beware of judging others for making suboptimal decisions if you don't know what they're optimizing for. If you saw the world the way they see it, you might make the same choices they are making.

A final note on optimization is that exercising choice presupposes having those choices, which isn't always true. Not all economic agents have the same choices available to them, even if they have the same amount of money. Culture, laws, and social norms have a huge impact on the range of options for optimization.

> The set of choices that individual and collective agents face, however, is far more complex than that implied by economic models of utility maximization that assumes perfect information, exogenously given preferences, and sovereign self-interest.
>
> —NANCY FOLBRE[6]

The Foundations for Optimization

> In evolutionary systems, history matters; where you can go in the future depends on where you have been in the past.
>
> —ERIC D. BEINHOCKER[7]

You can only optimize based on your foundation. When trying to optimize your purchases, for example, you can only use the money you have to buy what's available. If you're currently employed in the service industry, and it collapses, you can't just go be a carpenter tomorrow to better optimize for the changing job market. Some training will be necessary, because you don't have the foundation for carpentry. Thus there are constraints on optimization.

In *The Bare Bones*, paleobiologist Matthew F. Bonnan charts vertebrate evolution. A critical point in the eventual evolution of humans was when vertebrates left the ocean to explore land. In order to be successful on land, extensive evolution of the vertebrate skeleton first had to take place. Consider that "water is eight hundred times denser than air. . . . On land, gravity is a much more powerful force.... Resisting gravity and moving under its force led to selection of fewer, sturdier bones and strengthening of the skeleton."[8] The changes were numerous. Some vertebrates developed longer snouts or more dexterous tongues, and necks evolved for the first time. New joints developed to support the spine, so it didn't get pulled down in the middle by gravity in animals walking on all fours. Eyes dry out on land, so evolution produced and selected for tear ducts and eyelids. There were changes for breathing in the atmosphere and to help creatures better cope with a greater daily range of temperatures.[9]

The most fascinating part of this process, however, is that evolution could only work with what it already had in existing vertebrates. Animals slowly optimized to function on land, but that optimization was achieved by evolving from the foundation they had developed in the water.

Here is a great example. Sound travels more slowly and over shorter distances, and loses intensity faster, on land. So for the vertebrate species coming out of the ocean, "a way must be found to convert the high-frequency vibrations of the eardrum into pieces strong enough to overcome the viscous fluid of the inner ear." Modern tetrapods (land vertebrates) solved the problem by adapting a part they already had, the hyomandibula, into a sound transducer through a complex process of adaptation in skull structure.[10]

If you were designing a land vertebrate from scratch to be optimally suited to its environment, would you choose and organize these parts in this way to produce sound for the brain? With a total blank slate, probably not. There are likely more effective and powerful structures you would use. But evolution is a process of continual optimization that can only work from what it's already got.

The concept of being constrained by your existing foundation applies to companies as well. That doesn't mean that companies have to keep producing the same goods or services in perpetuity, but it does mean that they evolve from their existing infrastructure. A company that prints books today cannot make vaccines tomorrow. It can, however, look at what it currently has and identify what and how to evolve to optimize its business in a changing environment.

One company that has experienced and worked within the constraints of an existing foundation is Nintendo. An incredibly successful Japanese company, Nintendo is an example of how ongoing attempts to optimize are constrained by your immediate past.

Nintendo started in 1889 as a shop that manufactured and sold playing cards decorated with colorful flowers to gamblers. Within five years, writes Jeff Ryan, it "had craftily shifted over to the toy market to capitalize on [its] existing distribution route for cards."[11] When longtime president Hiroshi Yamauchi took over from his grandfather, in 1949, he "tried out various new business models—rice, taxicabs, 'love hotels' rentable by the hour. None clicked until he decided to utilize his network of card and toy shops."[12] Nintendo found it easier to optimize using the foundation it already had.

Later, Nintendo built on its gaming foundation. It developed arcade games and small, portable electronic games that could run off watch batteries. It was very successful in Japan in both of these endeavors. In the early 1980s, Nintendo wanted to grow further by breaking into the lucrative American market. It started with what it knew, what it was already good at: arcade games. The first, and soon massively successful, Nintendo game in the United States was *Donkey Kong*. Early *Donkey Kong* arcade games were actually a rewire of a bunch of old shooter games that Nintendo couldn't sell, which were repurposed and reprogrammed. *Donkey Kong* was everywhere, and it gave Nintendo a solid presence in the United States.[13]

Donkey Kong is notable in the story of Nintendo for another reason, though. The game included the first appearance of the Mario character—albeit not with all the details that would come later. But *Donkey Kong* set the foundation, the beginning of Mario's becoming the Nintendo mascot. He began to appear as a side character in many Nintendo games and eventually became a critical component of Nintendo's first home gaming system, the Nintendo Entertainment System (NES).

Going forward, Nintendo found it hard to break away from its foundation. For example, the company tried a couple of educational games, but "after swinging 0 for 2, Nintendo gave up on the NES being a learning machine."[14] There was no technical reason for the games' failure. The NES was technically a computer, and computers are now a ubiquitous part of learning. But Nintendo was constrained by its "games as entertainment" foundation. People saw their function as games and didn't support the attempt at education. In a sense, the consumer performed a natural selection function and did not select for any of Nintendo's attempts at something different.

In the quest to optimize, foundations can be both a burden and a source of opportunity. For Nintendo, the gaming image restricted the company in terms of developing new product lines, but it allowed them to define the key electronic gaming experience: fun. Nintendo is still a very successful company, continually figuring out how to leverage its heritage and capabilities to entertain people. Building on what you already have, evolving from there, is one way to optimize.

Utility

> All men know the utility of useful things; but they do not know the utility of futility.
>
> —ZHUANGZI[15]

In economics, utility is defined as the underlying reason for a person's choice. Jeremy Bentham coined the term and argued that "the pursuit of self-interest [is] a rational activity based on a calculus of pleasure and pain." It is this calculus that he aimed to cover with the concept of utility.[16] Utility, then, is a broad, general concept that aims to capture why people make the choices they do in how they buy.

There is thus a relationship between utility and value, in two ways. First, a product or service's utility is what makes it worth paying for (i.e., gives it value). As Karl Marx put it, "Nothing can have value without being an object of utility."[17] Second, something's utility is tied to what we value and varies from person to person.

To the first point, regarding quantifiable economic value, something's utility indicates what people might be willing to spend on it. Utility is directly related to how much things cost—or, as Thomas Edison put it, "Anything that won't sell, I don't want to invent. Its sale is proof of utility, and utility is success." If people are willing to allocate some of their finite money for what you sell, then by definition, they expect it to maximize the utility of their expenditure.

The usefulness of additional units of any good tends to vary with scale. Marginal utility allows us to understand the value of one additional unit, and in most practical areas of life, that utility diminishes at some point. On the other hand, in some cases, additional units are subject to a critical point where the utility function jumps discreetly up or down. As an example, giving water to a thirsty man has diminishing marginal utility with each additional unit and can eventually kill him with enough units. Utility as traditionally conceived thus contains its own end. As Eric Beinhocker writes, "Diminishing marginal utility keeps consumers from consuming an infinite quantity of donuts."[18]

It becomes trickier when we start thinking about something's utility in terms of what we value. For example, why do I choose tea over coffee? Because tea has higher utility for me. This utility can be explained in a number of ways and is usually a combination of many factors. Maybe tea is cheaper, so I can afford more of it. Maybe the pleasure I get from the first sip in the morning is one of the best moments of my day. Maybe drinking tea is an activity I can do with others who have similar tastes. All of these reasons add up to me placing a higher value on tea than coffee. Given the choice between the two, I will choose tea due to its higher utility for me.

However, our perception of utility is also influenced by what society considers useful or valuable. While some expenditures are survival necessities, if you're reading this, you probably have income to allocate on the basis of different kinds of utility, such as how it reinforces your identity. Utility, then, is also influenced by marketing, which is often about connecting intangible benefits to products. My tea drinking may be influenced by cultural stereotypes that suggest intellectual people drink tea (if I consider myself an intellectual) or persuasive advertisements that convince me I will have anything from more energy every day to less of a negative impact on the environment (if I value those things).

One common criticism of utility is that it is too broad a term to have real explanatory powers. Julie Nelson discusses the limitations of utility by saying that in traditional economics, the utility one gets from having children is comparable to the utility one gets from eating ice cream. Juxtaposed like this, it seems absurd to treat utility as a simple unit of measurement. "People in households act from a variety of motives and are organized in a variety of complex ways," Nelson writes. "People face real dilemmas in their choices about where to work, what to purchase, how to form their families, and how to participate in public decisions."[19] Often, the decision leading to the most utility isn't clear, and really, the things that provide us utility are often complex and unique to us.

Therefore, when considering utility and the associated light it shines on value, we need to remember that not all of the things that satisfy our wants have a price tag or even can be priced.

The Tools of Optimization

If optimization is "the action of making the best or most effective use of a situation or resource,"[20] then an obvious question is, How do you know what you're doing is most effective? You need some way to measure.

Measurement comes in many forms. It can be something as informal as reflecting on two different experiences and evaluating which one felt better. Most often, measurement means statistics: investing with firm A brought 5 percent returns, while with firm B the returns were 7 percent. Maybe shopping at grocery store X is about fifty dollars cheaper per week than grocery store Y, or commuting on route 1 is ten minutes faster than route 2. If we only have four free hours in a day, we may want to spend a maximum of only one of them at the gym. The truth is, we tend to optimize only what we can measure. It stands to reason, then, that what we optimize for is influenced by the tools of measurement we have.

When humans first started spreading around the planet, there was no clock time. We experienced the arrow of time through occurrences such as the setting and rising of the sun and the growth of children. But there was no concept of looking up at the sky and saying that it was 3:00 p.m. and that the sun would be setting in four hours and forty-five minutes. It's hard to know what optimization looked like for early humans, but making the most effective use of resources possibly was measured in ways such as, "Does everyone in the group have enough food?" or "Is this location close enough to water sources that I can be back in my shelter before dark?" Making the most out of one's day was measured by the likelihood of survival.

The invention of clock time led to, among other things, a new vector for optimization. We could now know how many hours were available to us every day, we could measure how many of those hours we spent farming or praying, and we could watch their passage no matter what we were doing. The passage of time ceased to be something that happened in the background. It was codified into clock time and had great impact on how we organized our day.

In Verona, in the year 507 CE, the Gothic leader Theodoric erected a large tower just outside the city walls that housed a water clock. Set to the sun, this was an acoustic clock that auditorily announced the passage of time to the citizens of the city. In *About Time*, David Rooney writes, "Theodoric himself explained the purpose of the clock: to let the people of Verona 'distinguish the various hours of the day and thus decide how best to occupy every moment.'"[21] The clock helped the people of Verona optimize their time by reminding them of the pace at which it was passing. Now, humans could know how much time they were spending on any particular activity. Instead of, say, the question of farming wheat versus cows being evaluated solely on survival measures, with the advent of clock time it was possible to measure precisely how long each activity took and to compare the time investment involved with the outputs produced.

Clock time allowed us to measure our productivity in more precise units. Thus, it also became a feedback mechanism, notifying us when our productivity had increased or decreased.

Once time could be measured, that measurement was here to stay. Clocks got smaller, cheaper, and more ubiquitous, until people could have personal timekeepers of their own. Awareness of clock time became part of life, so much so that most of us probably don't think about it anymore. However, fundamental inventions that change how society is organized tend to have unplanned effects. In this case, "with clocks always in view, we started buying into the idea that time could be wasted."[22]

This shouldn't surprise us. After all, "deciding how best to occupy every moment" of time means that some occupations are deemed better than others. And being able to measure how long it takes us to do anything means that some occupations are more efficient than others. So if it's possible to be productive with our time, that suggests it's also possible to be unproductive with our time.

Notions of productivity tend to be culturally and socially driven. The phrase "time is money" became famous after it was used by Benjamin Franklin in 1748.[23] One way to determine productivity was to measure how much money you were making in a given unit of time; an activity that made you one dollar in an hour was more productive that one that made you nothing. Other thinkers spoke more about how much one saved per unit of time. For example, Rooney notes, some thought that "by carefully measuring and using the time that had been given to us—by being disciplined, by restraining our excesses—we would be living virtuously."[24] In both cases, how time was considered best spent reflected what was most valued.

Clock time didn't standardize time's value; it only helped us measure it. This continues to be a conundrum that is resolved differently depending on the interpretation of how best to use clock time, an interpretation that's usually culturally inflected. For some people, a walk in a forest is a waste of time that could be spent producing something useful; for others, walking in nature is a valuable use of time that makes life more meaningful.

As clock time became more and more precise—able to be measured in minutes, then seconds, then nanoseconds—more options for optimization opened up. Global positioning systems (GPS) are essentially satellite clock systems that allow us to optimize our driving routes. Fitness watches provide all sorts of data measured over time (steps, sleep, heartbeats) that gives us the information to fine-tune our days to optimize whichever health vector we choose.

Right from the first sundials through hourglasses, pocket watches, and atomic clocks, embedded within the notion of clock time is precision. As clocks have developed, our ability to mark time has become more precise. One way we've used that precision is to measure more and more of what we've done, to optimize what we're going to do.

Clock time is now so ubiquitous that most of us never go for very long without knowing what time it is. Clock time is what tells us when to start work, to pick up our kids from school, to meet friends. In many cases, it's also what tells us when to eat and sleep. Clock time structures our days, and there is no longer any way of getting away from it. Planes fly, stock trades get processed, billions of deliveries get made, all because of clock time. Even many of our laws are based on clock time. The synchronization needed for our world to work depends on standardized clock time.

Because it's so available, clock time is a go-to measurement when we want to optimize: we know we're better at something because we can do it faster or because we see rising outputs in a certain time frame. Even spending time with people we love becomes optimizable by the very notion that we can track the time we spend. There is no value judgment here about clock time being a tool for optimization. Most of us make allocation decisions every day; better tools help us make better decisions. But sometimes, it's just as important to remember that just because you can measure something doesn't mean you need to optimize it. Some of the most valuable things in life are intangible.

Conclusion

Optimization is about making the most of what you have. It's like solving a puzzle in a clever way, finding a trick to skip steps and get to the answer faster.

In a world of scarcity, optimization is powerful. It allows us to make the most of our limited resources, whether that's time, money, or energy. But like any tool, it's only as good as the hand that wields it. Used wisely, optimization unlocks hidden potential and drives extraordinary results. Used poorly, it leads to wasted effort and missed opportunities.

Optimization often works for you until it doesn't. It's like the student who writes the answer but doesn't show their work. Knowing when to use it, when to let it go, and when to avoid it entirely can give you a key advantage.

Trade-offs

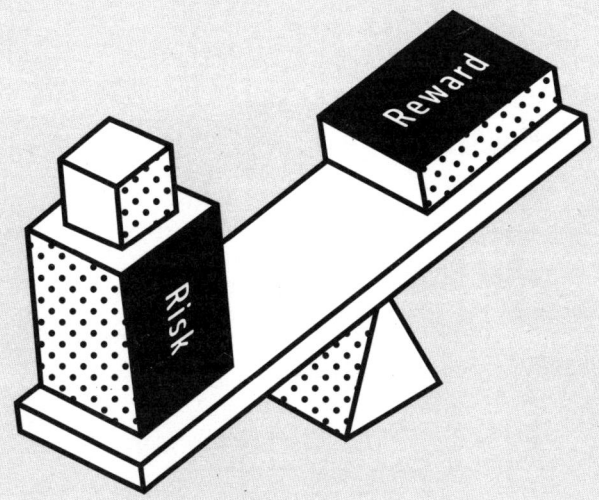

The cost of a benefit.

Economics teaches you that making a choice means giving up something.

—RUSS ROBERTS[1]

verything is a trade-off. To allocate scarce resources and meet our needs, we must make trade-offs. Choosing one course of action means giving up numerous things. Going to a party with one friend means you can't go to the movies with another on the same night.

A trade-off is any situation where making a choice means we must forgo something else, usually some kind of benefit or possible opportunity. Investors trade off risk and reward. Doctors balance a drug's potential to help with the possible harm of its side effects. Parents choose between their kids' momentary happiness and their long-term well-being. Customer service departments in fast-growing companies must make trade-offs between hiring new employees fast enough to keep up with the growing demand for support and taking the time to train everyone to handle support requests appropriately. Students face trade-offs between continuing their studies and getting a job. Whatever you spend your days doing, it involves trade-offs.

For example, buying unassembled furniture is usually much, much cheaper than buying premade. The company producing it can ship far more items in the same space and doesn't need to pay for labor or machinery to put it together. Also, for the consumer, it can sometimes be taken apart for transportation when moving house, again resulting in cost savings. The trade-off is that you need to spend time building it yourself and deal with associated risks, like striking your thumb with a hammer or spending an hour figuring out where to put that last screw.

All choices mean making trade-offs because they involve finite resources. We make trade-offs based on what we value the most. Someone with lots of free time but scarce funds may prefer unassembled furniture because it's the best way of allocating their resources; someone with more money but less time may opt for premade because it's the best use of what is available to them.

We also make trade-offs based on alternatives and opportunity cost. Someone who moves to the suburbs to save money increases their commute time. If the alternative use of the time spent commuting would be to earn significantly more money, it could be a very expensive move indeed.

Given that our time is finite, the opportunity cost of your time should increase every year. When you are young, it might make sense to trade time for money by moving to the suburbs or assembling furniture, but as you get older, these trade-offs become more expensive.

The optimal course of action is to choose the path with the greatest net present value—after considering all things, whether they are seen or foreseen. Making trade-offs involves opportunity cost.

Opportunity Cost

Trade-offs go hand in hand with the concept of opportunity cost. Every yes is also a no to something else. The opportunity cost of a decision is the potential benefit of the best forgone alternative choice. Every choice we make, every action we take, comes with an unseen price tag: the value of the opportunities we forgo. Sometimes those opportunities are immediate and sometimes they are in the future. Sometimes they are easy to quantify and sometimes they are hard to quantify.

Opportunity costs are often invisible. We see what we choose but not what we lose. Opportunity cost may be financial, but not always; it can include more nebulous costs like satisfaction or love. Consequently, opportunity costs are often hard or impossible to measure. It takes a disciplined mind to weigh unseen costs against visible ones.

Opportunity cost is the ghost of the path not taken. As Robert Frost so poignantly illustrates in "The Road Not Taken," we can never truly know what might have happened if we took a different option. This is the core challenge of factoring in opportunity cost to our decisions. For instance, a chain coffee company may face a choice between developing a new product to release or improving its existing products. If it funnels time, money, and other resources into the new product—say, a fizzy iced coffee—the venture may be a great success. Or, the new product may distract from the company's existing offerings, and the company may lose customers who switch to other brands that continually improve their coffees. But whichever path the company takes, it cannot know for sure what the outcome of other available choices might have been.

We can make better choices by learning to consider opportunity costs. Often, we choose things without evaluating them against the best possible alternative. While we can't perfectly weigh up every detail of our lives, a general awareness of opportunity costs can highlight the notion that some things are far more expensive than they seem.

Opportunity costs invite us to consider the full implications of our choices, to weigh the trade-offs with eyes wide open. They're a reminder that life is a series of forks in the road, and every step we take is a step not taken on another path.

Changes in the associated trade-offs of a particular decision can lead to large-scale changes in groups of people. For example, over the last century, more employment opportunities have become open to women in many countries. This is believed to be one reason for dropping birth rates; time spent caring for children now carries greater opportunity costs for women due to the forgone income.[2]

If we don't know what we value the most, we can't be sure we're getting the most out of the scarce resources we have available, like our time and money. When we know what we value and what we want to get out of life, we can pick the paths that offer the most of what we want. The irony here is that those who know how to make trade-offs can get so much more out of life than those who try to get everything. When we look at other people, we often end up getting the impression that they are managing to do everything: they are fantastic parents, their relationships are novel-worthy, they look amazing, their careers are epic, they get enough sleep, and they feel good all the time. This, however, is usually far from true. We're just not seeing the hidden trade-offs they're making.

Trade-offs can take awhile to become apparent; they sometimes only show up in the long term. Someone who eats a chocolate bar today will not become unhealthy tomorrow. Someone who eats a chocolate bar every day, however, will eventually see effects on their health. Just because the consequences do not happen immediately does not mean they don't happen. We also see this in complex adaptive systems: try to optimize one area, and there's likely to be a price elsewhere. Sometimes it's an obvious negative equation, as when steroid abuse leads to organ damage or when a fancy house masks crippling debt. But often, trade-offs are hard to evaluate. Choosing monogamy means you forgo other romantic partners, and many parents sacrifice career advancement to raise their kids. We all have to make sacrifices to be able to invest in what is important to us. Trade-offs imply that to get really great at a few things, you have to accept being mediocre at a lot more. Picture a dog pleading for someone to throw its toy but not wanting to let go of it in the first place. That's a good representation of wanting to attain something without paying the price for it.

Each of the myriad decisions we make on a daily basis involves trade-offs. If we don't consider them, we easily find ourselves stuck in situations where we're forgoing things we'd rather prioritize. We end up lamenting what we're missing out on against our will, unsure how this happened. But if we first consider the trade-offs associated with the decisions we make, we can end up with far more satisfying choices. According to Paul Dolan, professor of behavioral science at the London School of Economics, "The fundamental reason why most of us aren't as happy as we could be is that we allocate attention in ways that are often at odds with experiencing as much purpose and pleasure as we could."[3]

Although all choices in how to spend a resource, be it time or money or something else, involve trade-offs, there are certain factors that influence how and whether we evaluate those trade-offs. In their book *Scarcity*, Sendhil Mullainathan and Eldar Shafir argue that it is critical to put trade-offs in the context of slack. Slack is simply having enough of a resource that you can easily handle an unexpected demand on it. Having slack in your income means that you can easily absorb emergency expenses such as a new car battery or roof repair. The more slack we have in resources, the less critical trade-offs appear in our calculations.

Trade-offs are thus relative to the overall amount of a resource we have. For someone with a lot of income slack, spending ten dollars on a latte is no big deal. Yes, technically, there is a trade-off, because that ten dollars now cannot be spent on something else, but the person still has enough money to buy much of what they want. As Mullainathan and Shafir explain, "With slack, we do not feel compelled to question how really useful an item will be. . . . Since slack frees us from trade-offs, it licenses us to buy items that on their own, devoid of any other considerations, have some appeal."[4] However, to someone with no income slack, considering the trade-offs involved in spending ten dollars on that latte is much more critical. It may very well be a choice between that latte and dinner.

A general awareness of the existence of trade-offs can highlight that some things in life are more expensive than they seem. Getting what you want can be a matter of being good at knowing what to give up.

Trade-offs Are Everywhere

If you look around the world and consider the decisions that people have to make, you will see trade-offs everywhere. It's very rare that we are in situations of such total resource abundance that making one choice will not take some other choice off the table.

Consider designing a building—a situation that is fraught with trade-offs. All construction must consider trade-offs, because there is no way any particular building can have and be everything everyone wants. We must answer questions like: Who are we designing for? What is the purpose of the building? What kind of functionality does it need to have, now and in the future? These kinds of questions will force us to make choices, some of which take away other options. For example, durability and cost are often two competing parameters. "If we make the structure too weak, we may save weight and money, but then the chance of the thing breaking too soon will become unacceptably high," writes J. E. Gordon in *Structures*. On the other hand, "if we make a structure so strong that, in human terms, it is likely to last 'forever'—which is what the public would like—then it will probably be too heavy and expensive."[5] The useful trade-off is: cheap enough to get built now, durable enough to last some useful amount of time. We make, for example, a wood-frame house so that it is affordable for more people immediately, but we trade off the durability to have it last for untold generations.

Some people still build stone houses, bunkers, and other dwellings that are meant to last beyond a couple of generations. People evaluate trade-offs differently, so although trade-offs are often objective (such as certain materials impacting the amount of time a building is likely to be usable), they can sometimes be subjective (such as the value of living close to work or family, or buying in an older building that has historic appeal). When it comes to buildings, "There are no 'optimal' solutions applicable to all projects. Solutions can only satisfy certain people at certain times."[6] That's why all houses aren't the same. We all weigh each decision factor in construction uniquely, in accordance with our needs, resources, and desires.

Let's break down cost versus longevity in construction a little more. Bundled in with the idea of longevity is adaptability: Can your building adapt with the times? In a practical context, answering this question might require looking at something like occupant capacity. If we are designing an office building for today, and our organization has one thousand employees, should we design for exactly that amount? What if we grow? What if a recession hits? How adaptable can we be without creating too much waste or driving up the initial cost too much? If we design for two thousand employees, there's going to be a lot of empty space at the beginning, unless we can figure out some productive but temporary uses for it. But then we have to design for those too.

The number of trade-offs we have to make in a situation like this can seem overwhelming. So, another lesson about trade-offs is to not consider them so extensively that we get into analysis paralysis.

Take adaptability in building construction. Some factors are likely to make a building more adaptable, such as space that can be reconfigured and materials that will withstand a range of environmental changes. Adaptability, though, does not need to be (and cannot entirely be) planned. We humans are fairly adaptable ourselves, and if the structure is still standing and its condition is sound, we'll probably be able to find a use for it. The Parthenon started as a temple to the goddess Athena. In its 2,500-year history, it has been a church, a mosque, and a storehouse for munitions. None of these uses was intended by its original designers, but the Parthenon has proved highly adaptable.

This discussion of adaptability leads us to another complexity of trade-offs: they are not always easy to identify and quantify. The costs of one material versus another are clear, but the trade-offs between functionality and enjoyment of a space are less so. Furthermore, any built structure is "highly contextual, responding to constraints specific to geographic location, built environment, the immediate site, occupant characteristics, and the availability of resources."[7] Thus, trade-offs are not two-dimensional; often many dimensions have to be considered. If we innovate in a building's design to keep future costs down or increase future adaptability, what effect do we have not only on structural utility but on ongoing maintenance? A great design may cost less in the building phase but require expensive upkeep. Certain functions may be sustainable but impact the enjoyability of the environment or limit the building's potential uses.

It is therefore important to realize that in reality, trade-offs are not usually a simple "item A or B but not both" equation. They tend to be more complex: *If this, then not that, so then this other thing, which means maybe more or less of the original, plus something new that reduces the ability to do something else later on . . . maybe. If all these other variables stay consistent, which they won't.* (Possible throwing up of hands at this point.)

But we can't let ourselves get upset by the trade-offs we have to negotiate, because trade-offs provide us with variety. Think of it this way: if a building could have everything we wanted, optimized along all possible parameters so that nothing required sacrifice or compromise, then all buildings would be the same. Each building, by virtue of being everything to everyone, would be no different from the one beside it, which also had to make no trade-offs.

It's trade-offs that give us difference, including cityscapes with tall skyscrapers made of steel and glass next to stone churches and three-story brick buildings. They are what give us log cabins and wrap-around porches and treehouses and the odd geodesic dome. Each building is designed to meet the needs of people who have a unique perspective on what trade-offs they are willing to make in environments with local parameters that influence what those trade-offs look like.

Using trade-offs as a model shows us that they can operate on many variables simultaneously, and it is impossible to get away from them. But thinking about trade-offs also shows that there is a reason to embrace them, for they are responsible for a lot of the variety in our world.

> Abundance does not just allow us to buy more goods. It affords us the luxury of packing poorly, the luxury of not having to think, as well as the luxury of not minding mistakes.
>
> —SENDHIL MULLAINATHAN AND ELDAR SHAFIR[8]

No Paths without Challenges

True trade-offs cannot be mitigated by careful planning. They are factors where no amount of wheeling and dealing will let you have both. "For something to be called a trade-off, we should have evidence that it is at least difficult, if not impossible, to increase one thing without decreasing another."[9] You increase your donut consumption, you decrease your cholesterol health. The trade-off for the pleasure you get from donuts is less healthy cholesterol levels. Going for improved cholesterol means trading off the satisfaction and enjoyment of eating a donut. If you love eating donuts, trade-offs with your health must be navigated. You cannot have both good cholesterol and a serious donut habit.

When it comes to situations with trade-offs that must be considered, chosen, and lived with, one that has impacted humans since the dawn of the species is migration. Ever since the first *Homo sapiens* decided to leave the Great Rift Valley, every year, some human, somewhere, calculates the trade-offs involved in leaving home and trying to make a life somewhere new.

Although the particulars change and are unique in every circumstance, deciding whether to migrate involves trying to figure out the trade-offs between staying and going. What are we giving up, and what are we gaining? Do we think the net gain will be worth it? Because we are looking at migration through the lens of trade-offs, here we are not going to examine forced migration but rather those situations that involve some choice on the part of the people doing the migrating.

Given that humans have been moving around forever, obviously sometimes there is a net gain to moving. Harder to find are statistics regarding how many people consider emigrating but don't, but we can assume there are just as many of those. Why? Because migration is rarely, if ever, a win on every front. Something is always lost in the leaving, whether it's a physical home, career status, or people who share your memories. Immigrants always have to sacrifice something when they choose to move. What's really incredible is how often those sacrifices are deemed worth it.

Why do people immigrate? There are, of course, many different, complex reasons, but at the core there is the idea that something "there" is better than what's "here." In the anthology *Alien Nation*, Dr. Hisla Bates, who left Guyana for the United States when she was six, says, "I think that's the story of most immigrants—they leave their home and places they love, they leave family members behind, and that doesn't make sense to a lot of people. They do it because they want a better future for their children and grandchildren."[10]

For most migrants, it's not that everything they leave behind is terrible, nor that everything they're going toward is great. The potential of the new place simply outweighs the value of what they're leaving behind. It's important to acknowledge that the trade-offs involved don't have objective value, so another person in the same position might make a different choice. Such is the nature of trade-offs.

Sometimes, the choice for migrants is between two dismal circumstances. Writing about German migrant workers with the Dutch East India Company in the seventeenth and eighteenth centuries, the authors of *The Age of Migration* write, "The mortality of these migrant workers through shipwreck, warfare, and tropical illness was very high, but service in the colonies was often the only chance to escape from poverty."[11] Leaving for economic reasons is a common migration story, but people also migrate to escape violence, persecution, or situations in which there is no hope for autonomy and freedom.

No matter what the situation we are leaving may be, there are usually very few guarantees in the place we are going. The life we are living contains known quantities. The life we embark on is full of unknowns, suppositions, desires, and hopes. The new place might be a lot better, worse, or only slightly improved. Is marginal improvement in terms of safety or income worth being alone and isolated, away from family and everything that is familiar? The uncertainty of the possible payoff is what makes the trade-offs of migration hard to evaluate.

Not all migration is permanent. Some people migrate with the intention of making enough money to eventually return home and improve their situation there. Other motivations for migration could be education, marriage, or adventure. In terms of permanent relocation, family reunion is a huge factor in why many people choose to migrate.

As varied as their reasons for migration are, most migrants know that it's unlikely to be all sunshine and rainbows in the new place. There are often many challenges, ranging from learning a new language to making new friends. In addition, "many migrants discover that they can only enter the labor market at the bottom, and that it is hard to move up the ladder later."[12] There are many engineers driving taxis in New York and many doctors working delivery jobs in Toronto.

Migrant experiences in different countries are by no means

standard, and part of the decision of migrating is carefully considering which country might be the best choice. Do you know people
there? How hard is it to get citizenship? What programs does the
country have for newcomers that may offer the best chance of success? There are trade-offs that must be considered within the choice
of where to migrate to. For example, "A research project carried
out in six European countries emphasized the varying experience
of migrants. They had lower unemployment levels but less qualified jobs in Southern European countries, while they tended to
have more qualified jobs but a higher risk of unemployment in
Northwestern Europe."[13]

Deciding whether to migrate, to pick up and move somewhere
new, is an emotional calculation. Leaving family, or considering
professional opportunities for our children—these are personal
evaluations that pull in our fears and hopes. The emotional content
of many of the factors migrants consider means that the optimal
trade-off is neither obvious to outsiders nor the same for everyone.
Journalist Mazin Sidahmed, whose family fled Sudan when he was
eighteen months old, says of immigrating, "In a search for prosperity, we sacrificed stability. Moving from city to city, from country
to country building resilience but leaving pieces of ourselves behind."[14]

Writer Kay Iguh, a native of Nigeria who immigrated to the
United States, explains that for an immigrant, "in building a future, you dismantle a past."[15] Many migrants speak of never quite
feeling at home in their new countries but also not quite fitting in
when they return to their country of origin, even if just for a visit.
One of the trade-offs, then, is potentially never feeling a sense of
complete belonging again.

Outcomes of migration for immigrants are just as varied as their reasons for migrating. Some integrate well into their new country, finding a stable income and other measures of success. Others don't find work easily and struggle to survive. Some decide the trade-offs aren't worth it and go home. Others end up being deported.

Migration remains a popular choice globally. Every year, millions of people make thoughtful calculations regarding the trade-offs involved and decide to move. The point of looking at migration through the lens of trade-offs is to demonstrate that trade-offs cannot always be resolved with more time or more money, nor are they all always known in advance. There are many situations in life in which trade-offs exist and will impact your outcomes—when you can't have your cake and eat it too.

Conclusion

Life is full of trade-offs. Every choice has a cost. When you say yes to one thing, you say no to others. This is how the world works. It's like gravity. You can't escape it.

Opportunity cost is what you give up when you make a choice. It's the thing you can't have because you picked something else. Say you have a free evening. You can work on your startup or go to a movie. If you work, you miss the fun. If you go to the movie, you miss the chance to make progress.

Every choice has an opportunity cost because every time you say yes to something, you're implicitly saying no to a bunch of other things. You need to know your opportunity costs. This helps you make good trade-offs.

A trade-off is giving up one thing in order to get something else. It's choosing between options. Each has good and bad points.

Trade-offs are about priorities. When you make something, you face trade-offs. If you want it fast, you might lose some features. If you want it cheap, you might use lower-quality materials.

In life, we face trade-offs all the time. Do you take the high-paying job with long hours? Or the low-paying one with more free time? Do you spend money now or save for later?

Making good trade-offs is about weighing the opportunity costs and benefits of each option and choosing the one that aligns best with your goals and values. It's not always easy, but being conscious of the trade-offs you're making can help you make better decisions.

Wisdom is anticipating the consequences of your choices. In life and business, success is about making good trade-offs. It's not about having it all. It's about having what matters most. We all value different things. That's what makes life rich.

Opportunity cost is what you give up when you make a choice; trade-offs are the balancing acts you perform when deciding between competing options. They're two sides of the same coin—whenever you make a trade-off, you're incurring an opportunity cost for the option you didn't choose. The key in both cases is to be thoughtful and intentional about your choices.

Specialization

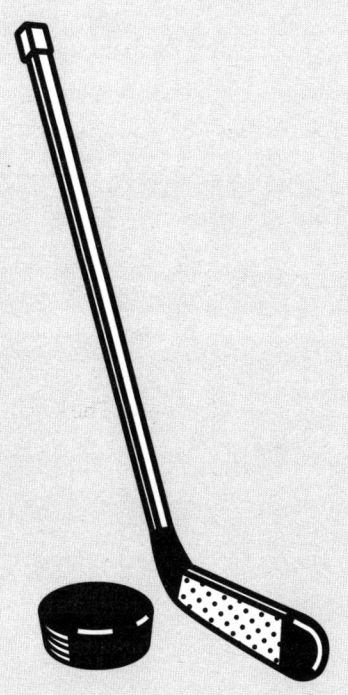

Focus is key.

Warren and I avoid doing anything that someone else at Berkshire can do better.

—CHARLIE MUNGER[1]

I f you try to do everything, it's hard to do anything well.

As economies develop, people's livelihoods become increasingly specialized. Greater division of labor tends to lead to increased efficiency and lower costs.

"Specialization" is when a person, group, or nation focuses on producing a particular good or service, intending to be able to do it in less time, at a higher quality, and/or at a lower cost. For an individual, it's microeconomic specialization; for a nation, it's macroeconomic specialization. Specialization in one thing involves a trade-off because it means not specializing in something else.

"What do you want to do when you grow up?" is a common question people ask children. Whatever the answer, it's expected to be something specific—not "whatever mixture of skills I need to survive." The reason for choosing a specific job is that specializing in our careers is the norm. Most people choose a particular area to work in and study or train accordingly; then, they get steadily better at that work over time, building up resources like contacts or respect within a field.

Adam Smith famously summarized the benefits of the division of labor in *The Wealth of Nations* when he described a pin factory. A single, untrained worker could never manage to make even twenty pins a day and would be more likely to complete just one. But the pin factory's productivity increases by several orders of magnitude if several workers each take on one part of the process. Then, ten workers can make 48,000 pins a day. One worker draws out the metal wire, another makes it straight, another cuts it into lengths, and so on. No one involved needs much training or skill. And the more the labor is divided up, the greater the overall production per person. Smith also believed that there is a direct correlation between how economically developed a country is and how specialized the typical job within it is, with this relationship being a feedback loop, both a cause and an effect.[2]

How many of the objects you touch on an average day did you make yourself? There's a good chance the answer is zero—or at best just a few. Yet this is a recent development in human history. Most of the people to have ever lived made most of their possessions themselves, or owned things that were made by people they knew personally. And if you've ever learned how to make yourself a dress or a table or a wooden spoon, you can appreciate the sheer range of skills required for each item.

It's worth noting that specialization, as in Smith's pin factory, has been criticized as creating work that is boring and mind-numbing. Specialization also creates a sense of alienation from the products of our labor, because we don't see them consumed, and from the labor of others, because we don't see them produce what we consume. So there is a balance between the benefits we receive from being able to specialize (more variety and cheaper goods) and the sometimes unappealing conditions that extreme specialization produces. There is no doubt, however, that on balance, specialization has maximized the effectiveness of the resources we have and was a critical component of the significant, though uneven, rise in global living standards over the last two hundred years.

Specialization goes hand in hand with trade; the two create a feedback loop. Eric D. Beinhocker writes that "one of the great benefits of trade is that it enables specialization"[3]—you can't specialize if you can't trade for the other things you need but don't produce. Specialization, in turn, reinforces trade: once you specialize, you can produce goods that you don't need for yourself, making them available for trade.

We must remember, however, that solving problems often leads to new ones. One of the aspects of increased specialization that must be managed is that it leads to increased coordination costs and requires ever more effort to avoid cascading failures. In his book *Human Capital*, economist Gary S. Becker states, "The cost of coordinating a group of complementary specialized workers grows as the number of specialists increases."[4] It's much easier to organize the work and exchange of a small group in, say, a kitchen—where the chef, sous-chef, pastry chef, line cook, and dishwasher can all figure out how to adjust their actions to complement the others' roles—than to map out the most effective intersections in a multinational organization.

The increased interdependence created by specialization is both a benefit—it encourages cooperation—and a cost, as it results in vulnerability. The more you need others to do what you can't do yourself, the more you need to produce something yourself that others need. But the problem is obvious: your inability to produce everything you need creates a dependency. If your needs stop being produced by others, you're in trouble. At the extreme of this problem come cascading failures: you can't meet your needs, so you stop producing your specialization. Those who rely on you are thus themselves jeopardized. If a society has too many gaps, in terms of requirements that can't be produced, the result is widespread instability.

Specialization also requires trust. The more specialized people's jobs become, the more specialists are required to bridge communication gaps. When trust isn't possible, because people don't personally know one another, specialization also requires legal frameworks and enforcement mechanisms.

Overspecialization leads to poor nonsense detection. The more narrow our own focus is, the harder it can be to know if someone else is being honest or even knows what they're talking about. Overspecialization can also lead people to put up barriers to protect their specialization, such as by requiring expensive licenses to practice the skill. Indeed, specialists may be incentivized to exaggerate how distinct their knowledge is in order to protect their advantage.

Consequently, the mental model of specialization illustrates the value of cooperation. We're usually better off doing what we do best and working with someone else for the rest. We just have to be mindful of the vulnerabilities that specialization creates and not put ourselves in a position where we can't adapt if we need to.

> The more complicated the whole structure becomes, the more important it is that each element fits in its appropriate place.
>
> —FRIEDRICH A. HAYEK[5]

Computers to Programmers

There is a path-dependent element to specialization: if and how you adapt to changing circumstances depends a lot on the skills and abilities you had before the changes. If world events lead to a demand for a new kind of medical specialty, chances are the people developing that specialization will already have experience in the medical field. It's less likely that your new medical specialist will have previously worked as a lawyer.

One of the most interesting things about specialization is that although we can reasonably predict it is going to occur, as new technologies develop and new events impact our environment, we don't know exactly where those lines of specialization are going to be drawn.

If we think back to Adam Smith's pin factory, it seems fairly easy now to identify various needed job specialties. But that's because we know how pins are made, and we also know the general components a business needs to operate and be successful. We can imagine there is someone to punch a hole in the metal and someone to scoop a set amount of pins into a box. We also acknowledge there is likely a sales team to find customers for the pins, and someone in accounting to track the money coming in and money going out.

But on the front end of development, when a technology is both new and disruptive, it's not easy to see how specializations will fall out. These unknowns create opportunities—and the people who get there first can have a lot of impact, as the skills and knowledge they have end up shaping development.

Using specialization as a model can show you how it can grow from the bottom up. Instead of thinking of specialization as top-down—wherein you identify in advance the roles you need—you can use the model to remain flexible. It can show us how to take advantage of the opportunities that present themselves when people address new problems using previous experiences, making nonobvious connections to spur development.

In the 1940s, women were employed in significant numbers in

many countries to do mathematical calculations. They worked for government agencies, universities, and in support of the war effort as computers. They computed data.

During World War II, significant advancements were made in the engineering of hardware that could process information faster than humans. One of these machines was ENIAC—the Electronic Numerical Integrator and Computer—located at the University of Pennsylvania's Moore School of Electrical Engineering. It was a giant machine made up of about 18,000 vacuum tubes, each with switches to communicate electrical pulses and signals. When a new problem came in for the computer to crunch through, the links between the tubes and switches had to be adjusted.[6]

Nowadays, most of us are familiar with the distinction between hardware and software, the difference between constructing the machine and programming the code that runs on it. But when these first computers came on the scene, this distinction wasn't so obvious. In her book *Broad Band,* Claire L. Evans explains, "The distinction between hardware and software at that time was blurry, even nonexistent: every calculation called for switches to be flipped, cables to be patched."[7]

The men who designed and built the ENIAC, John Mauchly and J. Presper Eckert Jr., were brilliant at constructing hardware. But once the ENIAC was up and running, the day-to-day programming, which included adjusting the connections based on the problem sets to be solved, fell to a team of women. "Six women handled the time-consuming and intellectually demanding job of readying mathematical problems for the computer, plugging them in, the executing, debugging, and executing again to achieve the final results." Called "the ENIAC Six," Kathleen McNulty, Betty Jean Jennings, Elizabeth "Betty" Snyder, Marlyn Wescoff, Frances Bilas, and Ruth Lichterman had all worked as computers at the

Moore School. It was their experience as human computers that gave them the opportunity to work on the new machine computers.[8]

It was, in a lot of ways, a good fit. Not only did the women possess the skills and experience to tackle the development of what was essentially computer programming, but because it was seen as an offshoot of work they already did, it was socially acceptable as well. "Nobody thought much of assigning women to this job," Evans writes. "It seemed only natural that the human computers should train their own replacements. Further, the ENIAC looked like a telephone switchboard, reinforcing the assumption that its 'operators' should be women."[9]

These women effectively became some of the first computer programmers in the world. It was not an easy task, partly because the concept itself was so new. "Programming, the six learned, would not be a desk job. The women would stand *inside* of the ENIAC to 'plug in' each problem, stringing the units together in sequences using hundreds of cables and some three thousand switches. There were no instructions to read, no courses to take."[10] So the women wrote the instructions and developed the courses for those who would come after.

Their work was part of the early efforts that led to the specialization of programming. When the machines were first built, no one knew that the skills to build them and the skills to instruct them were completely different and would lead to two specializations. Women were able to participate at the beginning due to their former employment as human computers, and their experiences influenced how programming would develop. Evans explains that many of the early female programmers saw the necessity of creating a programming language that would be accessible, one that people could learn and would be easy to use. Other early programmers— most notably Grace Hopper, another woman with a mathematics background—pushed for the development of standards in programming language. Hopper also coded the world's first compilers, instructions that let the machines do some data processing on their own.[11] Evans writes, "Hardware may be static, but software makes all the difference. And although it took some time to settle in, that truth came with a corollary: those who write the software make all the difference too."[12]

The story of the early female computer programmers is a valuable one to consider through the lens of specialization. Diving into some of the details, we can see first the path-dependent component that often characterizes much specialization: human computers, essentially working as data processors, were on the right path to apply their experience to the new world of machine computing. The work they did made them a logical fit to take on the operation of computers.

The experience they brought with them influenced how programming developed. The specialization did not come about overnight, and it would be years before programming was its own specialty, with required education. But that is one very useful insight about specialization: it's not always possible to know, at the outset of something new, how specializations will break out. Often how the lines are drawn has a lot to do with the past experiences of those working on the new problem set in the early years. Allowing for a more evolutionary-type process can take development to places impossible to imagine at the outset.

Comparative Advantage

> All competitive advantage is temporary. Some advantages last longer than others, but all sources of advantage have a finite shelf life.
>
> —ERIC D. BEINHOCKER[13]

The principle of comparative advantage, also known as the Ricardo principle, states that as long as one party in an exchange has a higher opportunity cost for producing something than the other, it makes sense for each to specialize and trade. This holds true even if one party is better at everything else. Economist David Ricardo first put the concept into words in the eighteenth century, and it remains a powerful argument for unrestricted international trade. In theory, the most efficient global economy would be one where every country specializes and produces the goods it is best at compared to everyone else.

Some economists have debated whether the principle of comparative advantage and associated free trade is really always that mutually beneficial for both parties. Raúl Prebisch argued that trade between two countries with disparate wealth can actually limit growth for the poorer nation and reinforce the wealth of the richer nation. The poor country becomes even poorer if it specializes, because poor countries usually export primary products, like food, and wealthy countries usually export secondary products, like manufactured goods.

Often, specialization is a consequence of the resources

available in a particular country. That country can focus on producing goods related to its resources, then sell them to the rest of the world. Countries with an abundance of valuable natural resources can get locked into a cycle of selling those resources in their unprocessed form to other nations, which then process them and resell at a high markup.

Why does trading in these circumstances reinforce income disparity between the two countries? Niall Kishtainy summarizes Prebisch's reasoning:

> When the economy of a poor country grows, its demand for the cars that it imports from rich countries rises. But when a rich country grows, the country's demand for the sugar that it imports from poor countries rises much more slowly. In consequence, the price of cars rises faster than the price of sugar: the poor country's "terms of trade" worsen.[14]

The solution proposed is for the poorer country to diversify, protecting homegrown industries as they develop while creating incentives to make sure that development will allow them to compete internationally—much as the United States did early in its nationhood, and countries like Japan and South Korea did in the latter half of the twentieth century.

Nancy Folbre also cautions readers when taking the thought experiment of comparative advantage and applying it in the real world. Even in Ricardo's time, the reality of trade rarely fit the theory. She writes of Ricardo:

While his reasoning was correct, it was incomplete. All else equal, free trade could make everyone better off. But little else was equal. Countries could use their military power to force trade on their own terms, as the British did in India—where they virtually prohibited handloom weaving, and in China—where they sent their battleships to expand the opium trade.[15]

Comparative advantage suggests that specialization and free trade can offer real advantages, because no one country can be good at everything forever. But it really only works in terms of creating mutual prosperity when the advantages aren't exploited.

Modern expertise comes partly at the expense of narrowness, and of ignorance about what other people do.

—GARY S. BECKER[16]

The Best Teams

Specialization requires trust. You pursue your specialization each day because you trust that others are pursuing theirs. When you need something that you can't produce on your own, you trust that it will be there, available to you to trade for.

Sports teams function the same way. Everyone on the team is free to specialize because they know that everyone else on the team, in pursuing their own specialties, is covering all the elements needed to perform.

On professional hockey teams, there are multiple layers of specialization. First, players have different roles on the team; at a macro level, these are forwards, defense, and goalie. But not all forwards are the same; neither are defensive players. They all have different skills, capabilities, and strengths that impact the precise role they are expected to play. Depending on elements such as which way they shoot the puck, how big they are, and with whom they have chemistry, players might be assigned to play right wing or left defense on a particular line.

There is also specialization that occurs on the ice. This specialization is more fluid, because it reacts to the real-time events happening in the game. It's not very useful to have five players chasing after the puck. Instead, one player will go after the puck, and the other four players on the team will try to anticipate the best position to be in for what comes next. To do that—to know where you should best go based on where it's best for your teammates to be going based on their skills and strengths, and knowing they have the same expectation of you—requires an incredible amount of trust.

The National Hockey League championship trophy is called the

Stanley Cup. The oldest North American sports trophy, the cup is awarded to the team that wins a best-of-seven series, after four rounds of playoffs. Wayne Gretzky, one of the best to ever play ice hockey, says, "If you ask anybody who's won the Stanley Cup, he will tell you it's the ultimate team accomplishment. Everybody has to participate.... Every guy on the team has to play his heart out to win."[17] One or two superstars isn't going to win a team a Stanley Cup. There's too much going on in a game of hockey for it to come down to the performance of one player.

Some people might say that the goalie is the one player whose individual performance can make or break a game or playoff series. But this isn't true. Hockey requires both defense and offense; even if your goalie has an amazing night and stops every shot, someone on your team has to score in order for your team to win. Plus, good hockey from your team means fewer shots on goal by the other team. The chances of a win increase when the number of shots you ask the goalie to stop decreases.

Mark Messier, another hall of fame hockey player, has said, "Every player on your team, man for man, is valuable." Gretzky agrees: "From your top player to your bottom player, all have to be pulling together."[18]

In *99: Stories of the Game*, Gretzky tells the story of the winning goal in the 1987 Canada Cup, in which the Canadians were playing the Russians. Mario Lemieux scored the winning goal off a Gretzky pass. But Gretzky talks about what else was happening on the ice to make that goal possible: "It wasn't so much what Mario and I did. Had Larry [Murphy] not gone to the net and had Dale [Hawerchuk] not taken the backchecker out, we may never have scored."[19] Figuring out how to win means figuring out where you should be on the ice—and it's not always in front of the net, trying to score. It's more about what you can do to give your team the best chance of scoring. And that's about knowing your role and what your teammates expect of you.

In a hockey game, trust is paramount, because there isn't time on the ice to hash out what everyone should be doing. "In hockey," Gretzky explains, "there is so much going on, so fast, that even the most skilled player is going on instinct."[20] To build the instinct needed to execute well, specialization is required. You focus on the elements required of you. If you're on defense, you clear the puck out of your zone, knowing that one of your forwards will be in position to receive it. If you're a center, you build chemistry with your linemates to increase your scoring chances and you don't worry about stopping the puck from going in the net. You focus on executing your specialization flawlessly and trust that everyone else on your team is doing the same.

To be really successful, that trust has to be organization wide. "If you consider the most successful organization in every team sport . . . there's a defined culture that runs through every part of them. Trust, teamwork, accountability, sacrifice. They put in place the pieces that follow the culture and they live within it."[21] In hockey, trust on the ice is reflective of trust off the ice. The players trust one another because they trust the system they are playing in.

Hayley Wickenheiser, five-time Olympic medalist and member of the Hockey Hall of Fame, explains that it's ineffective to become an expert in every aspect of the game, because you have to get really great at what you're meant to do. That means sacrificing expertise in the things everyone else does. "When I was playing," she says, "I focused on offense. I knew what my responsibilities were in the defensive zone, but I didn't focus on what was required of goalies and defensemen."[22]

Most of us work in teams, and most of us specialize. Letting go of trying to be perfect at everything is how we really take advantage of the power of specialization. Wickenheiser also explains the value of knowing how you can best contribute when she talks about her endeavors off the ice. In speaking about her work in business, she says, "I am careful to hire people smarter than me who have expertise that I don't, and I trust them to do the work—the same way I trusted the defense to protect our zone."[23] Succeeding as a team, in hockey or otherwise, means being great at your specialization and trusting the other team members to be great at theirs.

That's one thing that every good team has in common—everyone has a role.

—WAYNE GRETZKY[24]

Conclusion

Specialization is a trade-off: pursuing one course means not pursuing another. It's narrowing your focus to broaden your impact. In a world of infinite knowledge and finite time, specialization is the key to unlocking mastery. It's about going deep, not wide.

Specialization has risks. If the world changes, what was once a valuable specialty can become obsolete. And yet, we need specialists. You wouldn't want a generalist doing your brain surgery or a root canal.

Here's the catch: the more you specialize, the more you see how much other fields can teach you. The most exciting finds often happen at the edges between areas of knowledge. The trick is to specialize without getting stuck. To go deep, but also reach out.

In the end, specialization is about where you spend your time and effort. It's how you stand out. It's choosing to be great at one thing instead of okay at many.

Interdependence

Mutual reliance, intertwined fates.

It is not the similarity or dissimilarity of individuals that constitutes a group, but interdependence of fate.

—KURT LEWIN[1]

Specialization leads to interdependence. The two models are closely related, enough insight to consider them separately. The more specialized an individual, company, nation, or other group is, the more reliant it must be on other specialists to meet its needs. We can't do everything on our own. We are all dependent on one another, in webs of various sizes and complexity. It's like playing a game where everyone needs one another to win. These interdependencies create both opportunities and challenges.

As economies become more specialized, complex networks form among economic agents. In a famous 1958 essay, "I, Pencil," Leonard E. Read encapsulated the astonishing interdependence of the world by positing that no one on earth knows how to make a pencil from start to finish.[2] Even such a simple device, Read wrote, involves numerous specialists: loggers to harvest the wood, workers in a sawmill to cut it, designers of machines used to work the wood, and so on.

Read's essay was intended to illustrate the concept of economic interdependence: how individuals, companies, and nations all become dependent on one another, forming complex trade networks. Global economic interdependence is considered beneficial for giving people more opportunities, disincentivizing war, and improving standards of living by reducing the cost of goods and services. If we all had to produce the ingredients to make a chicken sandwich ourselves, few people would be eating them. If we value our ability to buy chicken and buns, we will stay on friendly terms with at least two producers of each. The jobs we create in bringing together dozens of specialties to make and sell a chicken sandwich increase both the diversity of jobs available and the places in which people can do them.

There are a couple of downsides to economic interdependence. The first is that it can lead to dependencies that can be manipulated. If a country is dependent on another country for something it needs, it may be forced to tolerate bad behavior, not to intervene in the other country's affairs, and to bow to demands to keep the relationship going.

In addition, if one part of a supply chain breaks down (such as if one country faces a natural disaster or war), it can be difficult or impossible to find alternatives. This means that catastrophes now have more of a global impact. When the Chūetsu offshore earthquake struck Japan on July 16, 2007, Riken Corporation, an automobile parts manufacturer, suffered serious damage and briefly shut down production. Riken held a very large market share in the production of piston rings, which are necessary for the production of cars. Since most Japanese auto manufacturers use just-in-time inventory (meaning they carry no additional stock on hand), they were dependent on Riken's consistent production. When Riken stopped sending piston rings, they also had to shut car production down.

When everything works, interdependence works well. When things don't go as planned, however, interdependence shuts everything down. When you're dependent on it, the failure of even the smallest part can shut down an entire industry.

Interdependence can also lead to cascading effects. In the 1950s, Kenneth Arrow and Gérard Debreu looked at the far-reaching and nonobvious ripples that interdependence can produce in an economy.[3] For example, Arrow traced some of the cascading effects when new oil fields were discovered in the 1930s. First, oil prices went down all over, and because none of us collect and refine our own oil, there was widespread reaction to the windfall our dependency created. Homes started to heat with oil instead of coal. Great; it's cheaper! But then employment in coal mines fell, and the price of steel went up as because coal became more expensive. We drove our cars more. Railway usage declined. Highways grew. Towns caught in the wrong location or dependent on the wrong resource stagnated or died out, while other towns boomed. New oil produced effects that cascaded far outside the oil industry.

Another note on interdependence is that we can only appreciate the ripple effects our actions might create if we're honest about where we are truly dependent. Historically, economics has only focused on goods and services that are exchanged for money. The field has not been great about acknowledging, for example, how the whole economic system is dependent on the unpaid labor performed in the home, mostly by women. Although that is starting to change, the legacy of early economists such as Alfred Marshall, who argued against counting work in the home as part of the economic equation of a country, means that some dependencies are still overlooked.

The mental model of interdependence teaches us that problems can be enmeshed in a way that prevents them from being solved separately. It also demonstrates that being mindful about our interdependencies can reveal to us how to leverage them for mutual benefit.

Coordination Failures

In game theory, a coordination game is one where players get the best possible payoff by all doing the same thing. If one player chooses a different strategy, they get a diminished payoff, and the other player usually gets an increased payoff.

When all players are carrying out a strategy from which they have no incentive to deviate, this is called the Nash equilibrium: given the strategy chosen by the other player(s), no player could improve their payoff by changing their strategy. However, a game can have multiple Nash equilibria with different payoffs. In real-world terms, this means there are multiple different choices everyone could make, some better than others, but all only working if they are unanimous. If everyone is already making the same suboptimal choice, it can be difficult to change anything.

Many of the major problems around us are coordination failures. They are solvable only if everyone can agree to do the same thing at the same time. Faced with multiple Nash equilibria, we do not necessarily choose the best one overall. We choose what makes sense given the existing incentives, which often discourage us from challenging the status quo. It often makes most sense to do what everyone else is doing, whether that's driving on the left side of the road, wearing a suit to a job interview, or keeping your country's nuclear arsenal stocked up.

Building Interdependency
for Group Cohesion

Interdependence can be a good thing. One theory is that interdependence can be advantageous because it creates a need to remain on good terms, creating a more integrated and peaceful world. If your fortunes are tied up in the fortunes of everyone else, why bother fighting? Hurting you will ultimately result in hurting myself. Interdependence creates incentives for us to work together to pursue actions of mutual benefit.

In her book *The Old Way*, Elizabeth Marshall Thomas details the lives of the Ju/wa people in the Nyae Nyae area of Africa, now straddling the border of Botswana and Namibia. In the 1950s, Thomas and her family lived with and chronicled the lives of a group of Ju/wa people, some of the last humans on earth who maintained an ancient hunter-gatherer lifestyle.

Thomas makes it clear that among the Ju/wa, group cohesion was critical for survival. It was not an environment where anyone could go it alone—and, realistically, that's true of all human environments. We *need* one another. Even someone living off the grid in a forest is still dependent on other people to make the supplies they buy.

For the Ju/wa, interdependence was a survival tool. The more they were connected with one another, the more they shared resources with one another. Resources in that part of Africa, like water and meat, could be hard to come by. Being able to rely on receiving resources from a variety of people within the larger group was often the difference between life and death. Thomas describes the Ju/wa people as having a fear of marginalization and exclusion, because being all alone suggested both a deathlike state and a lack of support in times of trouble.

Some bonds of interdependence are natural, such as those commonly found between parents and children. Close kin relationships may have to be nurtured but often have a natural foundation as well. But developing connections outside the immediate family group isn't as automatic. One of the ways the Ju/wa people created and nurtured these connections was through sharing. "Sharing," Thomas says, "was perhaps the most important element in the social fabric. Fear that others would not share was the constant preoccupation of many people." Sharing was critical to survival, not because it increased access to resources but because it reduced anxiety and created a social network. In the challenging environment of the Kalahari Desert, "the goodwill of the group was one's most valuable asset."[4]

One of the sharing mechanisms Thomas describes is that of *xaro*, the practice of giving gifts. Xaro was practiced widely, and gifts would travel hundreds of kilometers as they passed from hand to hand. Rules included the fact that you could never refuse a gift, and that receiving one obligated you to make a gift in return. Critical to the system was that the reciprocation was spread out, so it was clear the gift was not meant to be a trade and that it came from the heart.

Thomas explains, "Almost every object in Nyae Nyae was subject to xaro, and . . . almost every person had a set of partners with whom he or she exchanged gifts. Thus xaro was one of the most powerful bonds within the social fabric, because a xaro partnership could last for life."[5]

The dispersed populations of groups of Ju/wa people meant that xaro was a significant time investment, far more involved than dropping a cake off at your neighbor's. "The average man or woman had fifteen xaro partners . . . and spent three or four months a year visiting these partners."[6] Thus, xaro was an investment of time and energy in a life in which resources could sometimes be limited. But investing in xaro, versus, say, investing in more gathering of nuts, was valuable over a longer time horizon. If those nuts were ever not available to you at all, your xaro partners, primed by years of giving, would gladly step in and help you out.

Thus, xaro provided widespread benefits on multiple fronts. As Thomas explains, it increased the resources available to each person, it was a method of transmitting information, it gave people social options so they weren't confined to socializing with the same people all the time, and it "spread happiness and decreased jealousy and ill will."[7]

Xaro ensured that no person needed to suffer from loneliness and isolation. By increasing unity and creating and maintaining bonds, "xaro strengthened the social fabric."[8]

The Ju/wa had another practice that increased their interdependence. Hunting was an integral and well-respected part of Ju/wasi life. The meat it provided was tasty, nutritious, and life-giving. Hunting itself was prestigious, and a man's ability to marry was directly tied to his ability to hunt. Thus, hunting could have easily become a source of exploitable power, as not everyone was able to hunt big game.

The Ju/wa people developed a system to distribute the power and prestige that came with hunting. Thomas says, "When dividing big game, the hunter did not distribute the meat. That role belonged to the person who provided the arrow that actually killed the antelope." She further explains, "By the Ju/wa system, anyone could own an arrow or arrows (although only the hunters used them)." This practice meant that anyone "who had little chance of ever being much of a hunter could give an arrow to a hunter and become the distributor of important meat."[9] The practice of providing arrows to hunters was widespread.

Why do this? Why would a hunter do all the work, without being given the power of sharing meat? Similar to xaro, this system of interdependency strengthened the social fabric by minimizing opportunity for resentment and conflict. Thomas says, "Without the formal system of sharing, the same people, the strongest people, would always be distributors, and over time, unfairness would emerge."[10] That unfairness could undermine the stability of the whole society.

This story of the practices of the Ju/wa people provides a different way of using interdependence as a model. Frequently, we think of interdependence as a by-product of specialization, and it often is. But the story of the Ju/wa shows that sometimes, interdependence can be used deliberately to promote benefits—in this case, increased social cohesion.

Conclusion

Interdependence is the web that ties us all together. It's the recognition that no person, no company, no country is an island. We're all connected, all reliant on one another in countless ways, big and small. Interdependence is the reality that underlies the illusion of self-sufficiency. No one is entirely self-made.

Interdependence can be both a vulnerability and a strength. When we recognize our interdependencies, we can leverage them for mutual benefit. We can form alliances, partnerships, ecosystems. We can create value that no single entity could create alone. Interdependence is the foundation of synergy, the alchemy of the whole being greater than the sum of its parts. On the other hand, if we are dependent on others for something critical, it can leave us exposed if they fail to deliver. It's easy to be a good partner when things are going well. But you want to be careful upon whom you are dependent in a crisis.

Interdependence isn't just a macro concept. It's deeply personal. We're all interdependent with our families, our friends, our communities. We rely on one another for support, for love, for meaning. Interdependence is the fabric of our social lives.

Efficiency

Maximum output, minimum waste.

Markets weed out inefficient processes, but only when no one has sufficient power to manipulate them.

—HA-JOON CHANG[1]

Efficiency is the optimal path toward achieving your end. In a video game, if your goal was to get the maximum points possible, efficiency would be earning those points in the least time, so nothing was wasted.

In economics, "efficiency" refers to how well resources are distributed. Economic theory suggests an economy is fully efficient if there is no way to reallocate resources without any loss of benefit. If we can make one person better off without hurting anyone, then the existing market is not efficient. The greater the gap between perfect efficiency and reality, the less well we consider an economy to function. When a good or service is inefficiently allocated, economists call it a "market failure."

Sometimes called Pareto efficiency (in a nod to Vilfredo Pareto, who first conceptualized this type of market efficiency), this conception of efficiency rests on the idea that there should be no wasted resources in an economy.[2] Wasted resources hurt everyone: they drive up prices for consumers (because businesses have to make more per transaction to compensate for the goods that don't get sold) and costs for producers (because they spend money making products that no one buys).

Within a hypothetical efficient economy, companies earn the

highest possible revenue at the lowest possible cost. Consumers receive the greatest possible quality in what they demand at the lowest possible cost—the cost closest to what they are willing to pay. Whoever wants a good most gets it. All needs get met.

Through the interplay of supply and demand, the goal of a market economy is for suppliers and consumers to reach a point that is desirable for everyone, where all consumers have the best possible living standards and all firms are as profitable as possible. Realistically, this is an impossible state for any economy to achieve or maintain. Efficiency is more often a question of degrees.

It's important to note that efficiency is not a moral judgment, as there are many different distributions that would qualify an economy as Pareto efficient. In an efficient economy, not all people have everything they want or have perfect lives, nor are all firms infinitely profitable. Efficient economies may have a majority of their resources allocated to a small percentage of people. Pareto efficiency says nothing about fairness or equity—it is a theoretical aim for an idealized market scenario.

Maintaining efficiency is inherently tricky. Again, if we were to conduct a thought experiment to imagine a simple market where Pareto efficiency is possible, it would do no good to confine our experiment to a world that doesn't change, because such a world doesn't exist. So, in our little efficient market, we can imagine a severe drought that destroys all the apple trees. I was perfectly happy with my access to apples before the drought, but now there aren't any. I need fruit, so where do I get it? If I take fruit from you, you're going to be unhappy, so I need to look for a market that has a surplus right now, maybe of oranges. But what if I don't like oranges? Can we all make adjustments in our fruit consumption to get back to Pareto efficiency?

As this quick thought experiment demonstrates, efficiency is not a static state that, once achieved, can be perpetuated forever. The world is dynamic, and adjustments have to be made. If we want to maintain an efficient state that we've stumbled across, it's going to take some work—and it will still end eventually.

What hinders Pareto efficiency in an economy? Markets become more efficient through the spread of information, allowing people to make better decisions about what to demand or supply. No single economic agent can know all of the information that might be relevant to their activities, but the more we amalgamate knowledge in markets, the more we can see by considering them as a whole. We have to be careful, when we think we're making something more efficient, that we're not removing valuable sources of information. Markets work because there is a plurality of views, which cancels out anomalous ones.

> The Internet moves us closer to "perfect information" on markets. Individuals and companies alike can buy and sell across borders and jurisdictions wherever they find the best match of supply and demand.
>
> —MILTON FRIEDMAN[3]

Another challenge to Pareto efficiency is the actual economic practices of humans. If we were to expand our thought experiment and imagine a nicely efficient economy, we might suppose that enough food is produced for people to eat what they need for a satisfying life. There are enough shoes and coats, and nothing goes to a landfill because it can't get sold. Everyone has the ability to purchase what they need, because a company somewhere has produced it. What we probably wouldn't imagine is an efficient economy that doesn't meet some people's needs because there's more profit to be made in filling other people's wants.

Humans don't just buy what is needed; we also purchase what we want. Sometimes we want to show off. The problem with this type of signaling, however, is that it can lead to a reinforcing feedback loop that challenges the drive for efficiency. Thorstein Veblen, he of the Veblen goods (see sidebar), called it "conspicuous consumption" and considered it a waste. He thought that it "diverts economic energy from the production of what people really need into what they can show off with."[4] An efficient market thus may also be one that meets the economic desires of the segment of consumers who are only about signaling value via the wealth they can display.

Economic efficiency, then, is about not only the binary of waste or no waste but also the range of options to achieve efficiency. As a model, it helps us consider where we can improve at getting people what they need as well as consider what is really involved in maintaining an environment where the actions of one group don't make anyone else worse off.

Veblen Goods and Giffen Goods

Veblen goods are items that are perceived as more desirable because they have a high price, even if it involves unnecessary markup. The higher price makes the item a signal of wealth and prestige, which people wish to show off. Thorstein Veblen discussed the concept of goods that typically have minimal practical use and little additional practical value compared to cheaper versions of the same thing in his book *The Theory of the Leisure Class*. He suggested that being expensive makes these goods a meaningful signal of wealth, because only a person with income to spare can access them. Because being wealthy is often considered something worth signaling, Veblen goods don't follow the usual model of supply and demand. Higher prices don't temper demand but instead drive it higher because people are paying for the signal more than the product.

Giffen goods (named after Scottish economist Sir Robert Giffen) are an overlapping, though distinct, concept. They include any product for which demand increases as the price does but that is not purchased as a status symbol. For example, if the price of a basic staple like bread increases in a region where poor people heavily rely on bread as a staple of their diet, they may end up purchasing more bread instead of less. While counterintuitive, this situation can happen because the rise in bread prices renders these consumers unable to afford other food with a higher nutritional content, so they buy more of the cheaper food to maintain their caloric intake. As a result, the demand for bread increases as the price increases, which is characteristic of a Giffen good. In economics, there are always exceptions to any rule—even seemingly inviolable ones like "demand always decreases as price increases."[5]

Keeping Everyone Happy

One of the basic ideas underpinning the concept of economic efficiency is that an efficient market exists when it is impossible to make someone better off without making someone else worse off. So, if you and I are the only two people in a market in which a hundred oranges are available, and I have sixty and you have thirty, that market isn't economically efficient. There are ten unsold oranges, and you can get more oranges without impacting me at all. However, if I have ninety-nine oranges and you have one, despite the lopsided distribution, the market is economically efficient. All oranges available for sale have been bought. You cannot improve your share without making me worse off.

Thus, economic efficiency doesn't necessarily equate with fair or even logical distribution. Having an efficient market might produce undesirable outcomes. So, what can we learn by using efficiency as a model?

The truth is, the world is full of situations that might not be the best for everyone, but there is no obvious way of fixing them without some people becoming worse off. Sometimes, that's okay. Really, it shouldn't be a hardship for me to give up ten oranges, going down to eighty-nine so you can have eleven. But sometimes it's desirable to maintain the status quo: by ensuring that no one loses, in a sense, everyone wins.

Using economic efficiency as a metaphorical lens, let's explore how maintaining the status quo in order to not make anyone worse off worked in the Mexican comic book industry from about 1940 to 1970.

The comic book industry in Mexico started in the late 1930s. By the mid-1940s, comic books were immensely popular, widely consumed and shared by Mexicans from a variety of backgrounds. Mexican comic books were very different from the typical American comic book. As Anne Rubenstein describes in *Bad Language, Naked Ladies, and Other Threats to the Nation,* comic books in Mexico did not focus on superheroes and were not primarily consumed by young men. The stories featured regular Mexicans, often in melodramatic situations, navigating the exaggerated complexities and challenges of a Mexican culture that was quickly modernizing. Each comic book contained multiple stories, some of which would go on for years. The books contained contests, letters from readers, some reproductions of American comics, and artwork. Comics were read by Mexicans of all ages and economic backgrounds.

However, not all Mexicans were comfortable with the content of the comics. Some people felt they were indecent and immoral, a corruptive influence on readers. Rubenstein explains that the development of comic books occurred against a backdrop of large changes taking place in Mexico, including movement from rural to urban areas, expanded education and literacy, increased work opportunities for women, and a modernizing communications and transportation infrastructure. As such, comics often contained stories that were at odds with perceived traditional experiences and values.

Not surprisingly, groups of protestors organized to demand the government exert more control over the content of comic books. Some, like the Catholic church, wanted an outright ban on comic books because of their immoral subject matter, especially concerning premarital sex. But there were also groups that wanted to ban comic books because they felt the books encouraged a breakdown of family values and were thus a threat to national unity. Still others resisted comic books because the borrowed American content was seen as a form of cultural imperialism that would negatively impact the development of Mexican culture.

In response, the Mexican government created a commission charged with overseeing and approving comic book content. However, the design of the commission was not an unqualified win for those who opposed comic books. Rubenstein explains that when designing the commission, "the government acted in an attempt to satisfy both supporters and opponents of mass media. . . . The new Commission had no clear powers of enforcement: it could levy fines, but not require that the judiciary collect them; it could ask that publishers submit to interviews, or even be arrested, but could not compel the police to make these arrests."[6]

The commission functioned as a government-sanctioned mediator with those who wanted to ban comic books or at least substantially change their content. The way the government designed and supported the commission through the years ensured that the efforts of protestors "were met with just enough success to prevent them from giving up, but not nearly enough to satisfy them."[7]

This commission was the principal tool the government used to make sure there were no outright losers in the debate on comic books. Publishers could still publish. The Mexican public could still consume comic books. And those who heavily opposed the comics had a place where they could go to vent their frustrations and have the assurance the problem was being dealt with.

The situation was a tricky one for the government to navigate. Some of the opponents of comic books were quite powerful, such as the Catholic church. And there were enough individuals disgusted by the content of comic books that to ignore the issue completely could have been destabilizing for the government.

On the other hand, comic book publishers were powerful economic agents in Mexico. They also often owned newspapers and were thus in a position to offer direct and visible support to politicians. Comic books were an important source of revenue for thousands of vendors, since they sold by the millions. There was clearly a large audience for them.

The commission became the government's way of maintaining a balance among all the opposing factions, ensuring that no one completely lost out. It is in this sense that the model of economic efficiency provides some insight: among all the interested parties in the comic book economy, it was impossible to make someone better off without making someone else worse off. To heavily censor or ban comic books would hurt publishers and vendors and have a negative economic impact on the state. But not to acknowledge the many people who opposed comic books' content by giving comic book publishers free and unsupervised rein would hurt them and, by extension, undermine the government by eroding their support for it.

In the end, more than thirty years of protest did relatively little to change the comic book industry. The commission, as a vehicle of the government, did an excellent job maintaining an environment where everyone could pursue their desired ends without making anyone else worse off.

Equalizing Spaces

Economic efficiency requires widespread access to and sharing of information. People can't make good economic decisions if they don't have a sense of what is happening in the economy, and economies are often so large that one person cannot have firsthand knowledge of everything going on. So, people share information. They talk about what they paid for their house. They talk about how the harvest went on their cousin's farm. They talk about how hard the blacksmith is working to keep up with demand. Gossip seems frivolous, but it enables more efficient decision making.

Considering the role information plays in economic efficiency is a great lens to use to evaluate how information sharing might impact efficiency in other situations. Common spaces, such as bars and coffeehouses, have played a large role in the economics and politics of societies, such as by enabling protest movements or organization for political change, because the sharing of information increases when there is an environment that facilitates exchange.

Why would places where people go to drink in their limited leisure time play such a role? Historically, taverns and similar establishments were the only places where people of varying social ranks would frequently mix and be free to express their opinions. Therefore, varying ideas would develop and spread in these spaces.

In his 1989 book *The Great Good Place*, Ray Oldenburg wrote about "third places," places that are neither home nor work where we can go to experience companionship and community. A third place is "neutral ground" and "a leveler" where "the main activity is conversation." No one is in charge, and "those gathered are on equal footing."[8] Third places produce a dynamism that is often absent in other places because of the diversity of the people gathered. In the other places where we spend time—including home, work, and places of worship—we are much more likely to be surrounded by people similar to ourselves. Third places offer the opportunity that comes with exposure to different lives and lifestyles.

Taverns and pubs were the original third places. Groups could congregate, strangers were welcome, and as long as you could pay for your drinks, you could stay as long as you wanted. There were no restrictions on who could talk to whom. "The common people enjoyed a freedom of speech and action in their drinking places that was denied to them elsewhere," Author Iain Gately explains, "and these institutions became the nucleus of a popular culture."[9]

Taverns were all over the colonies of the United States, with some places achieving a ratio of one drinking establishment for every twenty-five men. Given that many early settlers were Puritans, there was some unease about the ubiquity of drinking establishments, but "most colonists, however, continued to reconcile the use of drink . . . with the patterns of fellowship so vital to the conduct of everything from the transmission of news to the execution of business transactions."[10] Furthermore, what taverns could charge for a drink was often fixed, so establishments couldn't cater to narrow groups of patrons.

In early American society, the benefits of the information-sharing service the taverns provided outweighed the potential negatives of drinking itself. Information about what was happening, to whom, and where, helped the economy to run, culture to develop, and perhaps most critically, political change to incubate.

With very little limit on what information could be shared and which ideas explored, taverns opened up all sorts of possibilities. In the American colonies, taverns, as Steven Johnson argues, "were the seedbeds of the rebellion that would ultimately become the Revolutionary War."[11] Where else could people from all walks of life discuss and collaborate on such a sensitive topic? The tavern provided the only space that allowed for that kind of exchange. This is not to say that all taverns promote political unrest and produce political changes. But information is always shared within a context, and in the colonies, that context was "a decisive independent streak [that] ran through the tavern culture . . . many taverns were used by British smugglers trying to evade British taxes."[12]

Johnson is careful to note that taverns didn't cause the American Revolution. But, he says, change that one variable, and the buildup to the War of Independence has to, at the very least, unfold along a different path, since so much of the debate and communication around it relied on the semipublic exchanges of the tavern, a space where seditious thought could be shared, but also kept secret.[13]

Places like taverns and pubs enable people to make full use of the information they have because, in those settings, it becomes common knowledge. People both know the information and know that others know it. Information around collective action can be used fully only if people know it's common knowledge, because then there is less risk to individuals taking action. If you want to empower people, make it easier for them to share and aggregate information.

Conclusion

Efficiency is about getting the most done with the least waste. It's not always about finding the perfect answer, but the one that works well enough without too much fuss. Efficiency matters because in real life, you never have all the time or resources you want. You have to make do with what you've got.

But efficiency isn't just about speed. It's also about effectiveness and doing the right things. There's no point in doing something fast if it's not worth doing. True efficiency is about focusing on what matters most. It's about saying no to the small stuff so you can say yes to the big stuff.

Like everything, efficiency has its limits. There's a point of diminishing returns, a threshold beyond which further optimization yields little gain. The key is to find the sweet spot, the point of maximum efficiency before the costs start to outweigh the benefits.

Efficiency works until it doesn't. The more perfectly efficient a system, the more vulnerable it becomes to any change. While the idea can be hard to appreciate, maximal efficiency in the short term rarely leads to maximum long-term efficiency. A common benefit that gets eroded in the quest for efficiency is a margin of safety. Through the lens of efficiency, the opportunity cost of holding something like extra cash, inventory, or even people may come to be seen as too high. However, excess cash, inventory, and people can become more valuable with supply shocks or other changes in the environment. Inefficiency in the short run is often very efficient in the long run when it leaves you better able to adapt to an uncertain world.

In a world of trade-offs, efficiency is a balancing act. It's about making the most of what you have, but also leaving room for what you might need. It's about being prepared for the future, not just optimized for the present.

Debt

Borrowing against the future.

Debt defines your future, and when your future is defined, hope begins to die.

—KENT NERBURN[1]

The benefits of debt are visible, but its liabilities are often hidden. Taking on debt is borrowing something to use now, usually money, that must be paid back in the future. We have an intuitive sense of debt beyond straight financial transactions: If we don't get enough sleep or eat enough, we say that we have a sleep debt or caloric debt, which our bodies nudge us to repay. When someone helps us, we may feel a "debt of gratitude," the need to help them in return.

The total cost of repaying financial debt tends to be higher than what was initially borrowed. Lenders charge interest to compensate them for the risk of nonrepayment. If the interest rate is too high, it can lead a debt to grow faster than is possible for it to be paid off. Another downside of debt is that we tend to value future expenses differently from immediate ones and may spend more if we can pay later.[2]

A default occurs when a person or an entity fails to pay off a debt. If an asset for which someone owes money suddenly loses value, and the remaining debt is greater than that asset's current value, a debtor may make a deliberate choice to default, regardless of whether they *can* pay or not. If a person, company, government, or other group accrues a level of debt beyond their ability to ever pay back, they can, in most countries, declare bankruptcy.

Debt is inevitably a complex, sensitive topic. While most people tend to generally believe that what's borrowed should be repaid, there are numerous situations where things aren't that simple. For example, "odious debt" is debt accrued by a government regime that acted so far out of the interests of its nation that it is considered a personal debt of that regime rather than of the nation. In some cases, international legal frameworks may decide that odious debt does not need to be repaid by the people of that country, because the money should not have been lent to a repressive and corrupt regime in the first place.[3] The concept of odiousness highlights how debt can serve as an instrument of control.

Interestingly, according to economist Michael Hudson, "Nowhere in antiquity do we find governments become chronic debtors. Debts were owed to them, not by them."[4] It is, however, currently the norm for countries to issue debt for various purposes. When countries take on debt, it is referred to as "public debt," since the public is ultimately responsible for paying back the debt, and not all public debt is odious. It's another sensitive topic, for sure, but debt has been employed by countries in the past to develop public infrastructure that facilitates economic growth, such as banking and transportation systems, and to successfully defend themselves against invasion. The general idea behind public debt is that the money is used to develop infrastructure, so that the economy grows and the future revenue generated by that infrastructure (either directly or indirectly) will be greater than the debt incurred.

The Meiji government in Japan, circa 1873, is considered an example of the benefits of public debt.[5] The Meiji governed during the transition from the country's traditional samurai culture to the beginnings of what became modern Japan. They borrowed to create a central bank, a commercial banking system, and railroads, and to fight a war. They were able to successfully defend themselves while simultaneously building a financial and transportation infrastructure that spurred development and economic growth. They were also able to pay back the original debt within thirty years.

Debt both enables and requires us to do things that wouldn't otherwise be possible. Yuval Harari writes in *Money* that the European colonization of other countries was enabled by the creation of a banking system that provided credit. Harari says, "This was the magic circle of imperial capitalism: credit financed new discoveries, discoveries led to colonies, colonies provided profits, profits built trust, and trust translated into more credit."[6] Of course, just because something is possible doesn't mean it's good or even necessary.

But borrowing now with the intent to pay back in the future is still often advantageous if it allows us to build assets with greater value later on. For example, a loan to pay for a university degree that increases your income after graduation is generally considered good debt.

Debt, as a model, prompts us to consider whether the actions we will have to undertake in the future to compensate for what we do now are worth it.

Future Costs

The core premise of debt is that someone pays for something in the present by borrowing. To have what I want now, you give me money, and I commit to repayment later. Debt is undesirable when the cost of repayment exceeds the value gained by the present expenditure.

Sometimes our current needs seem so great that they blind us to the invisible reality of the cost of repayment. The use of land mines is an example of how borrowing to address a current perceived need can cost us more than we can ever repay.

Land mines have been used in war for centuries, but as with all weapons, the technology was subject to ongoing development. Modern land mines began to be deployed in large quantities during World War II. The contemporary image of a land mine is of a small explosive device buried in a field that detonates when pressured by a foot or wheel. The resulting explosion kills or maims the person who stepped on the device, or blows up the vehicle. The use of land mines in an active battle follows a simple logic: you place them in an area that you then manipulate your adversary into crossing. The result: a bunch of adversaries are blown up and removed from the fight. Land mines are relatively cheap compared to a lot of other weaponry. Although they are sold commercially by weapons manufacturers, they also can be easily improvised in local, small-scale settings.

If you know your enemy will be taking a particular path or occupying a certain territory, the use of land mines might appear to make immediate sense. You can cause a lot of harm for very little cost. The problem with land mines is that using them now requires repayment in the future. They may help win the battle, but they essentially make it harder to win the war. Why? Because the cost of repayment is often more than can be gained from the immediate benefits of using them.

There are two types of debt created when land mines are used. The first is short-term debt. Using land mines in a war may seem like a great idea, until you consider that your adversary is likely using them too. That means each new territory you find yourself in that the adversary has previously occupied must be treated as if it contains land mines. This is a serious problem.

As one account by a United States military veteran describing the reality of land mines in war explains, "When someone stepped on a land mine and set it off, often everyone around him would freeze for fear of stepping on land mines themselves." This is a reasonable fear and one that incurs costly delays. Furthermore, "it's harder to get mine victims off the battlefield, and they generally need more blood, more surgery, and more resources than those with other types of combat injuries, which can overwhelm military medical teams."[7] Thus, using land mines creates a debt that must be repaid out of future resources.

The second type of debt created by land mines is a long-term debt. Using them creates a global obligation of repayment over decades, if not centuries. Using land mines leads directly to civilian deaths, they restrict the movement of humanitarian aid, and they limit postwar recovery and development. Jody Williams won the Nobel Peace Prize in 1997 for her work leading the campaign to ban land mines. She explains in her memoir:

Land mines violate the important provisions of international law: proportionality and distinction. . . . The effect of land mines is disproportionate, which means the long-term impact of the weapon on civilians outweighs the benefit to the military of using it. . . . The violation of distinction is obvious because, by land mines' very nature, they are indiscriminate. No land mine can tell the difference between a civilian and a soldier.[8]

Describing the experience of the nation of Vietnam after the Vietnam War, Jody Williams explains:

The war was over, but land mines hadn't gone home with the soldiers like guns and other weapons. Once in the ground, they waited in deadly silence until the unsuspecting stepped on them or picked them up. Then the mine exploded, shattering not only the individual, but also the victim's family and community."[9]

After a war, most of the victims of land mines are civilians: farmers trying to grow crops, women going to rivers to get water, kids playing.

Dealing with land mines thus consumes an incredible amount of resources. It costs money to try to clean them all up. It costs money to treat the wounded. There is a loss of productivity, because land can't be farmed or otherwise utilized, land mine survivors cannot contribute to society at full capacity, and those who are killed cannot contribute at all. There is emotional trauma and negative social impact. Development slows or stagnates. Winning a war is all about neutralizing a threat, but the legacy of land mines means that threat often grows. No one looks favorably upon the country that causes such negative long-term consequences.

Under international law, any use of land mines is supposed to be mapped so they can later be removed, but the reality is the maps are rarely created and the cleanup is almost never done. Although 164 countries have signed the treaty to ban land mines, there are still a handful that have not. In addition, land mines are often used by nongovernmental groups.[10]

The United Nations website says, "The presence of land mines continues to impede social and economic development."[11] According to a BBC news video, as of 2016, there were approximately 110 million antipersonnel land mines still underground in about sixty countries, and one person was being killed or maimed by them every hour.[12]

Although not an example of debt in the traditional monetary sense, using debt as a lens to look at land mines helps us consider the long-term costs of our actions. Debt as a model prompts us to consider whether we can afford the cost of making right those wrong actions we embark on today.

Debt Forgiveness in Ancient Societies

Most of us think of debt as something that must be repaid. After all, you decided to borrow the money; you should have to deal with the consequences. However, historically, there has been an awareness that there are different types of debt, some of which are regarded as corrosive to social functioning.

As economist Michael Hudson explains, in many different Bronze Age societies in the Near East, including Babylonia and Assyria, rulers often practiced widespread debt forgiveness. Records of such practices "have been excavated in Lagash, Assur, Isin, Larsa, Babylon and other Near Eastern cities as far west as Asia Minor."[13]

Debt cancellation was not for all debts, such as those incurred by merchants for capital growth purposes or by wealthy landowners for their townhomes. Rulers forgave the debts of the agrarian population and aimed for nothing "above the basic subsistence needs of citizens. . . . The aim was not equality as such, but the assurance of self-supporting land and production for the citizenry."[14]

Hudson continues, "Rulers sought to check the economic power of wealthy creditors, military leaders or local administrators from concentrating land in their own hands and taking the crop surplus for themselves at the expense of the tax collector."[15]

Why would rulers do this? Essentially, to be able to continue their rule. Hudson writes,

> When harvests failed as a result of drought, flood or pests, there was not enough crop surplus to pay agrar-

ian debts. In such cases rulers canceled debts owed above all to themselves and their officials, and increasingly to private creditors as well. The palace had little interest in seeing these creditors force debtors into bondage.[16]

It was better to have a loyal population that could feed itself than one indebted and indentured to a small, wealthy class, for two reasons. One, rulers needed a free population to join the army or to help build public infrastructure, such as temples and city walls, when called upon. Two, a population that was in debt bondage to anyone other than the ruler would be a threat to their rule. Thus, as Hudson argues, "For thousands of years, economic polarization was reversed by canceling debts and restoring land tenure to smallholders who cultivated the land, fought in the army, paid taxes and/or performed corvée labor duties (what we would now call public works projects)."[17]

Canceling debts so that people could continue to survive, pay taxes, and fight for the military was a strategic move on the part of the ruler. It acknowledged that not all debt is a result of uncontrolled spending; sometimes natural events such as droughts and challenges such as war put excessive strain on populations.

Debt forgiveness by rulers faded away during the Roman Empire. In this period, instead of protecting debtors from losing their property and livelihoods, governments began protecting creditors from loss. The general attitude toward debt became more like what we're familiar with today: "Moral blame is placed on debtors, as if their arrears are a personal choice rather than stemming from economic strains that compel them to run into debt simply to survive."[18]

But not recognizing the different kinds of debt and their potential impacts on the stability of leadership can have negative consequences. According to Roman historians, including Livy and Plutarch, "Classical antiquity [was] destroyed mainly by creditors using interest-bearing debt to impoverish and disenfranchise the population. Barbarians always stood at the gates, but only as societies weakened internally were their inventions successful."[19]

Conclusion

Debt is a double-edged sword. It's a powerful tool that can help you grow a business, buy a home, or seize an opportunity. But it's also a chain that can bind your future or destroy you.

When debt spirals out of control, it quickly turns dreams into nightmares.

Debt isn't just about money. It can be a favor you owe, a social obligation, or anything that creates a future obligation. We even have sleep debt.

It can be hard to appreciate just how fragile debt makes you. It's a bit like driving across a huge desert without a spare tire. If everything goes just perfectly, you will reach the other side, but the smallest hiccup will leave you stranded and desperate.

Use debt wisely. Respect its power, but fear its edge. Remember, the more you borrow, the less room you have to weather life's storms.

While debt might seem cheap in the moment, the future often proves it to be more expensive than we imagined. The more you borrow, the less room you have to deal with uncertainty.

Debt can give you leverage, but it can also take away your freedom. Respect its power but fear its edge.

Monopoly and Competition

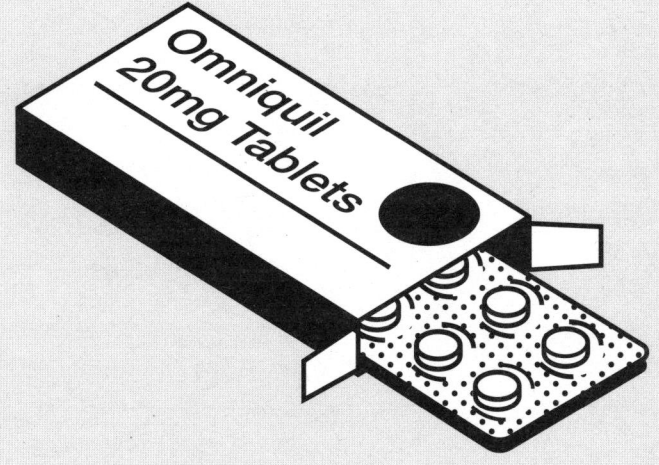

Monopolistic might, competitive fight.

Nature hates monopolies and exceptions. The waves of the sea do not more speedily seek a level from their loftiest tossing, than the varieties of condition tend to equalize themselves. There is always some leveling circumstance that puts down the overbearing, the strong, the rich, the fortunate, substantially on the same ground with all others.

—RALPH WALDO EMERSON[1]

Markets become efficient through competition. Buyers compete to get the goods and services they want at the lowest possible prices. Sellers compete to sell at the highest possible prices. In a monopoly, a single company controls a market; there is no competition. Imagine a bridge that crosses a body of water, with no alternative. If you want to cross, you must use the bridge.

When there is competition in a market, consumers are free to choose the best providers and firms compete to serve consumers. Monopolies are often considered harmful because they interfere with this process, letting monopolists set prices higher than they could if they had real competitors. That's why many countries try to prevent monopolies.

What is more common is oligopolies—markets with only a small number of competitors and limited room for new entrants. Markets tend to favor unequal distribution of market share and profits, with a few leaders emerging in any industry—what's known as a "winner-takes-all market." Winner-takes-all markets are hard to disrupt, and they suppress the entry of new players by locking in market share for leading players. When we say a market is "winner-takes-all," what we mean is that a single company receives most available profits. A few others have at best a modest share. The rest fight over a minuscule remnant and tend not to survive long.

Monopolies can be positive, though, when significant investment needs to be made to develop and supply a product in the first place.[2] One example is utility companies. It costs a lot to create the infrastructure needed to provide sewage treatment or electricity. Giving a company a monopoly for service to an entire city justifies the initial upfront investment required and increases the possibility the resulting infrastructure will have a certain longevity.

This type of monopoly often develops into a natural monopoly, which occurs when an industry has steep barriers to entry. These barriers—such as significant physical infrastructure requirements—make it daunting for new competitors to take on established players that are already operating at a large scale. When natural monopolies of providers of essential goods or services occur, governments may intervene to ensure prices remain affordable. With restrictions on prices in place, a natural monopoly can continue to benefit consumers, especially with an undifferentiated product, by reducing the overall cost of required infrastructure.

Sometimes, markets have mechanisms in place to deliberately create temporary monopolies, to incentivize desirable economic activity. Economist Joseph Schumpeter believed that "monopolies were especially important for bringing about innovation because they give entrepreneurs big rewards for the risky activity of trying to create new things."[3] For example, pharmaceutical companies typically receive exclusive rights to sell newly developed drugs for a few years, allowing them to set high prices to recoup the costs of research and development. Although this may initially restrict access, in the long run, pharmaceutical patents are intended to incentivize the development of drugs that would otherwise be unprofitable to create.[4]

We can use the mental model of market monopolies to help us understand many situations involving unequal distributions: Most of the books sold each year are written by a handful of authors. Most internet traffic goes to a few websites. The top 100 websites get more traffic than ranks 101 to 999 combined. Most citations in any field refer to the same few papers and researchers. Most clicks on Google searches are on the first result. Each of these is an instance of a winner-takes-all market.

Monopolies can perpetuate themselves; sometimes things are famous for being famous or popular because they're popular. Robert H. Frank writes of such things in *Success and Luck*: "Although we often try to explain their success by scrutinising their objective qualities, they are in fact often no more special than many of their less renowned counterparts.... Success often results from positive feedback loops that amplify tiny initial variations into enormous differences in final outcomes."[5]

Monopolies interrupt evolution because of their lack of competition. In a monopoly, there is less room for trying new things, for diversity, and for overall resilience.

Extreme Monopoly

People tend not to like monopolies. A monopoly means you don't have a choice of who to buy from. And that feels threatening, because if there's only one seller, they have power over you.

Monopolies can also be scary because of the lack of competition inherent in the model. In some monopolies, the barriers to entry are so high that no one can compete by bringing different goods or services to market. Saying we can't compete seems unnatural; the entire history of humanity is predicated on some humans, some of the time, coming up with better, more effective ways of doing things. Monopoly can discourage us from doing what really comes quite naturally.

So, let's explore what an extreme monopoly might look like. If a monopoly is characterized by lack of competition and therefore being the sole option for consumers, then we can consider totalitarian governments as a monopoly.

Here, we will look at two leadership periods in the twentieth century that are generally considered to be totalitarian: the Soviet Union under Joseph Stalin and Germany under Adolf Hitler. The particulars of each regime are not as important here as what the general aims of each leader were. Neither achieved an absolute global monopoly, but we're going to use the lens of monopoly to look at totalitarianism in theory, with examples from the Soviet Union and Nazi Germany to provide context.

First, what is totalitarianism? Totalitarianism is an all-encompassing system of rule. In the words of historian Stephen J. Lee, "Totalitarian regimes possessed a distinctive ideology which formed a body of doctrine covering all vital parts of man's existence."[6] These types of governments enlarge the state so that it covers absolutely everything. Nothing exists that is not under the purview of the state.

Totalitarian leaders try to achieve a monopoly on all functions of society and all relationships between people by eroding anything that they do not control. "Totalitarianism is at bottom simply the internal invasion by the state of its civil society," writes Robert Nisbet. "It represents the desire to subjugate, and where possible exterminate, the groups, associations, statuses, and roles that are the building blocks of a civil society and, ideally, to replace them all by relationships entirely of the state's creation."[7] Therefore, totalitarian leaders undermine and eliminate groups like churches and unions, and replace remaining ones like schools and sports clubs with ones that are creations of the totalitarian state.

To achieve the complete destruction of civil society and the construction of a society completely controlled by the leader, totalitarian states are thought to have some commonly defining characteristics. Carl Friedrich and Zbigniew Brzezinski define that totalitarian state as having "a combination of an ideology, a single party typically led by one man, a terroristic police, a communications monopoly, a weapons monopoly, and a centrally directed economy."[8] In short, there is no aspect of day-to-day existence that a totalitarian leader is not involved in.

Humans are social creatures. We're biologically wired to participate in groups. The type and intensity of participation varies from person to person, but it's hard to imagine someone living completely alone, without being even a loose member of a group such as a family or work team, or part of a community of people with likeminded interests. Thus, totalitarianism must work hard to undermine and pervert our natural tendencies.

In her book *The Origins of Totalitarianism*, Hannah Arendt offers insight into how totalitarian states pursue their goals. One requirement is that they are run by a leader who has "absolute monopoly of power and authority," which means that the leader has "a monopoly of responsibility for everything which is being done."[9] No subordinate acts of their own free will; instead, they implement the desires of the leader.

There are a few techniques that remove the ability of anyone but the leader to act. One is the duplication of offices. One of Hitler's more effective totalitarian techniques was to have multiple, overlapping organizations whose aims were vague and conflicting, so that everyone had to look to him for leadership. Another is an ongoing and random purging of people from positions. Stalin killed thousands of workers in deliberate purges of state organizations, so that no cliques or challenges to his power could develop.

The terror of elimination based on random and arbitrary factors is also a means of undermining the strength and independence of the general population. Arendt writes often of totalitarianism seeking to "atomize" people to achieve control; atomization means "to deprive of meaningful ties to others."[10] When your actions have no impact on your experience, when you could be shot just as easily for what you did not do as for what you did, your ability to trust others and build social ties collapses. Random terror is thus a means of preventing the development of any credible alternative to the totalitarian state.

The problem with totalitarianism as a monopoly is that it goes against how the world works. The arbitrary use of terror may dull a population and inject suspicion into all social relationships, but it cannot eliminate the human propensity to create and seek out alternatives. Arendt writes that "total power can be achieved and safeguarded only in a world of conditioned reflexes, of marionettes without the slightest trace of spontaneity."[11] It's hard if not impossible to imagine a world in which all humans have lost the ability to be spontaneous, to have original thoughts, and to form connections with one another. Totalitarian regimes want a monopoly on history and the path to the future. However, to achieve this, they require a monopoly on thought, which is not possible.

In the desire to isolate people to control them, totalitarian regimes may also sow the seeds of their own failure. Regardless of one's ideology, societies need to have certain attributes in order to function. They must be able, at a minimum, to feed, clothe, and shelter their populations. But the tactic of "constant removal, demotion, and promotion makes reliable teamwork impossible and prevents the development of experience."[12] Without experience, all challenges are new. The same mistakes can be made over and over. There is no ability of a population to adapt to change.

The truth is, no one person can have everything figured out or know the best course of action in all circumstances. Stalin couldn't feed the Soviet population and created famines. Hitler destroyed the economic functioning of Germany to pursue terror-based ideological ends. Arendt explains:

> The reason why the ingenious devices of totalitarian rule, with their absolute and unsurpassed concentration of power in the hands of a single man, were never tried out before, is that no ordinary tyrant was ever mad enough to discard all limited and local interests—economic, national, human, military—in favor of a purely fictitious reality in some indefinite, distant future.[13]

Arendt's comment leads us to the problems inherent in a total monopoly: Life develops. Evolution happens. Environments change. Positive response—even if we define that simply as survival—requires people who can think independently and creatively interact with the challenges presented to them.

Totalitarianism seems to see the world as a giant machine, with all its parts identified and in place. Therefore, the logic goes, if the leader has control over everyone, they have control over the machine and can keep it running in perpetuity. But the earth is not a machine. Evolution is not predictable. We evolved the traits we did to survive and flourish in our ever-changing environment. To seek to eliminate those traits is to render useless the very capabilities we need to survive.

Conclusion

Monopoly and competition are the yin and yang of the business world. They're the opposing forces that shape the landscape of every market, the tides that lift and sink the fortunes of every firm. To understand business, you must understand the dance between these poles.

Competition is the default state of the market. It's the Darwinian struggle where many firms vie for the same customers and resources. In a competitive market, no one firm has the power to set prices or dictate terms. They're price takers, not price makers. They survive by being efficient, delivering value, and innovating.

If competition is the natural state, monopoly is the entrepreneur's dream. A monopoly dominates a market so completely that it becomes the market. Think of the only bridge that crosses a river. But monopolies inevitably sow the seeds of their own destruction. The question is how long they will last.

We need both monopoly and competition. Competition keeps firms honest and drives innovation. But we also need monopolies' deep pockets to fund big visions and moon shots. The ideal is a balance: enough competition to check monopolies, but enough monopoly to reward innovation.

Externalities

EXTERNALITIES ARE ONE FORM OF MARKET FAILURE. THEY OCCUR when someone either incurs a cost or receives a benefit without being compensated for or paying for it. Externalities, whether positive or negative, are inefficient because scarce resources are not being used in a way that confers the most utility. However, externalities are difficult to prevent and are consequently an accepted part of markets.

When costs spill over from one party to another, the solution is to create additional costs for the party causing the externality. But the cost must be at the margins, not the average. This means that the party responsible must pay for each additional unit of externality they cause.

For example, charging people each time they drive in the center of a city is more effective than charging a flat fee for driving in a city. This is because, subconsciously or not, people tend to aim to get their money's worth when they pay a flat fee. Each additional trip costs them nothing extra. But paying per trip makes the cost much more obvious.

An example of a positive externality is vaccines. Each person who gets vaccinated benefits other people who are unable to do the same, such as those with serious immune system deficiencies. Those who benefit do not pay for that. For that reason, vaccines against common diseases are often made free or cheap to obtain.

Creative
Destruction

How the mighty fall.

Yet technological creativity as an economic phenomenon does not require the creation of totally new knowledge: innovation does not require invention. Borrowing, extending, and adapting will increase the supply of goods and services just as well.

—JOEL MONKYR[1]

Most of us can easily recognize that change is constant. In our lives, we never get to a plateau where we can stop and never do anything different from that point onward. Our circumstances change. New challenges present themselves. And the world around us is always evolving.

Joseph Schumpeter describes the process through which the old order crumbles to make way for something better as "creative destruction." In *Capitalism, Socialism, and Democracy*, Schumpeter writes:

> The opening up of new markets, foreign or domestic, and the organizational development from the craft shop to such concerns as U.S. Steel illustrate the same process of industrial mutation—if I may use that biological term—that incessantly revolutionizes the economic structure from within, incessantly destroying the old one, incessantly creating a new one. This process of Creative Destruction is the essential fact about capitalism.[2]

Other economists have since referred to it as "Schumpeter's gale," comparing it to a wind sweeping across the land.

Creative destruction captures an evolutionary process, and we are going to use that broader context, expanding beyond Schumpeter's original concept, in this chapter. In volume 2 of *The Great Mental Models*, we looked at natural selection as a mental model. Traits that make an organism more likely to survive long enough to reproduce are passed on. The organisms that are best suited to their environment survive. It's a constant process of adaptation and improvement.

Revisiting the concept of evolution can help us understand creative destruction better. Any economy is an evolutionary system: the market is the ecosystem; the firms within it are the living things. Even if a company is doing fine and meeting the needs of its customers, a new one may come along that is more efficient in some way and able to do more for customers. A population of a species that can obtain enough food with less energy expended is likely to usurp one that requires more energy. In the same way, a company that can provide a service at a lower cost is likely to survive over one providing the same service for more money. In any evolutionary process, whoever survives, wins.

In an evolutionary economy, technology can be thought of as mutation. As in nature, not all mutations are beneficial, and not all of them stick around. But some provide such an advantage that they are reproduced throughout a population and become the new norm. Schumpeter emphasized the role of the entrepreneur in creating technological innovations and establishing them in the market, asserting that they are the disruptive force that both initiates change and capitalizes on it. But an updated understanding of the economy as an evolutionary system doesn't require such a defined role. Entrepreneurs are just one of many sources of change and development. Anyone can produce a change that impacts the system.

Creative destruction rests on the understanding that there are always better ways of doing things, and it's more effective technology that can really propel overall advancement. It also acknowledges, similar to the biological world, that economies must always respond and adapt to broader global trends and changes.

Even if creative destruction proves beneficial overall, it leaves chaos in its wake. People lose their jobs and may need to retrain, at great financial and psychological cost. Companies go bankrupt, and local economies can suffer. New technology may carry health or environmental risks. The number of available jobs may fall, or wages may drop. Schumpeter himself advised that when it comes to new technologies, or even capitalism itself, "you can only begin to reckon its achievements in the long run."[3] This thinking also resonates with the biological analogy: not all change benefits all individuals and species.

History is usually written by the victors. The history of technology tends to tell of improvement and progress, but these advances always come at a price. All leaps forward leave some people behind. With the benefit of hindsight, we easily forget the extensive periods of unease, confusion, and suffering that accompany technological progress. Even though we can appreciate overall gains that occurred in the past, when it's happening around us in real time, we may be less amenable.

Technology is always moving the goalposts for economics. Creative destruction tends to wipe out existing wealth, turning it into the raw material for new forms. For societies to remain creative, the forces pushing new ideas forward must be stronger than those protecting the established order. There never was a "good old days." The economy—and by extension the world—is always shifting due to changes in technology. If we try to stop creative destruction, we are essentially trying to stop evolution, an impossible task.

Using creative destruction as a model calls us to explore how to let go of our entrenched ideas and make way for new ideas. It also asks us to acknowledge that there are always better ways of doing things and we are always in a position of discovering and trying to implement them.

The Evolution of the Law

Evolution doesn't end; it keeps churning. And occasionally, a mutation occurs that spreads through a population and has a massive impact on all parts of the surrounding environment. This effect of a mutation is similar to what Schumpeter describes with the term "creative destruction": society is just chugging along, and then the car or the internet gets invented and spreads through society, and large changes occur that ripple outward. These technological "mutations" occur in part because there are always different ways things could be done, and some people are always working to explore what could be.

It's not only technology that produces change but also new ways of thinking. New ideas spread through populations and can cause significant structural shifts. One important component of creative destruction as a model is to see that it always keeps on going. Although Schumpeter was enthusiastic about the positive impact of creative destruction, he was more pessimistic about growth eventually stagnating and capitalism collapsing, because he worried creative destruction would become a codified process and thus stop being creative. This eventuality is, however, unlikely. A broader definition of creative destruction, beyond the activities of lone entrepreneurs, allows us to see that there will always be new ideas that shake up the status quo.

Exploring the history of law highlights how creative destruction lacks an endpoint; there is no state we achieve in which there is nothing left to improve or innovate. We just keep going, moving along from where we are to somewhere we think we might want to be.

For much of human history, we existed in groups without laws. We had norms that were enforced by the group, but no independent, codified laws as we understand them now. As our groups started to grow, as we got rulers and cities and empires, there came the idea in some places to compile a set of laws to be enforced by a class of people under the direction of the ruler. The birth of the law likely arose in the Near East, in city-states with large groups of people who weren't connected as kin.

First, what is the difference between rules and laws? "Rules and commands take on legal force only when they meet basic formal requirements," writes law professor David M. Beatty. For example, "They must be general, transparent, and prospective."[4] Laws are not arbitrary, nor can they change on a whim. For something to qualify as a law, it has to be developed or modified according to procedures that are set out in advance.

Second, what is the point of having laws? "The purpose of law is to encourage people to behave respectfully toward one another and to settle their conflicts peacefully."[5] This goes a long way toward explaining why laws first evolved in large city-states: The more people in one place, the more chances for conflict. The more unchecked conflict, the more unrest. The more unrest, the weaker the power of the ruler.

So, back to our evolution. One of the earliest legal codes in these city-states was that of Hammurabi, the king of Babylon from roughly 1790 to 1750 BCE. The Code of Hammurabi, as it is called, was easy for the average person to read and was posted publicly where all could access it. It does not lay out general rules but instead is a series of examples of something that happened and what the consequence was. For example, instead of saying "arson is prohibited," it would say something like, "If a man burns down his neighbor's house, then he is burned to death."

One key feature of the code was that "it was likely intended more as a teaching tool illustrating proper behavior in specific situations rather than as a binding precedent in future cases. It provided judges and juries with guidance rather than hard-and-fast rules."[6] There was thus an interpretive element, necessitating a legal structure to accompany the code.

The Code of Hammurabi provided the model for how legal codes were developed and implemented all over the region. There were variations, for sure, but the idea of the rule of law had come into being and would evolve from there. From its beginnings in the Near East, the idea of having a legal code, of a group of people adhering to a system of laws, began to spread. There are more innovations to the rule of law than we can cover here. But a few more milestones demonstrate the process of creative destruction in the evolution of the rule of law, whereby powerful new ideas fundamentally altered the way societies organized and developed.

Over a thousand years later, a new idea about the law came out of ancient Greece: the concept that laws were considered legitimate by the agreement of the people who adhered to them. Previously, under Hammurabi and those with similar codes, laws were justified by relating them to divine authority that came through the society's leadership. In ancient Greece, however, polymath and reformer Solon argued that society would be better served if people were responsible for the law. Beatty explains:

> By any measure, making the people guardians of the law was a bold decision. It was unlike anything that had been tried before. In creating the jury courts and giving them the power to overturn the decision of the magistrates, the peo-

ple were able to determine the force of the law and to say what it actually meant.[7]

Now, as with creative destruction in its conventional sense, just because something is new and useful doesn't mean its uptake will be widespread and immediate. Leonardo da Vinci conceived of mechanisms for flying machines more than five hundred years before they entered widespread use. The ancient Greeks encountered political turmoil and their circumstances changed, but the idea of a rule of law that could be bottom-up instead of top-down was now out there, and eventually it became a standard component of many legal systems. Most importantly, in terms of creative destruction and the idea that "the waves it creates never die down,"[8] legitimizing the idea that people can and should be involved with the rules that govern them is a cornerstone of democracy. And democracy, too, got its ideological foundation in ancient Greece.

Another big idea that appeared as the rule of law evolved was that rulers were also bound by the law. Early legal codes were part of a system of governance ultimately enforced by a ruler. As such, the law was part of the ruler's power, a tool of the state; laws did not exist higher than rulers. As time went on, laws were practiced and systems evolved. More and more, legal analysis started to argue for rulers being required to adhere to the same laws as their people. Schumpeter said that "capitalism is nothing but the constant change caused by restless entrepreneurs."[9] We might say that the rule of law is nothing but the constant change caused by restless legal analysis and application.

To be fair, rulers did not naturally and easily embrace the idea that they were bound by their own legal systems. But this big idea persisted. It was argued for by the ancient Greeks, encoded in systems such as sharia law, defended by jurists in seventeenth-century

England, and became a core pillar of the American constitution in 1787. Now, for a society to be considered a rule-of-law state, everyone in the state—including the leadership—must be bound by the law, and there must be a mechanism to enforce that compliance. No one is above the rules—another idea that rippled out, causing social change.

The law is constantly moving; it has no endpoint. It will always be changing and evolving. There will always be different ways of having, organizing, and interpreting the rule of law. Some will be better or more popular and become part of the idea's evolutionary story.

Creative destruction as a lens shows us that occasionally, a powerful idea comes along that instigates widespread change. These moments of creative destruction are inevitable. There will always be people trying to figure out a better way of doing things. Creative destruction can be hard to use as a model because the mechanism reveals itself best when one can take a long look over history. What's most useful is the notion of new ideas causing fundamental changes in the way we live and organize ourselves. Prepare for a world that is going to change and don't be afraid to contribute.

The End of "Clovis First"

Old orders crumble all the time: Gunpowder gets invented, and warfare changes. The telegraph comes along and revolutionizes how business gets done. Looking back over the history of technology, it's easy to see how some technologies fundamentally altered the way a lot of our societies operated.

It's equally easy to see how not everyone embraces change immediately. Often, technology must be further developed and refined until it is useful enough and cheap enough to be available to everyone. In those cases, we can understand the lack of instantaneous, overnight adoption. But when something comes along that threatens the existing order, resistance can persist for a while regardless of a technology's availability. The famous story of Ned Ludd and his Luddites trying to stop automation in the textile industry comes to mind. We should not, however, look back at people like Ned Ludd and shake our heads with pity, as if to say, *Poor souls; automation made everyone's life better in the long run,* or *Boy, were they on the wrong side of history.* A more pertinent lesson is to understand people's natural resistance to change when they don't see themselves as having a place in the new world order that is on the horizon.

Creative destruction wreaks havoc. People get displaced. Fortunes are lost. Entire ways of living get disrupted, and some even become obsolete. The model of creative destruction thus can also be used to help us understand resistance to new ideas.

Science is a field that has its moments of creative destruction. The world is understood to work a certain way—say, everyone believes the sun revolves around the earth—and then, *boom!* New information is discovered, and the old order crumbles. We change our thinking and now understand that the earth revolves around the sun. These creative-destruction-type moments in science are like the idea of paradigm shifts that Thomas S. Kuhn wrote about in *The Structure of Scientific Revolutions.*

In the science textbooks we read in schools, you'll find what Kuhn called "normal science": "research firmly based upon one or more past scientific achievements, achievements that some particular scientific community acknowledges for a time as supplying the foundation for its further practice."[10] The material of normal science is what Kuhn called a "paradigm." Looking at a particular field at a particular time, its paradigm should be simple to identify. An example of a paradigm is Newtonian physics, which is based on the three laws of motion. Once a field has a paradigm, normal science progresses along a predictable path for a while.

However, at a certain point in normal science, something goes wrong. An anomaly emerges—a phenomenon that contradicts the existing paradigm. It is this departure from what is expected that engenders the moment of creative destruction and that ultimately leads science to advance. At first, researchers often assume an anomaly is a mistake. When it proves repeatable, they may ignore or work around it, sometimes for long periods of time, expecting it to be resolved.

Paradigms are always imperfect, and therefore some anomalies are not unexpected. But unless there is a crisis, there is no reason to question a paradigm. Because individual scientists are reluctant to shake the foundations of their work, they are commonly able to deal with anomalies without being deterred. They may not even notice anomalies that later become significant.

However, during a period of scientific crisis, resolving the anomaly becomes the focus of the field. Many of the most talented researchers will devote themselves to it. Due to all the focus on this one subject, it will seem to grow in size. Once an anomaly proves insurmountable, one thing becomes apparent: the existing paradigm must be wrong. Attempts to resolve the anomaly begin to deviate away from the paradigm. It is time to replace the paradigm with a new one—only when a replacement emerges will scientists relinquish the old one, for science cannot exist without a paradigm. The unresolvable anomaly kicks off the gale of creative destruction.

The transition from the old order to a new paradigm is a scientific revolution. The resolution of scientific revolutions is always a gradual, slow process; it can take centuries. The field as a whole cannot, in one sweep, abandon the old paradigm. Therefore, two paradigms may coexist for a time, as Einstein's and Newton's did. At first, only a few people are convinced of a new paradigm. Early adopters work to improve the paradigm, making it more persuasive. This attracts other scientists, who in turn improve the paradigm further. Eventually, this feedback loop converts all but a few holdouts, who depart from the path of the developing science. Once enough time has passed, they die off or leave the field, and the new paradigm fully takes over.[11]

The Clovis theory of the migration of humans to the Western Hemisphere is a great example of the tension and struggle of a paradigm shift in science. In the 1930s, bones that were found in the desert near the village of Clovis, New Mexico, were determined to be human. This set off a flurry of activity, and soon, human artifacts similar to those at Clovis were found in multiple places in what is now North America. Carbon dating in the 1950s determined these artifacts were between 13,500 and 12,900 years old;[12] the humans associated with these artifacts came to be called the Clovis people. Because no earlier human artifacts had been found at the time, archaeologists proclaimed the Clovis people to be the oldest North Americans.

How did they get here? Well, right around the time the artifacts dated from, there was a land bridge over Beringia, connecting what is now Russia and Alaska. So, it was decided, these Clovis people walked over from Asia. They walked right down through Canada, which at the time was covered by two giant ice sheets except for one small path through what is now Alberta. These early humans got through this narrow passage, spread all over the rest of the continent, and made it down to what is now Chile. They also killed everything along the way, which is why we don't have mastodons or saber-toothed cats anymore.

This theory was plausible—considering the data available, it offered an explanation for what might have happened. Archaeologists bought into it hard. It was taught in schools. It became what Thomas Kuhn called a paradigm. Like all scientific paradigms, work continued to refine and develop the theory, filling in holes and making it more robust.

Then the anomalies started showing up. Soon, bones were being excavated all over the Americas that were older than the window provided by the land tunnel through the ice sheets covering what is now Canada. For example, human bones have been found in southern Chile that date to 18,500 to 14,500 years old, and others that possibly go back to 33,000 years before present (BP). Archaeological finds in the Yukon date human presence there to at least 24,000 years BP.[13] More and more precise dating "has challenged our understanding of the human past and supported the rewriting of early human history on a global scale."[14] Dealing with these anomalies was a textbook example of Kuhn's idea of replacing an old paradigm with a new one.

Widespread resistance occurred in the archaeological community. The "Clovis first" believers attacked the reputations, skills, and credibility of those uncovering older bones. Many scientists were marginalized and had to fight to maintain their careers. "There are very few recorded archaeological sites in the published literature that date to over 100,000 years BP in the Americas. This is due in part to bias and denial in the field over the last one hundred years. Those few archaeologists who did report on earlier than 12,000-year-old sites faced overly aggressive critiques and ostracism."[15]

It's the lens of creative destruction that can help us understand what happened. The new science coming in meant those who had argued for the Clovis people being the first in North America were wrong. And being wrong meant they were unlikely, like the Luddites, to have a place in the new order that was forming. So, they fought to keep it at bay. You might think this reaction inappropriate for a discipline that is meant to constantly discover what we do not know, that is based on the premise that you can never prove a theory right, only wrong. But when you've invested your time and reputation into a theory that is about to be dismantled, it's hard to remember the principles you're supposed to be working under.

In reality, the new theories of human migration weren't such an intellectual stretch. As archaeologist Paulette F. C. Steeves explains:

> Since the environmental history shows that a viable landmass area was available for most of the last 100,000 years and for a greater part of the last 64 million years, one has to question why discussions have not traditionally mentioned the possibilities of earlier hominin migrations to the Western Hemisphere.[16]

Still, today, there remain archaeologists who adamantly deny pre-Clovis hominid habitation of the Western Hemisphere. And still, in the face of these denials, the evidence for older occupation of the Americas continues to mount. Geologists have demonstrated that the ice-free corridor that humans apparently walked through was actually inhospitable. Bones from Clovis people have not been found in the corridor. The extinction of the large mammals on the continent seems to predate the Clovis timing. And within Clovis sites, there is evidence for only minimal hunting, suggesting that humans were not responsible for the mass extinctions that occurred.[17]

"The ultimate demise of the Clovis dogma was inevitable," Charles C. Mann quotes historian David Henige saying in his book *1491*. "Archaeologists are always dating something to five thousand years ago then saying that this must be the first time it occurred because they haven't found any earlier examples. And then, incredibly, they defend this idea to the death."[18] But the lens of creative destruction reveals this stance to be not so incredible after all. No one wants to get left behind as the waves of change push out the old order.

However, science is built on learning more. "No one should expect that archaeological theories of early human habitation anywhere in the world will not change."[19] Beyond archaeology, science as a whole will always have to contend with waves of creative destruction. "Archaeological goals are to study the human past; however, it is evident that we cannot possibly understand anything if we deny it exists before we even look for it."[20] This explains why creative destruction, or Thomas Kuhn's paradigm changes, are part of science: at its core, science is full of people who go looking for new things. And sometimes, those new things fundamentally change our understanding of our universe.

Conclusion

Creative destruction is the engine of progress in a capitalist economy. It's the process by which new innovations replace old ones, the cycle of birth and death that keeps an economy vibrant. It's the embodiment of the old adage: The only constant is change.

In a dynamic economy, nothing is sacred. Every industry, company, and way of doing things can be disrupted by newer, better ideas. The smartphone replaced the flip phone, online streaming replaced movie rental stores, cars replaced horses.

While creative destruction can be painful for individual companies, it's essential for the health of the overall economy. It prevents stagnation and ensures resources are always put to their most productive use. Without creative destruction, we'd still be riding horses and renting VHS tapes.

On one hand, creative destruction is the opportunity you're looking for—the chance to disrupt an incumbent, to build something new and better. But on the other hand, it's the threat you're always guarding against—the possibility that you will be disrupted by the next big thing.

Creative destruction isn't just about business; it's a metaphor for life. We are all subject to change, to the constant cycle of endings and beginnings. The key is to not cling too tightly to the old, but to embrace the possibilities of the new.

Gresham's Law

Incentives matter.

If the intrinsic values of coins are different it will become a source of profit for the wicked to collect the small (bad) coins and exchange them (for good money) and then they will take them to another country and shift the small (bad) money of that country (to this country).

—IBN TAYMIYYAH[1]

G resham's law is the economic principle that bad money will always drive out good money. In practice, this means that if legal coins have a varying metal value, people will tend to spend the cheaper ones and hoard the more valuable ones.

In historical situations in which Gresham's law was observed, coins with different perceived values led to currencies becoming unreliable as a medium of exchange. People started to regard the coins as a store of value equal to their metal content versus their face value as legal tender and either saved them or, if the metal was worth more overseas, exported them.

At its heart though, Gresham's law is about the consequences of asymmetry—specifically, when asymmetry isn't supposed to be there but is, like when the value of two coins is legally supposed to be equal, but people behave as if the coins have different values. Asymmetry can lead to a breakdown in trust, such as no one trusting the value of the currency they are exchanging—which is a problem, because human systems run on trust.

You can also apply Gresham's law to lending: bad lending drives out good lending. This caused the 1980s savings and loan crisis as well as amplified the great financial crisis of 2008. A borrower has an incentive to deal with the counterparty that has the fewest restrictions and the best terms, which leads to a gradual reduction of lending standards in the entire industry. The few companies that refuse to partake by lowering their standards make fewer loans and are, at least temporarily, punished as their share price goes down.

Gresham's law takes its name from the English merchant and financier Sir Thomas Gresham. As an advisor to Queen Elizabeth I of England, Gresham critiqued Henry VIII's decision to debase the English currency by using an alloy that contained 40 percent base metals instead of pure silver. While Gresham didn't codify the consequence of this action as a law, nor was he the first to notice it, his name was later attached to the principle by economist Henry Dunning Macleod, in 1858.

I's Law

The inverse of Gresham's law is I's law. In the absence of legal tender laws, the opposite occurs: good money drives out the bad. For example, in a new state that issues its own currency, people may prefer to receive payments in the form of an older and therefore seemingly more reliable currency from abroad. Even if this practice is illegal, if legal tender laws are sufficiently difficult to enforce, the imported currency predominates.

One of the problems that Gresham's law highlights is the potential for market failure if supposedly equal values skew too asymmetrical. At first you may think, What's the big deal if I'm keeping the good coins under the mattress at home and just spending the bad ones? But what if you don't have any bad coins on the day you need to buy groceries? You certainly aren't going to use your good ones, as they can only buy you the same amount as the bad coins. So you don't go shopping. You don't participate in the market until you can get ahold of some bad coins. The market then becomes distorted, because the prices of goods don't line up with the value of all the coins, both good and bad, that could be used to pay for them.

The mental model of Gresham's law highlights how asymmetrical value in entities that are supposed to be equal creates a feedback loop that reinforces all kinds of bad behavior and eventually drives out good behavior. Although the original coinage problem tends not to occur now that currency is generally not made of precious metals, it remains a useful concept for understanding human behavior. It can apply to any situation where there is asymmetry.

The asymmetry needed for Gresham's law to play out doesn't have to be just in the value of the commodities. It can also occur in the information we have about those commodities. Perhaps the best summary of the impacts of information asymmetry on market interactions comes from George A. Akerlof's influential 1970 paper, "The Market for 'Lemons': Quality Uncertainty and the Market Mechanism."[2] Akerlof considered the role of information asymmetry in the used-car market. Prior to Akerlof, this type of transaction would have been considered fairly symmetrical—I want to buy a car, and you have a car to sell. We both have the same information about what cars are and what they do. Our needs match. It's a fairly straightforward, even exchange.

But Akerlof pointed out that sellers of used cars have far more information than do buyers. There's an endless list of things that could be wrong with a car, and it's difficult for a buyer to know if the seller is hiding anything. The information available to each party in the transaction is actually very asymmetrical. Akerlof illustrated how the used-car market could reach the point of failure, with bad cars driving out the good, by using a thought experiment. Imagine there are two types of cars: peaches (ones without hidden problems) and lemons (ones with serious hidden problems). Buyers are willing to pay a thousand dollars for a peach and five hundred dollars for a lemon. Sellers are happy to sell both for those prices.

If a buyer can accurately distinguish between a peach and a lemon, they will pay the appropriate price for each. But what happens if they cannot distinguish between the two? In that case, they might only be willing to pay $750 for any car. Unable to make a profit, sellers will stop offering peaches. Buyers will realize this and stop paying more than $500 for any car. In the long run, the market fails because there are no good cars available. Sellers can't make a living, and buyers can't get good-quality cars. The lemons have driven out the peaches—the bad money has driven out the good.

Gresham's law demonstrates that we are less likely to participate in transactions if we feel there is too much asymmetry. It makes us feel as if we're getting ripped off because we can't verify that we're not. Even if having more good coins or knowing more than the other party in a transaction can give us an edge in the short term, in the long run, everyone loses out. Excessive asymmetry negatively impacts trust, which deters engagement. We're less likely to want to do business with one another. The more symmetrical our information, the higher the chance of developing trust, an essential component of any market.

Once a critical mass of people engage in a particular "bad behavior" without oversight or the right incentives, they can end up making "good behavior" not worthwhile for anyone. If we are hoarding the good coins, we can bet everyone else is.

It Can Always Get Worse

There is bad behavior going on all of the time; there's always someone trying to sell a lemon as a peach. A little bad behavior is to be expected, and there is usually enough counteracting good behavior to preserve our trust in whatever market we are engaging in. Using Gresham's law as a model is not as much about trying to understand when situations go from good to bad as about understanding when they go from functioning to nonfunctioning. How asymmetrical can the information get before trust breaks down completely? And do we really understand what happens when a group of people no longer trust each other?

In April 1971, a riot broke out at Canada's most notorious prison, the Kingston Penitentiary. The riot started out as a mostly peaceful protest against the treatment of prisoners and the conditions inside the penitentiary, which was by that time more than a hundred years old. Built on the water, it was damp and structurally degraded. It was also overcrowded, housing 50 percent more prisoners than it was supposed to. Inmates were housed together regardless of the severity of their crimes, and the institution was understaffed. In January of that year, the warden had written a letter to his government supervisors stating, "There is a high degree of tension at Kingston Penitentiary at this time. In fact it appears to be almost at the point of explosion."[3]

And explode it did. Writer and producer Catherine Fogarty tells the story in her book *Murder on the Inside*. Led initially by inmate Billy Knight, who instigated the riot by coordinating a surprise attack on the guards when a group of inmates was being led around the cell block, the riot took over the prison. The stated intention of those instigating the riot was to bring awareness to their appalling living conditions. Knight told warden Arthur Jarvis that no one wanted anyone to get hurt. Speaking to the inmates under the central dome where most of them could congregate, he "continued to stress the need for nonviolence."[4]

This being a prison riot, the idea of nonviolence needs a bit of explanation, because in the hours immediately following the takeover of the cell block building of the prison, there was certainly a lot of property damage. Windows were smashed, and furniture was ripped out of cells and piled in common areas. Pipes were broken, and the cell block was vandalized. But there was relatively little violence toward any person. The prisoners did not fight much among themselves; most importantly, a group of about thirty of them took it upon themselves to protect the six guards who had been taken hostage. The leaders of this small group recognized that "any chance of getting out of the riot alive would be gone if the guards were killed. They were their only insurance against an all-out attack."[5]

The leaders of the riot didn't want to deal directly with the prison or government administration, so they demanded the creation of a citizens' group to act as an intermediary between the two sides. Just as the negotiating got underway, another problem was brewing. In a prison social hierarchy, sex offenders and informants are on the lowest rung. In the Kingston Penitentiary in 1971, these two groups were separated from the general prison population. When the riot broke out, a couple of inmates used the opportunity to stage an attack on these "undesirables." At that point, however, there was enough trust in the goals of the riot to prevent the proliferation of that kind of violence. When Knight found out about the attack, he "was furious. He called for a general assembly in the dome area. Visibly shaken, he told the inmates the attack on [one of the undesirables] was precisely the sort of thing they didn't want to happen. It made the inmates look like animals and would seriously jeopardize their chances of negotiating with the administration."[6] So the instigators backed off, and the undesirables were left alone for the moment.

So, right from the beginning there was tension among the rioting inmates. Knight and the small group he led were focused on drawing attention to prison conditions; the riot was just a way of getting the message out. But there was another small group who saw the takeover of the prison as an opportunity for revenge and the redress of old grievances. And then there was the large chunk in the middle, who certainly didn't want to die for the cause of change but who were nonetheless nursing frustration and anger at the way the system had treated them. At the beginning, most inmates supported Knight, which kept the violence in check. But over time, the trust the inmates had in Knight began to erode.

A huge contributor to the breakdown of trust was the asymmetrical information environment. First, Kingston Penitentiary wasn't a high-trust environment to begin with. Inmates did not trust guards or the government administration, nor did they often trust one another. Second, the citizen intermediaries made it harder for accurate information to flow among all parties. These volunteer citizen negotiators did an amazing job, but ultimately they could not speak for the government, though they were nonetheless seen as the face of bad news. Third, the inmates had access to radios and television, and so also received whatever information the media was putting out, accurate or not.

Compounding the issue even further was the fact that the military had been called in and was surrounding the prison. Between inmate worries and media speculation, the presence of the military suggested that a peaceful resolution to the riot was not a government priority. Without any information to offer an alternative explanation for the military presence, behavior within the prison walls began to change.

Gradually, Billy Knight began to lose credibility with the other inmates. Stepping into the void was inmate Barrie MacKenzie. He had been keeping the guards safe, but he "knew the situation was becoming more volatile and the lives of their hostages were in danger. If more inmates go onside with the rebels he had just confronted, they could soon be outnumbered and outpowered."[7] If the bad behavior completely drove out the good, there was a chance that everyone in the cell block was going to die.

The inmates received information regarding the negotiations to end the riot via the four to five prisoners who met with the citizens' committee. They had but one small channel to balance the reams of unvalidated information they were receiving from the media.

The inmate leaders released one hostage "as an act of diplomacy and to dispel some of the ugly rumours being fed to the media by guards on the outside."[8] These rumors were particularly problematic because they made the already volatile situation worse, and the prisoners had no channel by which to counteract them.

Bad behavior was thus on the rise. "Rumours were flying and distrust was building. Fights were breaking out and inmates were showing up at the prison hospital with injuries inflicted on one another."[9]

The information asymmetry continued to worsen. The inmate group reached an agreement with the citizens' group, only to hear the government lie about the progress to the media. "The inmates had indeed heard the Solicitor General on the radio saying he was not prepared to negotiate with the rioters. They were fed up with being jerked around. They weren't being told the truth."[10] The government had all the accurate information. The citizens' committee had some. The inmate leaders had a little. And the rest of the inmates had almost none. Furthermore, the government would not let the citizens' committee communicate directly with the media to counter any rumors. The complete information asymmetry finally led to a total trust breakdown. The bad behavior escalated and almost completely drove out the good.

The prisoners began to fight one another over food and blankets. The prison infrastructure was completely destroyed. A group of inmates went after the undesirables; they assaulted all of them and murdered two.[11] The dream of a peaceful protest to change prison conditions came to an end.

Why did the situation not end in total disaster? At least partial credit was given to Barrie MacKenzie and the mutual trust he established with citizens' committee member Ron Haggart. Because these two men could communicate with each other, some accurate information was able to flow, allowing for the eventual release of the hostages and the peaceful surrender of all the inmates. The citizens' committee heavily criticized the government for the way it handled the riot, specifically calling out the lack of communication of accurate information and how it almost led to the deaths of the prisoners, the hostages, and anyone else caught in the crossfire.

It Can Happen to Anyone

Implicit in Gresham's law is the idea that "everyone is doing it." Money doesn't circulate on its own; bad money drives out the good money because everyone is spending the bad and hoarding the good. It's ultimately human behavior that leads to the breakdown.

One of the most important takeaways from using Gresham's law as a model is to understand that each one of us can become a person who hoards the good money. Despite our intentions, or even our values, we all have the potential to succumb to bad behavior. Why? Because we may think it is the only way to participate in the system.

In 2012, a scandal shook the world of professional bike racing when it was revealed that doping was widespread and had been for years. Racers were stripped of their titles, championships, and medals. The entire credibility of the sport was undermined.

One person taking performance-enhancing drugs is likely to be an individual issue. Everyone who competes at the highest level taking performance-enhancing drugs suggests a systemic issue. It's safe to say that very few athletes commence competitive sport with the desire to dope. Doping has health risks and career risks, and deep down you're always going to know you aren't really the best purely because of your skill. So how does it happen that the bad behavior drives out the good?

In the book *The Secret Race: Inside the Hidden World of the Tour de France*, authors Tyler Hamilton and Daniel Coyle quote cyclist George Hincapie as saying: "Early in my professional career, it became clear to me that, given the widespread use of performance enhancing drugs by cyclists at the top of the profession, it was not possible to compete at the highest level without them."[12]

Tyler Hamilton (himself an elite cyclist) describes races early in his career when he was racing clean, doing everything right, pushing his body through incredible pain, and yet watching other riders easily pass him. For years, he watched others dope, watched drugs like erythropoietin (EPO) be passed out by team doctors. He describes the moment in 1997 when he decided to join them:

> After the race, I felt a new level of frustration as I watched the white bags get handed out. Now I could measure the injustice. . . . I could count the number of seconds those white bags contained. I could see the gap between who I was and who I could be. Who I was supposed to be. This was bullshit. This was not fair. In that moment, the future became clear. Unless something changed, I was done.[13]

Doping in cycling was, at that time, systemic. Athletes had to get their drugs from somewhere. A few doctors would supply dozens of athletes. Elaborate clandestine operations would be conducted involving athletes, team managers, and support staff to get the right injection to an athlete at the right time.

Drugs, along with other means of cheating such as blood transfusions, were used both during training and races. Such shortcuts are most useful at certain points in races that take place over days, and trying to avoid getting caught takes a lot of planning. Racers needed to know, down to the hour, when they were clean and when they were not.

They were, however, still operating within a system that offered some predictability. Racers were going to get tested, and tests were much more likely at certain times than at others. The mechanisms trying to enforce the good behavior weren't strong enough to discourage the bad behavior. Cyclist Bernhard Kohl said, "I was tested two hundred times during my career, and one hundred times I had drugs in my body. I was caught, but ninety-nine other times I wasn't. Riders think they can get away with doping because most of the time they do."[14]

Hamilton explains that doping was so pervasive, figuring out how to dope better and what the next new drug might be were part of an athlete's regimen. "The rewards were too big, the punishments too mild, so the hunt for the next magical product was too tempting." When a new drug or new doping technique came out, everyone jumped on it. "My choice was simple," Hamilton says regarding when he was first approached about a new freezing technique for blood transfusions, "because it wasn't really a choice. I could either let my rivals use the new freezer while I fell behind, or I could join the club."[15]

To be fair, some riders chose not to dope. Those riders, however, did not win the big, multiday races like the Tour de France. For the most successful cyclists, the bad behavior of doping was institutionalized. It was part of the sport. No one felt like they were behaving badly. Author Daniel Coyle, who wrote with Tyler Hamiliton, explains it this way:

> Cycling history contains zero examples of high-level racers who, having tested positive from doping, offered an immediate and complete confession. . . . Part of the reason is legal, but the larger part seems to be psychological: they don't feel like they've done anything wrong, so there's nothing to confess.[16]

Such is the nature of widespread bad behavior. If everyone's doing it, how bad can it be? Isn't it simply the way things are?

Dr. Michael Ashenden, an Australian scientist who helped develop tests to detect certain forms of doping, admits, "Now I see [the athletes are] put in an impossible situation. If I had been put in their situation, I would do what they did."[17] The system that existed around professional cycling effectively removed all incentives for good behavior. Thus, the bad behavior could completely drive out the good.

After the scandal broke and the evidence piled up and previous cycling winners were stripped of titles and made to pay back sponsorship money, the sport began to change. It wasn't easy; it required years of investigations and depositions and confessions and corroboration in many countries. But gradually, enough consequences were levied and changes made that the system once again had a place for good behavior.

Tyler Hamilton, who actively participated in shining a light into the dark corners of the sport of cycling, makes an interesting point: "I'm happy to see my sport cleaning itself up over the past few years. It's far from 100 percent clean—I don't think that's possible, as long as you're dealing with human beings who want to win—but it's significantly better and slower."[18] There's always going to be bad behavior. What we really want is to not have so much of it that positive actions aren't possible. That means creating a system that supports and reinforces good behavior.

For Hamilton, part of his purpose in telling his story is so that "people might focus their energy on the real challenge: creating a culture that tips people away from doping."[19] This sentiment moves beyond cycling specifically to a need we can all identify with. We need to look at the systems in which we live, work, and play and make sure we participate in creating a culture that doesn't allow bad behavior to drive out the good.

Conclusion

Gresham's Law states that bad money drives out good. But it's not just about currency. The principle applies anytime there are two competing versions of something, one perceived as high quality and the other as low quality.

In a sense, Gresham's Law is the dark side of human nature. We're wired to optimize for the short term, to get the most value for the least effort. If we can pass off the less valuable thing and keep the more valuable one, we will. Without consequences, bad behavior drives out good. Bad lending drives out good lending. Bad morals drive out good morals. Overcoming this requires constant effort.

In the short run, bad often drives out good. But in the long run, true value wins out.

Bubbles

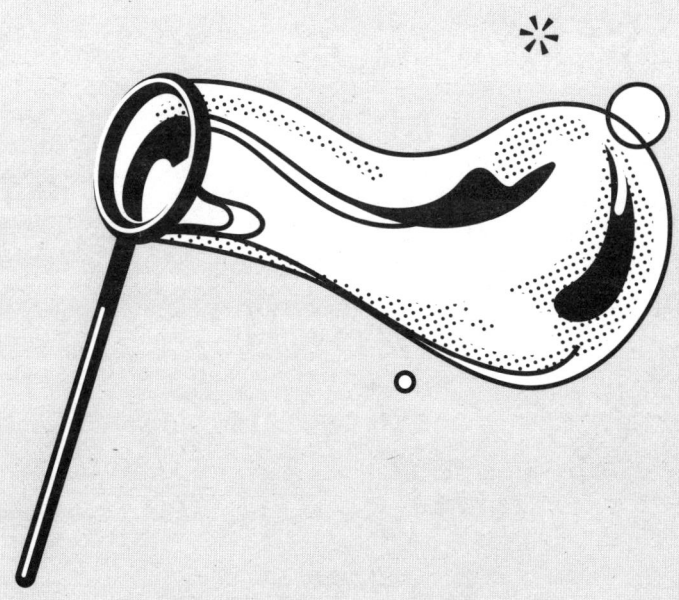

Don't get caught holding the bag.

Just what is a speculative bubble? *The Oxford English Dictionary* defines a bubble as "anything fragile, unsubstantial, empty, or worthless; a deceptive show. From 17th c. onwards often applied to delusive commercial or financial schemes." The problem is that words like *show* and *scheme* suggest a deliberate creation, rather than a widespread social phenomenon that is not directed by any central impresario.

–JOHN KENNETH GALBRAITH[1]

Bubbles are an emergent property of markets, tending to have no single clear cause or to be underpinned by deliberate fraud. A financial bubble occurs when the price of an asset increases an enormous (even exponential) amount in a short time due to buyers expecting continued price increases.

As with anything, the price of an asset, such as a stock, is set by supply and demand. The more people expect to be able to profit by speculating in the asset, the higher the demand, and the more the price rises. However, sustained price increases are not what makes a bubble. To be a bubble, it needs to eventually pop. Once people stop expecting further price increases—which tends to mean they expect the price to drop, not just stay the same—they rush to sell, to avoid losing money. Supply suddenly soars, demand vanishes, and prices plummet, causing even more investors to flee.

During the early stages of a bubble, many fortunes are made. But as knowledge about sharply rising prices spreads, more people enter the bubble on less favorable terms. Often, bubbles become truly divorced from reality once growing numbers of people who are far outside their circle of competence (a model we discussed in volume 1) start buying. People end up buying on the mistaken assumption that the immediate past is an accurate picture of the immediate future; there is a "contagious optimism, seemingly impervious to facts, that often takes hold when prices are rising."[2] People don't understand the economics of what they are buying; they just don't want to miss out on the gold rush.

> Beware of competing with those who have different time horizons to you.
>
> —MORGAN HOUSEL[3]

Even those who call out the bubble can get caught up in the excitement. "As a bubble expands, some skeptics begin to disregard their own judgment because they feel that everyone else simply couldn't be wrong."[4] Basically, it's really hard to sit on the sidelines while it seems that everyone else around you is making tons of money with minimal effort. However, any change in behavior by previous naysayers just serves to amplify the bubble, pushing it to its breaking point. Because "over time, the quality of information that can be gleaned from the behavior of others becomes worse and worse,"[5] a social proof situation is created, wherein it feels almost irresponsible not to jump on the bandwagon.

When bubbles pop, which they always do, later entrants into that market are worse off. Many people find themselves holding "assets" that are now worth less than they paid for them.

Irrational human behavior is a direct contributor to the life cycle of a bubble. Thus, they are partly a social phenomenon, with analogous applications outside of economics. Think of fashion trends: Every generation has to contend with a new look or style of clothing that appears out of nowhere and that, within months, everyone seems to be wearing. Then, one day, somehow that trend is no longer cool, and we're stuck with high-priced items that we no longer want to wear.

A couple of lessons you can learn about bubbles are, first, that your assumptions about the future influence your future and, second, that success can sow the seeds of failure. When you assume a good time is going to carry on indefinitely, you make decisions that can have far-ranging impacts on your lifestyle down the road. And when it comes to successful products, making something ubiquitous is not the same as making it indispensable.

Bubbles—however much we try to understand them—are not going away any time soon. In fact, there is a good argument to be made that in many ways, cyclical patterns drive development. Whether bubbles are necessary is subjective, but they certainly encourage investment. A short burst of wild speculation can be beneficial in the long run; if enough people are throwing spaghetti at a wall, some of it has to stick. A wide spectrum of ideas enables us to identify a healthy middle ground. Innovation and development can be impossible without an early dose of overconfidence.

As anthropologist Clifford Geertz writes in the essay "Thick Description," sometimes a new idea arrives in the intellectual landscape, and people try to use it to solve all problems in their fields.[6] They try applying it to *everything*. This burst of attention teaches us a lot about the idea and its limitations. Over time, we develop a narrower definition of it, which gives it long-term usefulness as a theory.

The life cycle of a bubble and the factors that contribute to its expansion and disintegration are what makes this model so useful. How to harness the exuberance, and not mistake it for a new, persistent state of affairs, is what we want to understand better by using this model as a lens.

Good Intentions, Bad Results

Good intentions and wishful thinking do not make a sound platform for investment. Whether we are investing our money, time, or reputation, it pays to be mindful of the information that underpins the structure in which we're investing. How reliable is the information? And thus, how much can we bet on it?

Bubbles can form and pop quickly. In the late 1990s, the dot-com bubble illustrated the perils of investing based on optimism rather than solid information. Eager to capitalize on the new economy, investors started pouring money into any company associated with the concept of "dot-com." The allure was based on a widespread belief that the internet would revolutionize business, providing new economic opportunities to those previously left out, and that absolutely any investment in this space would yield high returns. This enthusiasm led to a frenzy of overvalued stock prices as the demand for internet-company shares skyrocketed, with investors often disregarding traditional financial metrics such as profit and revenue.

The intention was to be part of a groundbreaking shift in the economy that would benefit the entire world. However, much of the information fueling this investment boom was unreliable and built on expectations of future growth with little evidence to back it up. In reality, many startups operated under untested business models. Their share price went up because the story they told was one of promise and hope. A few notable investors, including Warren Buffett, who opted not to participate in the bubble were cast as old and out of touch.

For a while, speculators bought the story, hoping there would be a greater fool later. As the results started to come in, and the underlying economic reality emerged, investors realized they could not be the one still at the ball when the clock struck midnight, and everyone wanted to exit all at once, causing a dramatic market correction. The resulting collapse wiped out vast amounts of wealth and underscored the importance of basing investment decisions on solid, reliable data, not hype.

What we can learn from this story is that investing in something with a shaky foundation comes with a big caution sign. Until that foundation is solidified by facts, we are taking a huge risk with our money, time, or reputation by investing in it. Structures built on the wishful thinking of others are ephemeral. Recognizing bubbles is a skill worth developing, because bubbles, by definition, always pop.

Keynesian Beauty Contests

When people speculate—meaning they purchase an asset intending to resell it later at a higher price—they engage in a Keynesian beauty contest. This involves assessing the price of something based on ever more elaborate estimations of other people's estimations of its value. Economist John Maynard Keynes used the metaphor of a beauty contest to explain how stock prices are set.[7] He asked readers to imagine a contest where entrants must choose six faces out of a hundred; those who pick the faces chosen by the most other people win.

Keynes believed stocks are priced not according to their intrinsic value but according to investors' perceptions of other investors' perceptions of their value. The reality is that, barring illegal insider trading, most investors have access to pretty much the same information. Predicting prices is less a matter of understanding a stock's value and more a matter of predicting how other people will react to the same information. First-order thinking is not enough. Second-order thinking—the act of thinking of the consequences of consequences—is necessary for useful predictions. (For more on second-order thinking, see volume 1 of *The Great Mental Models*.) In a Keynesian beauty contest, the more levels someone can think ahead to, the more accurate their decisions will be.

The Keynesian beauty contest contradicts the idea of markets as rational, with stocks priced per their intrinsic value. Consequently, it provides a means of understanding irrational behavior, like that which creates economic bubbles. If prices are rising fast, investors may think other investors will think they will keep rising and therefore may keep buying. This leads to out-of-control pricing. While Keynes only talked about stocks, the same concept applies in almost any asset market and is especially true now that markets are more accessible to nonprofessionals.

A Bubble in Space

When we think of a bubble, we might go to a classic like the Dutch tulip mania in the seventeenth century. Or we might think of something more recent, like the dot-com bubble of the late 1990s. But we probably wouldn't think of NASA's Apollo space program in the mid-twentieth century. After all, it put men on the moon— repeatedly. Everyone was on board, from the man in the street to the scientists in the labs to the president of the United States, and it succeeded spectacularly, right? Well, yes and no. The Apollo program, even by NASA's own reckoning, was a bubble that allowed for huge innovation and investment before collapsing.

To set the stage: In the early 1960s, the United States and the Soviet Union were deep into the Cold War, and tensions were high. In 1957, the Soviets had launched Sputnik, the first human-built satellite, into orbit. Then, in April 1961, they announced that Yuri Gagarin had become the first man to orbit Earth. Given the tensions between the two countries, the White House knew that the Soviets could not be seen to be winning the space race—and, by proxy, the Cold War. And so, President John F. Kennedy announced in May 1961 that the United States would land a man on the moon and return him safely to Earth.[8]

"The clarity of the goal, the amount of political support, the safety culture, the funding provided, and the prestige gained were far beyond all other human space programs," according to a NASA presentation. "The political will to go to the moon was so great because it was a response to the challenge of the Soviets, the cold war, missile race, and space race."[9] The political will was so great, in fact, that it completely overrode the will of almost everyone else— including the public and the scientific community. Polls of American citizens showed that they thought the money could be spent better elsewhere, and scientists thought that robotic space exploration would have a far better return on investment than sending humans into space. As the space race kicked into high gear, public opinion swung wildly throughout the 1960s from disdain to enthusiasm. In 1962, the press was almost uniformly on board with the program, but by 1963, reporting had become more skeptical. "Among scientists, the initial enchantment had faded before the mounting costs and they feared the heavy drain on other fields of scientific endeavor."[10] But by 1964, more than three quarters of American were saying that the Apollo program should continue apace or even move faster. Then, the fickle public-opinion pendulum swung back again, due to what author Neil Maher called "NASA fatigue,"[11] with nearly half of those polled saying spending on space exploration should be cut.[12]

While scientists worried that spending on the space race would suck up funds that could be used for other research, the public wondered why its taxes could fund sending a handful of men to the moon when people on Earth were starving, unhoused, and lacking healthcare. Poet and musician Gil Scott-Heron famously encapsulated this sentiment in his piece "Whitey on the Moon."[13]

So, the Apollo program was controversial, but it had the force of the White House and the threat of the Cold War propelling it forward. Enormous amounts of money and time were invested, and some of the solutions to space-exploration problems became well-known inventions that were then popularized back on Earth, like cordless vacuums and the reflective thermal blankets given to runners at the end of marathons.

And then came the big event: on July 19, 1969, "an estimated 600 million people—one-fifth of the world's population" watched the Apollo 13 mission land on the moon.[14] In this moment, almost everyone in the United States and many around the globe were firmly in favor of the American space program. It was an incredible achievement that further expanded the bounds of humanity's limits and justified its cost in time and dollars. It was also a decisive win against the Soviet Union in the Cold War.

But as soon as the lunar lander touched down, and the American people had a chance to come down off their infusion of patriotism and scientific wonder, the bubble burst. "It was one of the most exceptional and costly projects ever undertaken by the United States, and thus constitutes an excellent example of how bubbles function from within," according to one analysis. Undertaking this program posed a huge political, monetary, and of course safety risk. While the pendulum of public and scientific support swung back and forth throughout the 1960s, by the end of the decade, there was a kind of wild-eyed enthusiasm for the Apollo program. But the enthusiasm did not last. There have been other human space exploration programs since, including the shuttle missions of the 1980s and '90s, but they did not sustain the investment—in dollars or in hearts and minds—that the Apollo missions were able to create as that mid-century bubble grew. "As expected from our hypothesis on bubbles, it led to innumerable technological innovations, and scientific advances, but many of them at a cost documented to be disproportionate compared with the returns."[15]

The lesson to be learned from this model of creativity isn't that bubbles are necessarily bad. They have their uses. When the Apollo bubble popped, it did so in a halo of glory, and though it was an expensive mission, it did lead to incredible advances. That kind of investment isn't sustainable, though. If we use the excitement generated by an innovative and potentially risky idea to drive investment and innovation, then bubbles can foster outsize amounts of creativity. However, it's crucial to keep an eye on the bubble and note when it's about to pop.

Conclusion

Bubbles are a natural by-product of human nature. They happen when collective enthusiasm for an asset runs far ahead of its fundamental value. It's the moment when the market becomes untethered from reality, when prices are driven not by sober calculation but by mass delusion.

Bubbles are a fascinating study in human psychology. They're driven by greed and FOMO (fear of missing out). No one wants to be the sucker who sits on the sidelines while everyone else gets rich. But there's also an element of genuine belief, of conviction that this time is different, that the old rules no longer apply.

While ultimately destructive, bubbles also serve a function. They're the market's way of exploring new frontiers, of testing new possibilities. Many of the innovations we take for granted today—from cars to computers to the internet itself—were once the subject of speculative manias. Bubbles fund the infrastructure for future revolutions, even as they leave a trail of financial wreckage in their wake.

Bubbles are a reminder that markets are human constructs, driven by human emotions and beliefs. They're a mirror held up to our collective hopes, dreams, and delusions. The next time you catch yourself saying "this time is different," remember that all bubbles pop eventually.

Like a balloon that can only expand so far, bubbles eventually burst, and the game ends abruptly, without warning. Keeping yourself grounded in value and economic reality, not in story or hype, is key to standing alone as a bubble expands.

ART

Art evokes the mystery without which the world would not exist.

—RENÉ MAGRITTE[1]

Audience

Who is it for?

Write to please just one person. If you open a window and make love to the world, so to speak, your story will get pneumonia.

—KURT VONNEGUT[1]

The concept of an audience helps us explore the interaction between what we do and how it is experienced.

The relationship between the audience and the artist is a crucial aspect of art. Both parties engage in a mutual exchange that shapes the overall experience of the work. Iris Murdoch explains, "this ... is one of the deep attractions of art, that it gathers together the personality of the creator and the personality of the reader or spectator into a sense of unified significance which may, of course, be very momentary."[2]

Anticipating the audience greatly impacts what an artist produces. The audience is both the group for which the artist creates their work and the group that chooses to consume it. Although works of art may appeal to unexpected groups, artists tend to have a specific group of people in mind when creating, and they target their work toward what that audience is likely to enjoy and engage with. This means that when we encounter art we like, it may have been specifically created for people like us.

The audience also impacts the artist. Anticipating the audience can impact how art is developed. For example, when developing a piece of theater, the artist may need to consider whether the audience is likely to describe what they've seen or heard, and how they will engage with the performance, and adjust accordingly.

> Theatre must always be living in that dangerous moment of the unexpected; quite how is this audience going to respond? Is it indeed going to respond at all? Probably it won't; we've had experiences where people have just fallen asleep. What do you do in that situation? You've got to go through those two hours; how do you wake this person up?
>
> —JATINDER VERMA[3]

Audiences vary greatly in size and diversity. They can be one person or thousands of people; they can encompass one culture or many. Furthermore, audience engagement with art falls along a spectrum from a solo experience to a shared experience, wherein the audience participates in the art together. No two people experience art in the same way, and no one person experiences art the same way twice. It often happens that you read a book as a child and have vivid memories of the story and the tears running down your face. However, when you return to the same work as an adult, you read the same words and realize they have no impact on you anymore. You're a different person as an adult than you were as a child. As Heraclitus is credited with saying, "You could not step twice into the same river."[4]

> I reflected that public art looks futile without its power source: a crowd.
>
> —PETER SCHJELDAHL[5]

Engaging in art is a work of collaboration with the artist and, sometimes, even the audience. Reactions can be contagious. We participate in some forms of art as part of a group, and at least some of our reaction to these types of experiences is influenced by the group's responses: When one person starts to clap, we do the same. When someone starts to laugh, so do we.

The collective experience of theater and music has long served a purpose beyond mere aesthetic pleasure. These art forms have traditionally been performed for groups, to provide a platform for broader social, cultural, and political commentary. Philip Ball, in *The Music Instinct*, explains, "Music commonly happens in places and contexts in which it creates social cohesion, for example in religions and ritual or in dance and communal singing."[6]

Audiences both shape and are shaped by the art they consume; "we transform what we look at."[7] The feedback of the audience—their responses, their buying habits, and so on—impacts how artists work. A dialogue always exists, with information going both ways. The work changes the audience, modifying how they perceive the world and setting the tone for what they might consume in the future.

> Music is not a series of acoustic facts. [It] emerges from a collaboration in which the listener too plays an active part.
>
> —PHILIP BALL[8]

Some artists extensively study their audience to cater every detail of their work to them. Taken too far, this consideration can change the artist as they pander to the whims of the crowd. Other artists are less concerned with the public's reception and choose to create what they wish and hope it finds an audience. The prolific writer John Updike once claimed that when he wrote his books, he liked to imagine them being found—old and battered, with their dust jackets missing—on a library shelf by a teenage boy somewhere east of Kansas. To him, the reviews and the book shops were secondary to that very particular audience member he envisioned.[9]

There are two main ways to categorize audiences: by who they are (demographics) and by what they like (preferences). Audience demographics include factors like age, gender, socioeconomic status, occupation, location, and so on. Audience preferences cover whatever it is people enjoy in a work of art. So, an artist might target their work at people over age thirty with corporate jobs, or they may target people who enjoy fast-paced romantic fiction.

Artists frequently ask themselves, *Who will pay for my creation?* Thus, a consideration for some artists is creating art that will sell. In nineteenth-century Europe, there was a type of theater piece called the "well-made play." The best of the genre were well written and carefully plotted, but they were designed first and foremost to be entertaining. The plots were logical and the resolutions satisfying. Although they were sometimes attacked for being simplistic and saccharine, Neil Grant says, in *History of Theatre*, "Not all the practitioners of the 'well-made play' were artistically or socially worthless and, even if they did set their sights firmly on filling seats—and tills—they were hardly the first, or last, writers whose ambition was to give the audience what it liked."[10] One can view this notion of meeting demand as practical. Without an audience—and its associated money—to sustain an artist, it can become economically prohibitive to make art.

Throughout the centuries, art has been consumed by vastly different audiences. Sometimes it has been more like a public good shared freely among a group of people. Often, however, artists were looking for payment of some sort, and the art itself would be heavily influenced by who was doing the paying. The way you captivate someone on the street versus in a theater is different. Materials, such as paint, could be very expensive, and so the portrait of a wealthy patron might be imaginatively flattering versus technically realistic. And for centuries, artists created without the benefit of copyright protection, so being clearly and widely associated with a work was paramount.

Creating for someone influences what you create. Performing to someone can make us better, since knowing that we are being watched can help us focus.[11]

Once you start looking for audiences, you start to see them everywhere. There are two types of audiences: direct and indirect. Direct audiences allow for the creator and the consumer of a work to interact in a permissionless way. Indirect audiences, on the other hand, require a filter. Filters can be people, technology, or even culture. With an indirect audience, you need permission from someone, or something, to reach them. Depending on the message, these filters have the power to amplify or cancel it.

The well-meaning mother is constantly frustrated by the inability of her child to answer questions like "What did you do today?" (to which the answer is usually a muttered "Nothing"—a cover for "I don't know how to tell a good story about it, how to impose story shape on the events"). To tell stories, you have to hear stories, and you have to have an audience to hear the stories you can tell.

—SARA MAITLAND[12]

Influencing Your Audience

An audience might influence an original artistic creation if the artist has a specific audience in mind. It might also influence art in progress if people protest against a sculpture or heckle performers. Artists know their art is going to confront an audience eventually, so knowing who that audience is likely to be impacts what an artist develops.

If you want to sell art, you must craft it so that someone is willing to buy it—to pay for that portrait or those tickets to see your show. You can surprise your audience and throw a lot of extras into the expected package, but success requires an element of knowing what an audience desires and being able to deliver it. Not all artists give audiences what they want. Some provoke or challenge; some want to make people uncomfortable or thoughtful. But still, designing for a specific reaction means knowing your audience well enough to anticipate what will have the desired outcome.

The value of knowing an audience is not relevant only for artists. Trial lawyers know that figuring out how to most effectively communicate with an audience—a judge, a jury—is critical. Clarence Darrow was an American attorney who handled the defense in some of the most sensational and impactful trials in US legal history. It would be impossible to cover all these cases, so here we're just going to focus on how he handled his audience in three of them.

The first was the case of Leopold and Loeb. Richard Loeb and Nathan Leopold Jr., eighteen and nineteen years old at the time, were being tried for the brutal killing of fourteen-year-old Bobby Franks. Both killers had confessed to the crime. Neither their guilt nor their total lack of remorse was in doubt. The well-off families of the defendants hired Darrow to do one thing: keep their boys from receiving the death penalty.

When Darrow argued a case, part of the reason he was so persuasive was because he genuinely believed what he was arguing. In the case of Leopold and Loeb, Darrow thought that sentencing the boys to death would be a miscarriage of justice, both because they were too young and because capital punishment should not be used in a just and fair state.[13]

First, Darrow considered who would most likely be persuaded by the arguments he would make against capital punishment in this case. He decided that his best bet was to convince the judge, John Caverly, instead of a jury. Given the media coverage and both Leopold's and Loeb's incendiary statements regarding the murder, Darrow felt going in front of a jury was too risky. So, he instructed the defendants to plead guilty, and Darrow focused his efforts on the sentencing.

As John A. Farrell wrote in his biography of Clarence Darrow, Darrow developed his argument knowing that he "spoke to three distinct audiences."[14] The first, and most important, was the judge. He had to give Caverly a compelling legal reason to not give the death penalty. Darrow also spoke to America at large, seeking to put this trial in the broader context of the evil of capital punishment. The third "and final audience was Chicago. Darrow wanted to touch Caverly's heart, but he knew the judge was a politician and that this speech must move public opinion."[15]

So when Darrow spoke in the courtroom, he knew he had to convince more than just the man seated behind the bench; his audience was far larger. His argument couldn't be overly complicated or technical. He had to appeal to values and engage emotion if he was going to win over the larger public audience of Chicago—and

America. According to those in the courtroom, despite Darrow's speaking for hours at a time, "the crowd stayed with him, listening to every word."[16]

Farrell writes, "Darrow was, in retrospect, a uniquely apt lawyer for Leopold and Loeb. He had the audacity to treat judges and juries to original sermons on an intellectual plane far higher than the usual courtroom wrangling, and to do so in a captivating way." By the time he was done arguing for mercy for Leopold and Loeb, "women in the audience—including Judge Caverly's wife and sister—wept. The defendants had stopped laughing; he had touched even their cold souls."[17]

Darrow read his audience well. The papers were supportive of Darrow and uncritical in their coverage of his arguments. Darrow gave Caverly an out by focusing on the fact that no one so young had ever been given the death penalty in Illinois. So, in the end, "Darrow had read Caverly correctly. Precedent was the key."[18] Loeb and Leopold were given life sentences. Darrow had done his job.

Clarence Darrow "believed that the outcomes of trials rested on such elemental factors as likability."[19] In his next major trial, defending John Scopes's right to teach evolution in his science class in a school in Tennessee, Darrow again spent time considering how best to reach his audience. Although the trial would be publicly broadcast on the radio and reported across America, the jury would be composed of people from around Dayton, Tennessee. Those were the people Darrow most needed to connect with.

When Darrow first arrived, "he went to work wooing the locals."[20] He spent time learning about the town and how its residents thought about the particulars of the issue of teaching evolution in schools. During the trial, his delivery was accessible. He spoke clearly and eloquently, presenting himself as a man just trying to do what was right. Every day, the courtroom was packed, and when Darrow spoke, "the audience was mesmerized. The only sound, aside from his voice, was the clicking of the telegraph keys that were carrying his speech to millions of Americans."[21]

The prosecution in the case was led by former US secretary of state William Jennings Bryan. Darrow got Bryan to take the stand—a highly unusual move, but one Bryan accepted because he wanted to best Darrow in the argument. Darrow then got Bryan to admit parts of the Bible could not be taken literally, that God could have taken millennia to create the world, and that evolution could thus be an act of God. The faith of the jury in the mutual exclusivity of Christianity and evolution was destroyed.

While the Scopes trial was a legal defeat for Darrow and Scopes, it brought significant attention to the issue of teaching evolution and helped shape public opinion on the matter. The trial is considered a landmark event in the history of the American legal system and the debate over the separation of church and state.

In one of the final cases of his career, Darrow defended brothers Ossian and Henry Sweet, plus nine other black men, charged with the murder of a white man in Detroit. The killing had happened while the Sweets were being mobbed in their home, and thus, Darrow felt, was ultimately an act of self-defense. Darrow's main argument, while covering the history of race relations in America, was primarily about a person's right to defend themselves when under attack: the Sweets had been in their home. They were not provoking anyone. Everyone has the right to feel safe in their home, and thus the Sweets were well within their rights to stop anyone they didn't want to come in from entering. Darrow knew that the jury already believed this to be true for white people. His job was to make them accept that blacks had the same rights as well.

Journalist Jo Gorman, who attended the trial, wrote of Darrow's closing argument, "His voice went on and on, always interesting, always fascinating, always holding the attention of judge, jurors, and audience." He spoke to the jury for almost seven hours, and "it was wonderful," Gorman wrote. "Eloquent. Logical. People wept and jurors were moved."[22]

Again, Darrow read his audience correctly. He framed his arguments in terms that resonated with them and constantly adjusted his delivery to keep their attention. In the end, all nine defendants were found not guilty.

Using the audience model as a lens helps us see that we are often performing. While we may not be up on a stage, someone is always watching.

At its most basic, an audience can be understood as at least one person we're trying to communicate with. How we do that—through the words we choose, our tone, our body language, our medium, and more—often means the difference between a successful outcome and failure.

Thinking about how we reach, persuade, and build our audience is a powerful form of leverage.

Conclusion

The audience is the invisible participant in every work of art. They are the eyes that see, the ears that hear, the minds that interpret. Without an audience, art is like a tree falling in an empty forest—it may make a sound, but does it really matter? The audience is what gives art its meaning, its purpose, its very existence.

But the audience is not a passive. They bring their own experiences, their own perspectives, their own biases to the encounter. A painting of a sunset may evoke feelings of peace and beauty for one person and feelings of melancholy and loss for another. The artwork is the same, but the audience is different, and so the meaning is different. In this sense, the audience is a cocreator of the art.

This is why great artists are often obsessed with their audience. They aren't just creating for themselves—they are creating for the imagined eyes and minds that will encounter their work. They are trying to anticipate reactions, to provoke thoughts, to shape experiences. The audience is their silent collaborator and their ultimate judge.

But here's the paradox: the more an artist focuses on the audience, the more they risk losing their authentic voice. If you're constantly trying to anticipate what people will like, you end up creating something bland and generic. The true artist must walk a tightrope—respecting the audience but not pandering to them. Creating something that communicates but also something that is true to their own vision.

In a world where so much can be faked, the audience is something real. You can fake likes, followers, and reviews, but you can't fake the genuine human experience of engaging with art. The spontaneous laughter, the unexpected tear, the long, thoughtful silence—these are the honest reactions that both the audience and the artists live for.

Never forget your audience, but never let them dictate your creation. And always remember: in a world of illusions, the audience is your anchor.

Genre

Form shapes expectation.

I am more and more convinced that literature is made up of works, genres, schools, discussions, problems, collective work in order to solve certain problems.

—ITALO CALVINO[1]

G enre as a model helps us understand both the benefits and pitfalls of grouping things together.

Noticing similarities helps us make connections and process the world more effectively. But being too rigid in our classifications means we miss out on opportunities for new combinations and the insights they bring. There is a sweet spot to genre, and using it as a model shows us how to explore the power inherent in multiple types of connections.

Genre is an easy concept to grasp but a much harder one to apply. The *Oxford English Dictionary* definition is "a particular style or category of works of art; esp. a type of literary work characterized by a particular form, style, or purpose."[2]

To define the genre of an artistic work, we have to approach it from many different angles. Art critics use genre to describe categories of artworks, such as film noir, jazz, science fiction, and still life. Literature scholars use it to describe categories of text, such as biography, nonfiction, and newspaper editorial.[3] Early uses of the term, which we find in Aristotle's *Poetics*, merely divided artistic creations that used words into large buckets like "drama" and "lyric poetry." So, in this conception, a novel is a genre of writing product, and a mystery novel a genre of story.

The application of the term is thus by no means consistent. As

Catharine Abell notes in a paper on genre, "Even as used by critics, the term may pick out categories that appear to classify works on the basis of such diverse features as setting, content, medium, effects, tone, budget, or origins."[4]

At this point, it is fair to wonder why we should bother with genre at all. If it can refer to so many components of an artwork, then is there really any use in attempting classification? Diving into genre, however, reveals a few of its interesting facets.

First, genres change and develop over time. What is horror today is not what was considered horror fifty years ago. Scholars Tzvetan Todorov and Richard M. Berrong write, "A new genre is always the transformation of one or several old genres: by inversion, by displacement, by combination"[5]—which is how we get the space opera or art deco.

Because genres are not static, they are, note Wendy Bishop and David Starkey, "shaped by social forces and by the expectations of different readers (or audiences) during different historical periods."[6] Novels, for example, are a relatively new genre. The rise of their popularity in the eighteenth century coincided with the growth of a class of people who had both the money and time to spend on entertainment.

We can learn a lot about a society from the genre categories it uses. Blues music is very evocative of a certain time and place in American history, and many of the lyrics are an indirect (or sometimes direct) social commentary. Kabuki theater provides great insight into the cultural history of Japan. Tzvetan Todorov and Richard Berrong argue, "The existence of certain genres in a society and their absence in another reveal a central ideology and enable us to establish it with considerable certainty."[7]

Humans enjoy categories. *The Great Mental Models* series is based on the idea of chunking information into models and using them to understand the world better. Chunking information—putting like with like—helps us identify patterns and absorb new information. In this same way, genres are useful to consumers of art. Musicologist Nolan Gasser argues that "genre classifications unquestionably serve a valuable purpose in our understanding of and interaction with music, as with all art forms. . . . Without genre labels, most of us would have a hard time deciding whether or not to attend a concert or, for that matter, know how to discuss our musical taste."[8] Although genres are far from absolute in many cases, they allow us to make connections across a variety of categories. We understand both *The Age of Innocence*, by Edith Wharton, and *Pride and Prejudice*, by Jane Austin, as writings of manners, and *Dawn of the Dead* and *Get Out* as horror movies.

Genre helps us to narrow unlimited choices. In a world where seemingly everything ever created is available on demand in seconds, the number of options can overwhelm us (as well as the organizers of art). Picking a genre narrows our choices. If you've ever said to yourself, "I feel like watching a comedy tonight," you've used genre to tell yourself what to avoid and, in the process, significantly narrowed your options.

Understanding the greater context that genre offers both helps us understand the particulars of the art and limits what we experience. "A work's genre affects its evaluation because we evaluate works according to how well they perform the purposes for which they are produced,"[9] writes Catharine Abell. Knowing that *A Midsummer Night's Dream* is meant to be a comedy means we look for the humor in a character called Bottom and don't see that name as a tragedy.

We pick up on a work's genre through both internal factors, such as the first scene in a movie being set on a spaceship, and external factors, like what the sign above the aisle in a bookstore says.

In the words of literature professor Trudier Harris, "Genre is thus an umbrella concept that allows for many disparate, and often related, concepts to be conveniently divided and subdivided,"[10] defining the terms of engagement.

Each genre comes with a set of predictable conventions. Audiences anticipate these conventions when choosing to engage with a particular piece, whether it be a film, book, or painting. Writing specifically about music, Nolan Gasser says, "Hearing a genre label not only produces an instant impression about how a song or artist might sound; it also provides a code whereby artists and fans can build solidarity or division."[11] It's easy, though, to apply this thinking to all other arts. Genre is part of the contract between artist and audience.

Some artists feel that genre conventions are too binding and that they stifle creativity. If a romance always has to end happily, after a certain amount of turmoil, then how is an author meant to create something new, authentic, and different? The counterargument is that there are enough genres to cover everything, and a lot of room within each genre. Indeed, sometimes pushing at the boundaries of convention is what makes certain works of art so compelling. Theodor Adorno wrote, "The individual work that simply subordinates itself to a genre does not do justice to it. It is more fruitful if there is a conflict between them."[12] One way to achieve this conflict is to combine multiple genres, as many works of art do: jazzy rock music, historical horror movies, punk ballet dances. Any combination you as an artist can imagine, you can try to execute. Plus, conventions come into play at different points. Even if you don't want a happily-ever-after romance in your novel, you still need to follow certain conventions to be writing a novel. Freeform text without plot or character can definitely be art, but not a novel.

Neil Gaiman explains, "Genre, it had always seemed to me, was a set of assumptions, a loose contract between the creator and the audience."[13] The genre is the context in which you are operating. It allows us, as the audience, to understand what we're engaging with. We notice patterns and place them in reference to art we've already experienced. When it comes to books, Gaiman says genre is the "points in a story a reader would feel cheated without."[14] It's easy to argue that this description applies to all art. Engagement with art is active; it's a choice we make. Genre helps us make that choice so that we don't feel cheated by the experience.

The last interesting aspect of genre is that, by labeling what something is, genre also tells us what something is not. Jacques Derrida claimed, "As soon as the word 'genre' is sounded, as soon as it is heard, as soon as one attempts to conceive it, a limit is drawn. And when a limit is established, norms and interdictions are not far behind."[15] But right behind those imposed limits are artists who are deliberately flouting them: Go to see a zombie movie and end up in a Western. Pick up a novel and find yourself immersed in a memoir. Far from making genre irrelevant, art that steps over the lines helps us see those lines more clearly. "The fact that a work 'disobeys' its genre does not make the latter nonexistent; it is tempting to say quite the contrary is true. . . . The norm becomes visible—lives—only by its transgressions."[16] And eventually, these transgressions can lead to a new genre. Rather than limiting artists, Gaiman suggests that "the advantage of genre as a creator is it gives you something to play to and play against."[17]

Experiencing the creative interplay of genre can be rewarding for the audience, but it presupposes we understand genre in the first place. "Even when authors are madly mixing genres," Wendy Bishop and David Starkey explain, "the frisson we feel as one type of writing is juxtaposed with another can only occur when we can identify the different genres."[18] We don't need to have all of our expectations met, but we do need to appreciate genre to enjoy when those expectations are being thwarted.

Every Living Thing

How do you begin to understand yourself and your place in the world? To know what you are, you must know what you are not.

When it comes to your physical body, at first, this seems easy. You are a human; you are not a tiger. Looking around, you can differentiate between pumpkins and roses, flamingos and guinea pigs. Classification seems easy.

Scientific classification, however, has a lot in common with genre: start digging, and the edges become blurry.

We have billions of individual microbes, representing at least thousands of species, living on or in each one of us, many of which are critical to our functioning. At what point do they become *us*? If we can't live without them, are they separate, or are we just one component of a more complicated genre of being? Or, consider two ants that look alike but reproduce differently, or two beetles that reproduce the same way but look different. Does each difference get its own classification? How different can two organisms be while still belonging to the same group?

Something we learn from genre is that classification becomes a gray area at the margins. As new organisms are discovered, the distinctions become less clear. "The boundaries between organisms are at best fuzzy," biologist Rob Dunn writes in *Every Living Thing*, "the boundaries between species more so."[19]

Why is this all important?

In some ways, to name something is to bring it into existence. Not physical existence, because the thing still physically exists with or without being named. Rather, naming brings something into the collective consciousness. When we discover new organisms, we name them. We give them a place on the map of life. We decide how and where they belong and, in doing so, learn about them.

In his book, Dunn explains, "Every culture known names species, then groups them, and then builds them into knowledge and stories. Naming, and the learning associated with it, is part of what makes us human."[20] Historically, this learning has been very practical: We learn what tastes good and what can cause pain or make us sick. We learn what to avoid and what to seek out. And early on, we probably grouped things we encountered based on these types of categories. Instead of "insect" or "bird," we might have grouped the organisms in our environment based on their propensity to cause us harm.

If we can't classify something, if we can't label it and figure out where it belongs, we can't build relationships between individual units. If every animal and plant was considered only as an individual, the world would be overwhelming. Being able to group trees into the category "maple," or certain flying insects into the category "wasp," helps us navigate our world, making decisions about how to interact with it.

One idea the model of genre illuminates is that classification systems are only useful if they function as a common language. If we think about the arts, genres are essential for marketing. How am I going to attract you to my comedy show if we don't have a way of mutually understanding that comedy is a performance where I'm going to try to make you laugh? Centuries ago, scientists faced a similar challenge. If the same species had different names in different communities, then scientific investigation wasn't going to get too far. There would be no way to share information easily about a particular organism if everyone had different names and different ways of categorizing it. Carl Linnaeus started the modern species naming and classification system in the early eighteenth century; he gave us *Homo sapiens* and *Canis lupus*. Scientists have been building on and adding to his system ever since. Linnaeus's system set down not just names but also hierarchical classifications, similar to genres. It established a way of understanding where everything fits.

The challenge is that organisms can relate to one another in multiple ways. Hierarchical classification—whereby every organism is nested under ever larger parent groups—is useful sometimes, such as when making a guess about which tree you might try tapping to make syrup. But we can imagine—say, when trying to contemplate the relationship we have to the bacteria living on or in our bodies—that sometimes those hierarchical classifications set down by Linneaus aren't so useful. In the case of our bodily bacteria, a relational classification system might improve our understanding, such as one detailing the genre of symbionts. Does every human host the same bacteria? Is diet relevant? How about geography?

Thus, another insight that the model of genre helps expose is that classifications are only as good as their usefulness. Precision is subservient to function. There are classification guidelines for librarians that get incredibly granular. Urban fantasy or contemporary fantasy? Political thriller versus military thriller? It's easy to imagine a novel being both, and so the label a book ends up with will be influenced by things like who is doing the labeling and the audience the author already has.

When you go searching for a book to read, sometimes genre is useful. "Historical horror" might lead you to *Dracula* or *The Strange Case of Dr. Jekyll and Mr. Hyde*. But let's say you like books featuring elderly characters, or Ukrainian literature—searching by genre isn't likely going to be all that useful. When it comes to classifying species, "there are many different rules one could use to distinguish species, and because the category of 'species' is subjective, none is right, some are just more practical than others," writes Dunn.

The lesson here is to not be too rigid with your categories. It's impossible to be perfectly accurate anyway. Exploring the ways different elements connect can reveal whole new sets of possibilities. Classify for function, but don't demand only one function.

As a lens, genre offers us a common context—a loose blueprint for what to expect. When those expectations are not met, we feel wronged. No one wants to show up expecting a comedy only to find a horror movie. At the same time, genre expectations shape what we see and what we miss. If we think of something as this or that, we tend to see only what we expect and ignore what we don't.

Artists and Soldiers

Think of genre in the context of people. We don't want to pigeonhole or stereotype people—at best, doing so will stifle creativity in your organization, and at worst it can be offensive and damaging. Instead, we want to look at the roles people play.

Our instinct might be to find ways to get people in different roles to work together and cross-pollinate ideas. It's the same way that the occasional horror-romance, like *Pride and Prejudice and Zombies*, blends genres to great effect. But the true classics of any genre stick to their own, like *Bridgerton* as historical romance and *Dracula* as horror. Let's look to one of the best-known examples of organizational genres: DARPA.

In the early 1940s, engineer and inventor Vannevar Bush was

tasked with bringing the latest in science and technology to the military. The United States hadn't yet entered World War II, but the government considered it prudent to keep abreast of these things, as well as to supply the nation's allies in Europe with innovative technologies to help fight the German military. Bush served as an advisor to President Franklin Roosevelt, then as the head of the National Defense Research Committee. In 1941, on the eve of America's entry into the war, he became chair of the newly formed Office of Scientific Research and Development (OSRD). As author Safi Bahcall writes, the OSRD "would create the opportunity Bush sought for scientists, engineers, and inventors at universities and private labs to explore the bizarre."[21] The organization would eventually evolve into DARPA, the Defense Advanced Research Projects Agency that's famous today.

As you might expect, the military was not supportive of the OSRD when it was introduced, to put it mildly. Not only did top military brass not want to work with a bunch of eggheaded science nerds hunched over lab tables, they thought the OSRD was going outside the chain of command to usurp the military's power—and budget—for developing new weapons.

Bush knew that making these two camps work together was going to be like trying to mix oil and water. Think of it, Bahcall says, like ice turning to water: "One molecule can't transform solid ice into liquid water by yelling at its neighbors to loosen up a little." Bush's solution was to create "the unique conditions under which two phases can coexist."[22]

If the two genres—engineers and military leaders—were allowed to mingle, the military men would have quashed all the scientist's bizarre, out-of-the-box ideas before they ever got off the ground. The military leaders didn't realize that all the innovative, yet proven and reliable, weaponry they were using had started as weird projects in the mind of some engineer, who needed time and a lab to work out the kinks. As Bahcall writes, "People responsible for developing high-risk, early-stage ideas (call them 'artists') need to be sheltered from the 'soldiers' responsible for the already-successful, steady-growth part of an organization."[23] Keeping the artist genre separate from the soldier genre gives the artists space to develop new ideas, while the soldier genre helps shape that development according to the needs of real-world application.

This dynamic can be seen outside the military too, where efficiency systems like Six Sigma can risk keeping new ideas from growing into their full potential. Efficiency can be a huge help to the "soldiers" in an organization, like those on the factory floor, in the marketing department, or even on the C-suite team. It can enhance cohesiveness across the entire organization. But innovation is rarely an efficient process, involving many false starts and the need for multiple iterations before a product, a plan, or anything else is ready for the soldiers to implement it. The artists' process can look utterly foolish to the soldiers—until the ideas that work filter outward to those who know how to use them.

Today, Bahcall writes, "DARPA is run like a loose collection of small startups, with no career ladder. A hundred or so program managers each lead one project or field of research. They are granted an extraordinary degree of autonomy and visibility."[24] This structure has brought the world such ideas as the internet (first known as ARPANET) and the first mobile robot—named Shakey—to use AI to navigate a set of rooms.[25]

Treating both genres as equally important to the process is key for using this model in any organization. The soldiers and the artists both need to know that their contributions are valued. Neither romance nor horror—neither artist nor soldier—is better than each other or any other genre. They fulfill different requirements at different times, and recognizing their strengths while insulating their weaknesses will allow new ideas to flourish and become usable innovations.

Conclusion

Picture this: you're browsing a bookstore, scanning the shelves for your next read. You pick up a book with a shadowy figure on the cover, a magnifying glass in hand. Instantly, you know what kind of story awaits you within those pages. This is the power of genre—the unspoken understanding between creator and audience that shapes how we experience art.

But genre is more than just a label; it's a set of conventions, a understanding between the artist and the audience. When we pick up a mystery novel, we expect a crime, some clues, a detective. When we go to a rock concert, we expect loud guitars, driving rhythms, rebellious attitude. Genre sets the parameters of our experience, even as it gives the artist a foundation to build upon or rebel against.

Think of genre as a game with rules. The rules provide structure, but they also create opportunities for creativity. A sonnet has a strict form—fourteen lines, a specific rhyme scheme—but within those constraints, poets have found endless ways to express love, loss, joy, and sorrow. The rules of the genre game inspire ingenuity, challenging artists to create something fresh within the familiar.

But genres are not static; they are constantly evolving. Look at the way rock music has transformed over the decades. What began as a rebellious offshoot of blues and country in the 1950s has splintered into countless subgenres, each with its own distinct style and audience. From the psychedelic experimentation of the 1960s to the punk revolution of the '70s to the grunge explosion of the '90s, rock has reinvented itself time and again. What was once transgressive becomes mainstream, and new forms emerge to take its place.

Navigating genre is a delicate art. Stick too closely to the conventions and your work may be dismissed as formulaic. Stray too far and you risk losing your audience. The key is to find the sweet spot—honoring the expectations of the genre while also bringing something new and personal to the table.

Ultimately, genre is a tool—a way of framing the conversation between artist and audience. It provides common ground, a starting point for the journey together. But the true power of art lies in the way it can transcend genre, using convention as a springboard to take us places we've never been.

Contrast

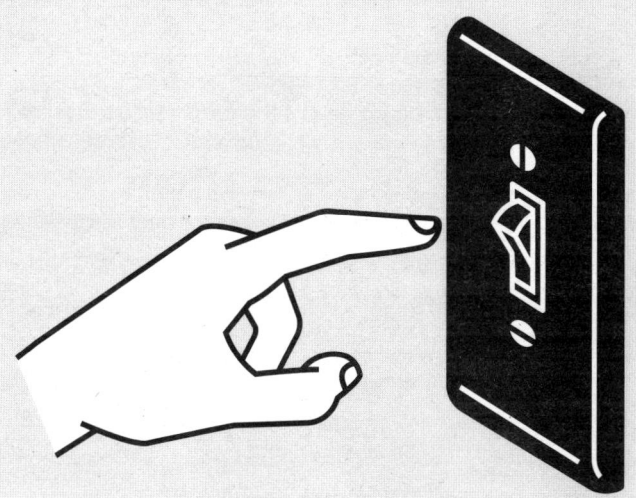

Difference defines.

To miraculously hold together contradictions and incompatibilities is a good definition of art.

—FRANK AUERBACH[1]

Contrast has an easy definition, but also a lot of nuances. It is one of the most important and useful concepts to understand and apply in life.

A pickpocket cleverly uses contrast to remove your wristwatch without you noticing. To remove your watch, he needs to touch your wrist and release your watch. Normally you would notice this touch, but while he touches your wrist, he creates a high-contrast touch somewhere else—like bumping into your shoulder. The contrast makes you feel the shoulder touch and ignore the wrist touch.

Contrast is a concept that underpins many techniques in the arts. It's juxtaposition, the placing of two things together to show how they are different. Often, you can see what something is more clearly in the context of what it is not.

Thus, contrast refers to the arrangement of opposing elements, effects, and/or content. In a painting by Cindy Sherman, *Untitled*, contrast is displayed on multiple levels, and quickly the viewer finds "the deluxe appearance of beauty and splendor, at first glance, disintegrates, upon a second, into the purely ersatz effect of tatty fabrics and obtrusive makeup."[2] By displaying and reconciling a spectrum of possibility for an element, contrast creates interest and meaning.

Contrast thus is stimulating and a great way to capture an

audience's attention. Describing a painting by Kitagawa Utamaro, Julian Bell captures the power of contrast when he writes, "the erotic heat comes from the interfaces of patterned and plain, of covered and revealed, of hair and the nape of the neck."[3]

In visual art, contrast can be achieved by using light and dark colors, smooth and rough textures, and/or large and small shapes, for example. Bell says of the painter Henri Matisse, "He discovered the power of clashing colour extremes—viridians and oranges, violets and lemons—to kickstart oscillations in the eye, pumping out a surplus of radiance."[4] Contrast produces emphasis, demonstrating to the viewer what we want them to look at. Think, for example, of a bright red apple set against a white-and-brown background.

Seeing the juxtaposition of dualities is also a way of telling the story in visual art. In describing a sculpture of the circa 1200 CE bust of a king from Nigeria, Bell explains, "West African cultures tend to *pair* their images. The pair to this, the king's outward likeness, would be not the queen's . . . but a diminutive upright cylinder, an abstraction poked with eyes—the likeness of the *inner*, the spiritual man."[5] By viewing these contrasting elements together, we get a sense of the whole meaning behind the depiction of the person.

Contrast is inherent in music as the progression through sound and silence. It is also seen in the pace of the musical notes (a range from fast to slow), their intensity (heavy to light), and their tone (high to low). Margaret Mary Barela explains in "Motion in Musical Time and Rhythm" that in music "tensions fluctuate in duration as well as in importance: driving or dragging, emerging in the foreground, or sinking into the background."[6]

In literature, contrast crops up in the juxtaposition of characters of varying intents. At the most basic level, the actions of the protagonist (likely a good person) are contrasted with those of the antagonist (probably a bad person). Authors will often have characters present different aspects of themselves and of humanity in order to highlight those aspects. We notice a character's virtue—such as a good temperament or intelligence—when they are in a scene with someone who is grumpy or quick to judge, or who doesn't understand the action of the scene.

Sherlock Holmes appears smart because he puts together the story of a crime faster than the others who are working on the same case (such as Dr. Watson or Inspector Lestrade). In Jane Austen's novels, the heroines Elizabeth Bennet or Elinor Dashwood spend many scenes in the company of characters who have opposing qualities. Putting Elizabeth in a scene with Caroline Bingley shows the former's wit and unpretentiousness and the latter's meanness and snobbery.

Contrast has a couple of different applications in theater. As in literature, it can often be found in the characters in a play. But there is also an element of contrast in staging: lighting is used to create areas of darkness, thus highlighting certain elements on the stage. Ever since the invention of powerful artificial lights, starting with gaslights in the early nineteenth century, performance lighting has become a critical tool in theater staging. The spotlight, which highlights one small area of the stage brightly to contrast with shadows everywhere else, was used as soon as the technology was developed to direct the light on stage. As Neil Grant writes, "Limelight, producing a brilliant, lens-focused light from a calcium flare, was introduced soon after gas. It was used chiefly like a spotlight, to illuminate the main actor—putting him 'in the limelight.'"[7]

A lot of art analysis considers what is happening in the foreground and the background of a work, which is often a type of contrast. In order to *have* a foreground, there must be a contrasting background. So we can ask: Where is the attention of an audience, reader, or viewer being directed? Where does the artist place emphasis? In paintings, the emphasis might be more literal: one's attention is often directed to the figure in the foreground. In other types of art, such as literature, foreground is better understood as the characters or situations that are described in the level of detail needed to capture the reader's focus. In theater, the foreground of both the characters' qualities that drive the story and the physical setting can be emphasized through lighting and other staging effects. Backgrounds are therefore often designed to help us see the foreground more clearly.

Contrast reminds us that we cannot see everything with perfect clarity all at once. We must focus on something, while the rest recedes from our attention. It also reminds us that we understand things more clearly when they are placed in juxtaposition to different elements.

Contrast as Context

How do you understand visual information? What is the difference between a pretty picture and one that conveys information? One answer is the context created by contrast.

We can often understand what something is in the context of what it is not. The things being considered don't have to be opposites; even something with several slightly different attributes provides enough contrast to convey information. Designing visual elements to educate or tell an information story is called "data visualization." A key principle of data visualization is to show comparisons, because only by accessing contrasting information can we begin to understand the story of the data.

In *Beautiful Evidence*, Edward Tufte explains the logic behind visual representations of data:

> The fundamental analytical act in statistical reasoning is to answer the question "Compared with what?" Whether we are evaluating changes over space or time, searching big databases, adjusting and controlling for variables, designing experiments, specifying multiple regressions, or doing just about any kind of evidence-based reasoning, the essential point is to make intelligent and appropriate comparisons. Thus visual displays, if they are to assist thinking, should show comparisons.[8]

Knowing there were one hundred car accidents last year tells you very little. But if these accidents were plotted within a geographical region, you would have a comparison with which to start understanding whether one hundred accidents was a lot for the area. Better yet, if this visualization included accidents over time in the same region, with easy-to-understand elements demonstrating intensity or type of accident, you might begin to form a picture of where the trouble spots are and what to do about them.

One of the classic images in data visualization is John Snow's plotting of cholera victims in London in 1854. It's simple but effective. The visual representation is clear and easy for the eye to process. The locations of cholera deaths are plotted geographically, and the contrast between regions of high mortality and low mortality is easily understood. The information conveyed by Snow's visualization allowed for clear and immediate action to try to remedy the cholera problem.

In *The Visual Display of Quantitative Information*, Tufte asserts, "Graphical displays should encourage the eye to compare

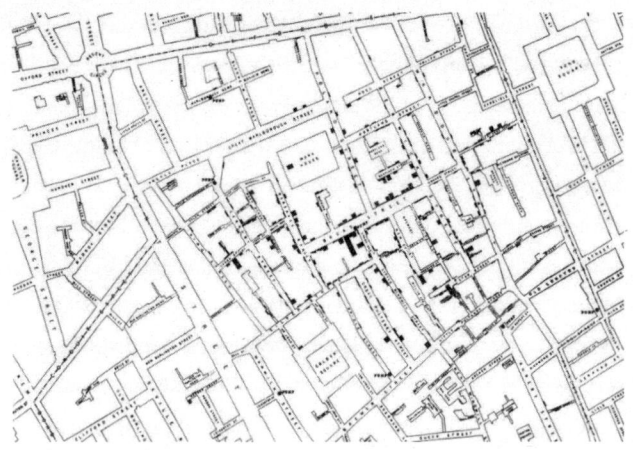

different pieces of data and reveal the data at several levels of detail, from a broad overview to the fine structure."[10] One of the key ways to accomplish this visual comparison is through contrast. We can only compare different pieces of data if they are sufficiently different to invite comparison.

When approaching data visualizations, Tufte argues that we shouldn't start with wanting to use a particular image or color. He says, "The first question in constructing analytical displays is . . . what are the content-reasoning tasks that this display is supposed to help with?"[11] If I am meant to understand the impact of commercial fishing on fish stocks in a certain region, what information do I need to contrast so that I can foster the comparisons that will augment understanding? Data must contrast with something in order for people to understand its context. And we need to have context if we're going to understand the story of the data. Tufte asserts that "data-rich designs give context and credibility to statistical evidence.[12]

Providing context requires avoiding clutter. Contrasting data with irrelevant information, designs, or images is useless. And simply making something a different color is not the kind of contrast we're talking about. According to scholars Tim Riffe, Nikola Sander, and Sebastian Klüsener, "Good visualizations enhance our understanding of the underlying data and grab the reader's attention without sacrificing truth for beauty"[13]—essentially, pretty is not the same as engaging. As Tufte stresses, ink should be devoted primarily to the data needed to tell the story. "If the intellectual task is to make comparisons, as it is in nearly all data analysis," Tufte writes, "then 'show comparisons' is the design principle."[14] Contrast information so people have a clear understanding of what something is—and what it is not.

It's surprising how many people don't understand how to apply contrast to their advantage. Hot business ideas that are attracting the best and brightest in an industry are seldom the most attractive field to enter. No matter how talented you are, your talent will always be compared with that of your rivals. In a room full of sneezers, it's hard to stand out. Unpopular fields, in contrast, can offer a better chance to stand out.

Contrast in the Universe

Sometimes we think of contrast only in the context of opposites, like the colors black and white or the attributes soft and hard. But a contrast doesn't have to involve a direct opposite to be effective. It could just be an effect that makes enough of a difference in a situation to change the landscape or, if we think of it in terms of thermodynamics, the entropy of an environment.

The second law of thermodynamics says that any system will settle into a state of equilibrium. Say there's a fish tank with a partition in the middle. One side is filled with hot water, and the other with cold. If the partition is removed, the water will reach a state of equilibrium, and the tank will be filled with uniformly lukewarm water.

The physical aspect of any thermodynamic system—in our very basic example, the water in the fish tank, along with its glass sides and the air with which it comes into contact at the surface—is called entropy. As chemist Peter Atkins writes, "We shall identify entropy with disorder: if matter and energy are distributed in a disordered way, as in a gas, then the entropy is high; if the energy and matter are stored in an ordered manner, as in a crystal, then the entropy is low."[15]

Atkins then gives another example of entropy at work in the world:

> A quiet library is the metaphor for a system at low temperature, with little disorderly thermal motion. A sneeze corresponds to the transfer of energy as heat. In a quiet library a sudden sneeze is highly disruptive: there is a big increase in disorder, a large increase in entropy. On the other hand, a busy street is a metaphor for a system at high temperature, with a lot of thermal motion. Now the same sneeze will introduce relatively little additional disorder: there is only a small increase in entropy.[16]

Atkins then goes into quite a bit of math, but for our purposes, the thing to note is the contrast: a sudden sneeze in a low-entropy environment creates high contrast. Everyone will notice, and it changes the "temperature" of the room by adding sound and visuals. People will react to the change because of the high contrast. Out on the street, most people won't even notice a sneeze. It doesn't change the "temperature" of an outdoor setting, where there's already a lot of noise, both audio and visual.

Sometimes, you want to change the entropy of a situation. A sneeze might not be enough to change the "temperature" of a busy street, but a chicken costume might. Or, more practically for many business owners, a sign advertising a sale at your shop or a billboard for your latest movie that stands out from the scenery could provide enough contrast to be noticed. Using entropy, or contrast, to change the temperature of a system works the other way too. A situation that seems to be teetering on the edge of complete chaos may need to be calmed down. We may not notice a sneeze amid all the other signals we're receiving on a busy street, but we may be relieved to see a spa or a city park full of trees that brings down the overstimulating temperature of the experience.

There are also plenty of times when we *don't* want to change the temperature of a situation. We probably want to remain quiet in the library, along with our fellow readers, as we contribute to the greater project of innovation and research. In that case, we would want to abide by the cultural norms of the library, to earn the respect of our colleagues and to show respect for their studies in return.

As with so many mental models, high and low contrast can both be useful tools. Wisdom comes in assessing any situation and knowing whether contrast—raising or lowering the temperature of the situation—might lead to a breakthrough.

Conclusion

Contrast is the spice of life and art. It's the clash of opposites that energizes a work and jolts our senses. Without contrast, the world is bland. With it, the world dances with dark and light, loud and soft, rough and smooth. Contrast makes us notice.

Contrast isn't just visual. In music, quiet moments make loud ones explosive. Gentle ballads set the stage for crashing anthems. In literature, calm before the storm makes extraordinary events remarkable. Contrast gives art emotional power.

Contrast creates interest and engagement. Our brains are wired to pay attention to changes, to differences. We tune out the monotonous, but we snap to attention when something breaks the pattern. Artists use contrast to manipulate our attention, to direct our focus and shape our experience of the work.

Contrast is a universal principle. Light and dark, hot and cold, life and death—the world is defined by contrasts. Darkness helps us understand light. Winter makes us appreciate spring. Contrast gives meaning to existence.

Framing

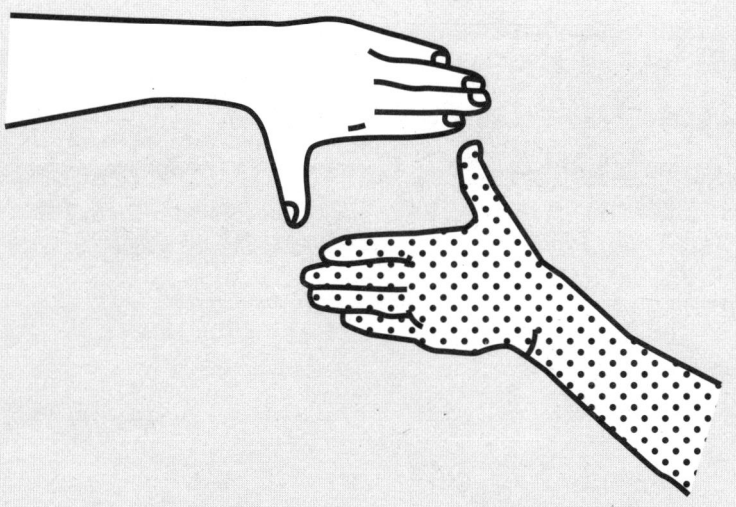

Context shapes meaning.

A good photograph is knowing where to stand.

—ANSEL ADAMS[1]

W e never see everything. We only engage with a small, often chosen part of the world. Framing helps us iden-tify the constructed frames around the information we receive. The frame decides what we see and miss.

Framing is a fundamental component of all art. Art may imi-tate life, but it selectively chooses what to portray. What gets in-cluded in the book, what gets edited out of the documentary, what is inside the boundaries of the portrait are all examples of framing. Framing conveys the intent, the story, and the focus.

The concept of framing also applies to more than art. One way to understand frames is as the mental constructs we use to make sense of our world. Mental models themselves could be considered a set of frames. Another way to think of framing is as the act of compressing something complicated into what you want people to see. People read *Farnam Street* (fs.blog) because they find the ideas interesting, timeless, and useful. But how do you position that in a way that can be shared with other people? We frame the idea with the tagline: Mastering the best of what other people have already figured out.

Some frames are specific to different types of art, and it is through these frames that the artist and audience interact. For example, whether we've given much thought to them or not, we all have frames for songs, paintings, and novels. Frames, in this sense, can be understood as a set of expectations. We know when we are looking at a sculpture or play, and we know when we are not.

Humans are generally good at figuring out what is meant to be within the frame of an artistic piece. We can easily tell when a character's aside is directed right at the audience within a play, whereas the crinkling of candy wrappers in the seats around us is not. In describing the Japanese bunraku puppet tradition, scholar Susanne K. Langer says it is "the most extreme example of such a channeling of audience perception because it asks the audience to ignore the visible presence of all these puppeteers in the act of manipulating a single puppet."[2]

Framing not only compresses an idea but shapes how you approach it. For example, the frames we have for art also tell us how we're meant to interact with it. We know that we're not supposed to talk during a symphony. We also know that we're meant to suspend our disbelief of events inside the frame of a movie or novel until the full artistic experience unfolds. You don't usually walk out of a movie just because you're dropped into the middle of the action in the first scene and have no idea yet what's going on. Part of the job of the artist, therefore, is to tell their audience what to look at, what to engage with. They need to put into the frame what is needed for a full artistic experience. What exactly is that? How much is required? There are no definite answers.

Art itself often tries to expand our frames, and frames evolve in response to artistic developments. Camille Paglia writes of artist Piet Mondrian, "Mondrian's lines hypothetically shoot out into infinite space, creating a charged new relationship between a painting and its surroundings. Hence his revolutionary step of discarding the frame, that heavy, ornate golden rim of traditional portable paintings."[3]

Not all artists want to work within the current framing conventions, but as Erving Goffman points out, "Certainly individuals exhibit considerable resistance to changing their framework of frameworks."[4] Sometimes, then, we may not like a piece of art not because it isn't good but because it's too far outside of our frame for what type of art the piece is supposed to be.

Social sensibilities with regard to how we're meant to experience art change too. For centuries, theatergoers would throw objects at the actors, interact with them directly, and even get on the stage to become part of the action. Now, in many places, for this same behavior, the stage action would be suspended, and you would be escorted out of the theater, if not arrested.

Normally, though, there is a successful collaboration between artist and audience. The artist gives us all the information we need to engage with the art, and we accept it. Goffman writes that there is "evidence of the great capacity of audiences to adjust and calibrate in order to get on with getting involved."[5] As audience members, we don't require a perfect rendering of our expectations in order to participate in the artistic experience.

Art is compression. When you write an email at work or an essay, you're compressing an idea and framing it for an audience. Compression necessitates choosing what to include and what to leave out. The artist focuses our attention on what they want us to engage with. A movie uses a close-up; a play uses a spotlight. Our eyes stop panning the museum wall when we hit the gilded edge around the painting. When we're listening to music, we easily distinguish the story of the melody from the embellishments of the harmony.

By choosing what is both in and out of the frame, an artist impacts our historical narratives. Paglia describes how in the painting *The Death of Marat*, the painter, Jacques-Louis David, "has reworked the scene. Marat is more muscular here than in real life and his raw blisters and scales have been erased,"[6] among other changes. It influences what we remember of Marat and so influences how we perceive history to have transpired. Movies are another example of how historical events can be reconfigured by how they are framed by the artist, in this case, the director.

Framing as a model encourages us to consider the frame of the person presenting information. An interesting approach to change your perspective is to ask yourself what has been left out of the frame. The framing model also pushes us to consider our own frames and how we go about changing them.

History as Frame

Historical records are frames. The person or people who compile the record decide what goes in or is left out. Historians consider many different records to produce a cohesive account of an episode or an era, but that account is still a frame. Information is excluded because it is deemed irrelevant, inaccurate, or incendiary—and historical accounts can never factor in information that is unknown or has never been included within a previous frame. Historical records also compress time. By definition, the record of history must be less comprehensive than all the actions, thoughts, emotions, and moments experienced by all the people it covers.

When people frame something, they're making a statement not about the objective truth but about themselves. Paying attention to the framing of a history is important. Something is always left out. Examining historical records through the lens of framing helps us develop our perspective by actively considering what has been left outside the frame. In her book *Empress: The Astonishing Reign of*

Nur Jahan, Ruby Lal openly confronts the challenges in navigating frames to build an authentic understanding of a subject. Nur Jahan was "the twentieth and favorite wife" of Mughal emperor Jahangir. Married to him in 1611, she quickly rose to an unprecedented level of power for a woman in Mughal society, which is reflected in undisputed biographical details such as her issuing orders, designing gardens and buildings, and having coins struck in her name.[7] However, to access an impression of who this woman was beyond these details is challenging because of the way she is framed in the historical record.

There are a few accounts of her reign by her contemporaries. Lal notes, "Some commentators pronounced her cunning and conniving." Other accounts by European men visiting the region characterized her as "manipulative and mysterious" and "haughty and stubborn." Their accounts of her explain that it could only be the emperor's love that gave Nur Jahan her position and power. Consequently, she was regarded as doing anything necessary to keep that love. Lal argues, "Faced with the reality of a de facto woman sovereign, most official observers of Nur's achievements, instead of acknowledging that she'd earned her position on the strength of her talents, explained it in terms palatable (to them) and conceivable (to them): she was a gold-digger and a schemer."[8]

As the years progressed, Nur's romance with her husband, Jahangir, continued as the main frame of the narrative of her story. Outside of India, "narratives of the royal romance became more extravagant in nineteenth-century British colonial histories that were steeped in the orientalism of the day, embracing exoticized stereotypes of Asia." Inside the country, the way Nur is framed is equally simplistic. Depicted in many popular films and comics, her story is often reduced to only the romance between her and the emperor, with everything she did and achieved being accomplished due to love. Despite her being a real historical figure, "the narration of her bold military and political endeavors is sketchy and tepid," and "she is not discussed as a leader."[9] Even into the late twentieth century, "academics . . . leaned on love as the explanation for her extraordinary rise rather than attributing it to her talents."[10] Love became the frame through which Nur Jahan was considered and evaluated.

When we deal with frames, we must ask ourselves what has been left out. In the case of Nur Jahan, if love is the frame through which she has been consistently depicted, then it stands to reason that anything that doesn't fit that frame might have been omitted. For the early chroniclers, the love between Nur and Jahangir was not the right kind. It wasn't selfless. Instead, it bewitched the emperor into allowing Nur to have an unprecedented amount of power for a woman. Of course, this may be true. But it's always suspicious when all of the information that's been presented perfectly supports the position. Did it all fit together so neatly, or was there more?

Even for more contemporary histories, the elements that don't relate to love don't tend to make it into the frame. As Lal writes, "There is no palpable sense of the anger or playfulness we'd expect of a living woman . . . her raw ambition, her vulnerability as well as her strengths, or the very human way in which she fought to build and preserve her husband's and her own sovereign rights."[11]

Nur Jahan's relationship with her husband isn't the only element of her life where there seem to be additions made to suit the person telling her story. We all do this—whenever we tell a story, we leave out details that don't fit what we want to convey. One example of the distortions that frames introduce is in Nur Jahan's birth story:

Besides her parentage and her name, only one thing is certain about [Nur Jahan's] birth: She entered the world outside Kandahar in the winter of 1577, on the road to India. During her time as empress and after, in chronicles and legends, several key embellishments were added to the tale. By the eighteenth century, three fascinatingly different versions of her birth story had been published, each revealing a great deal about the teller and his times (the writers were all men), including prevailing attitudes about politics, gender, and religion.[12]

If we want to be accurate, then what fits inside the frame of Nur Jahan's birth is quite small: a couple of sentences. But, as is often the case, contents get enlarged in order to direct focus. Later writers of the birth story wanted their readers to get more than just those few facts. They wanted readers to focus on Nur's mysticism, divine being, and childhood struggles—or the intervention of fate, the notion of destiny, or whatever. In order to accomplish that, they had to augment what was in the frame.

In terms of Nur Jahan's overall legacy, there are some clear contradictions between how she was officially written about and what survives in historical artifacts. Lal explains, "The official historians of Jahangir's son's reign (Shah Jahan) deliberately wrote Nur Jahan's merits and accomplishments out of Mughal history."[13] She goes on to justify this statement by pointing out elements that could not be written out but that demonstrate Nur did have extraordinary accomplishments to her credit.

Nur was the only Mughal woman to appear on coins, many of which have been found and displayed in museums. Nur also appeared in formal paintings depicting her exercising the powers of state. And there are inscriptions she wrote on monuments that she designed.

How Nur Jahan is depicted throughout history is a lesson that, quite often, history is framed according to the sensibilities of the one doing the framing. Understanding that there is always a frame, always someone who makes decisions on what to capture and what to leave out, is a great life lesson. We are always interacting with framed information.

On Caspar David Friedrich: "When human beings appear in his work, it is usually with their backs to us: they are looking at nature and thus directing our gaze."[14]

On *At the Café*, by Édouard Manet: "We are positioned almost as if we, like the waitress quaffing beer, were at work—behind a marble bar with glassware and a tap handle partly visible to the right."[15]

Updating Our Frames

The way you see something—that is, your framing—emerges from your experience. You are not born with any particular frames; you acquire them. Some are inherited, others are learned. Once you understand something in a certain way, that frame follows you.

We bring our previous understanding to each new situation we are in. How we frame events depends on our sensibilities, our knowledge, and our biases. When new information comes in, we often resist changing our frames because, in effect, we have to admit that we were wrong. It's both difficult and brave to process and share our changing frames.

When the Vietnam War broke out, Walter Cronkite was the much-trusted anchorman of the *CBS Evening News*. Cronkite had been a war correspondent during World War II, which shaped how he initially framed the Vietnam situation when reporting on it to the American people. He believed that journalists needed to be objective, but also that "reporters . . . needed to help the American military win the war, as he had done during WWII with United Press."[16]

Cronkite was a thoughtful journalist who knew it was critical to be objective, but he began covering the war with the utmost respect for the military position. It's important to understand that for Cronkite, supporting the American military went hand in hand with telling the truth about what was happening in Vietnam. Because if the Americans were ultimately doing the right thing in Vietnam, then reporting on their activities would help the war effort.

Cronkite made sure *CBS Evening News* put out balanced coverage. He reported on official White House statements, but he also covered actions such as the unnecessary destruction of Cam Ne by US marines. He interviewed members of the American military, yet also aired an interview with President Ho Chi Minh of Vietnam. Cronkite's frame in the first years of the war appears to have been that of someone who believed the Americans were essentially doing the right thing by being in Vietnam. As his biographer Douglas Brinkley writes, "Even after the Cam Ne incident, Cronkite remained a cautious hawk. He thought the Americans would, in the end, win over the hearts and minds of the Vietnamese people."[17]

The Vietnam War was the first US war to be widely televised, and so television broadcasts had a large influence on people's understanding of the conflict. Media coverage by people like Cronkite—not just government statements—shaped public opinion. By some accounts, a key part of the eventual shift in opinion in opposition to the war was the recognition that there could be discrepancies between the two.[18]

As the war progressed, Cronkite's framing in his broadcasts slowly began to change. He visited Vietnam for the first time in 1965 and was exposed to how the on-the-ground reality was far different from the reports put out by the White House. After that visit, he began actively seeking out a variety of sources to continually update and expand his understanding of the situation in Vietnam.[19]

Up until early 1968, Cronkite was careful to not take a public position on the war. It was his job as a journalist to report on it. But that was getting harder to do with accuracy from his position in the United States.

While the Tet offensive was raging, Cronkite decided he needed to go back to Vietnam. "When Cronkite was a United Press reporter, he learned an important lesson: be your own eyewitness. Worried about the proliferation of unsubstantiated rumors and deliberate misinformation streaming out of Saigon, he believed it was essential to now take in the Vietnamese situation for himself with 'mind wide open.'"[20]

So, in 1968, Walter Cronkite went to Vietnam again to see firsthand what was going on.

He and his producers decided that it was time for a network documentary on the war in Vietnam and for Cronkite to present an honest assessment—and to take a position on the war.

Writing in *Hué 1968*, Mark Bowden explains the question Cronkite found himself grappling with: Was it possible that the government line he had been fed, the one he had for years been delivering nightly, was a lie? If so, it was a betrayal both personal and professional; his reputation had been used. It made him angry. If it had happened, he needed to correct it—even if that meant abandoning strict journalistic neutrality, one of his core beliefs. And right away on his visit to Vietnam, Cronkite's worst suspicions were confirmed.[21]

The war was a disaster.

Wearing a helmet and flak jacket, interviewing soldiers at outposts, and touring all over South Vietnam, Cronkite chronicled what he was witnessing.[22] "After two days Cronkite flew out on a chopper with body bags and wounded marines. He had seen enough to be convinced that he had not been told the truth."[23] He concluded that there was little chance of a good outcome for anyone in Vietnam. Troop morale was in shambles, senior officers appeared to have little understanding of the North Vietnamese, and respect for the chain of command had broken down in multiple places. His experiences had pushed him to update his framing of the Vietnam War and to share that new frame with the American people.

Cronkite went back to the United States and prepared his half-hour "Report from Vietnam."

On February 27, 1968, CBS aired his damning verdict. Cronkite's change of opinion was a turning point toward majority dissent. It is worth quoting his conclusion in its entirety:

> We have been too often disappointed by the optimism of the American leaders, both in Vietnam and Washington, to have faith any longer in the silver linings they find in the darkest clouds . . . To say we are closer to victory today is to believe, in the face of the evidence, the optimists who have been wrong in the past. To suggest that we are on the edge of defeat is to yield to unreasonable pessimism. To say that we are mired in stalemate seems the only realistic, yet unsatisfactory conclusion. On the off chance that military and political analysts are right, in the next few months we must test the enemy's intentions, in case this is indeed his last big gasp before negotiations. But it is increasingly clear to this reporter that the only rational way out then will be to

negotiate, not as victors, but as an honorable people who lived up to their pledge to defend democracy, and did the best they could. This is Walter Cronkite. Good night.[24]

Cronkite's reporting was balanced and did not outright condemn the war as a mistake. But as Bowden writes, "Cronkite's cautious pessimism had tremendous impact and made it much harder to dismiss those who opposed the war as 'hippies' or un-American. It was hard to imagine an American more conventional and authentic than Walter Cronkite."[25] His broadcast was the tipping point to turning the tide of opinion on both the Vietnam War and, more broadly, the trust that Americans had in their political and military leaders.[26]

Losing Cronkite's trust and support was a huge blow for the Johnson administration, which remained committed to the war. His reputation for integrity and his previous support meant that when he decided the White House had been lying about the reality America's troops were experiencing in Vietnam, he had the ability to change the framing of the war for millions of people:

> Cronkite's nutshell editorial wasn't radical. Calling the Vietnam war a "stalemate" was a middling position. . . . But in the harshly polarized environment of early 1968, it placed Cronkite in the dove camp. Cronkite had lent his august name to the antiwar movement and thereby put it into the mainstream.[27]

In March 1966, just 25 percent of Americans viewed Vietnam as a mistake. By August 1968, 53 percent believed it was a mistake, and 60 percent believed this in 1973. In 1965, Gallup asked American adults if they'd ever felt the urge to join a public demonstration, and 90 percent said no. While the polling company didn't follow up on this survey, in 1990, one quarter of Americans said they wished they'd tried harder to protest against the Vietnam War.[28]

For someone with Cronkite's background as a journalist during World War II, the American political and military handling of Vietnam must have been devastating. It is a credit to him that he didn't let his past blind him to his present. Walter Cronkite thoughtfully and carefully updated his frame, sharing his new understanding via his wide reach on the *CBS Evening News*. It was not an easy thing to do.

Framing matters to not only how an idea is presented but how it's received. What you omit and what you include matters. How something is compressed and positioned can make the difference between ten people seeing it and one million.

Conclusion

Framing is the art of context, the craft of shaping perception. It's how we present information, the lens we invite others to view the world through. Like a photographer choosing what's in the frame, we constantly decide what to emphasize, minimize, or leave out. These often unconscious choices profoundly influence how others understand and respond.

In psychology, framing is a key concept in understanding decision-making. Present the same options in different ways, and people's choices change. Is it a muffin or a cake? The thing doesn't change, but its packaging does.

For marketers and advertisers, framing is a potent tool. A car can be framed as a status symbol, an adventure machine, or a sensible family vehicle. A watch can be about punctuality, or it can be about luxury and prestige. The product stays the same, but the story changes. The right frame makes the ordinary extraordinary.

But framing isn't just about persuasion. It's also about understanding, about making sense of the complex world around us. We all carry frames in our minds—mental models of how things work, cultural narratives, personal beliefs. These frames shape how we interpret information, how we explain events, how we imagine possibilities.

Framing's power lies in its subtlety. Unlike a logical argument, a frame doesn't need to be explicitly stated to have an effect. It works on an emotional, often subconscious level. A well-crafted frame can make an idea feel intuitive, even inevitable, without the audience quite knowing why.

Framing is the silent partner in every communication, the hidden hand shaping understanding. Like any powerful tool, framing can be used for good or ill. It can illuminate truth, or it can obscure it. It can empower people to see new possibilities, or it can subtly limit their thinking to narrow, predefined channels.

Rhythm

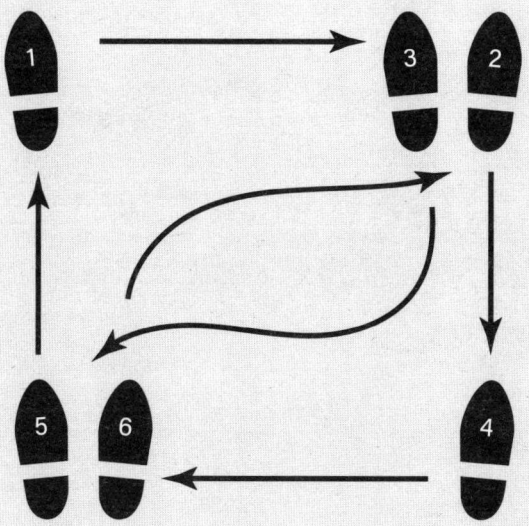

Pace yourself.

Why do we care about rhythm? It connects us to the world. It plays a role in listening, in language, in understanding speech in noisy places, in walking, and even in our feelings toward one another.

—NINA KRAUS[1]

Rhythm, in life, is like the beat of your favorite song. It's the pattern and pace at which things happen. Rhythm synchronizes us, gives us purpose and direction. Once we start looking and listening, we find the world full of rhythms.

In music, rhythm is the element of time. Most people easily identify and anticipate rhythm. Margaret Mary Barela explains, "Our perception of time is an integral part of musical experience. Once our attention is directed to that aspect, we can make comments about our perception of the way time-space has been filled."[2] To identify the rhythm in a piece of music, we pay attention to the recurring movement of strong and weak notes, and rests or silences.

> It is the relation between repetition and difference that allows rhythm to be both produced and perceived.
>
> —SARA ADHITYA[3]

In music, rhythm indicates when notes are played, how long they are played, and the intensity at which they are played. Think about any song you listen to: not all of its notes have the same intensity or pace. Some are louder or are played faster. If every note were played exactly the same way, a song would be very boring to listen to. Musical movement is like a wave, and "it is rhythm that determines the shape of the wave."[4]

Part of what makes music enjoyable is our ability to anticipate what comes next in a rhythm pattern, but as with incentives, we get a rush from uncertain payoffs when the stakes are low. Therefore, musicians play with both meeting and thwarting our expectations to create particular emotional effects, such as by changing up the tempo at an unusual moment, or by layering multiple rhythms on top of one another. Too much predictability is boring; too little is disorienting. "It's not just the stressing of some beats," writes Philip Ball, "but an asymmetry of events that creates a true sense of rhythm and avoids monotony."[5] If you think of how we speak, versus how we usually depict robots speaking, you can appreciate how a little uncertainty and anticipation can be exciting and engaging.

Thwarted rhythmic expectations in a piece of music wake us up. They make it harder to tune out. Research has demonstrated, as scientist John Powell explains, "we are equally surprised by increases or reductions in loudness (or even sudden silences) [which] shows that it's the change in pattern which is important. A pattern of sounds makes you expect a continuation of that pattern, and if your expectations are violated, your brain starts paying attention."[6]

Although not all music contains rhythm, it's rare to find music without it. There are examples of pieces of music that are written/designed/developed without a steady pulse underlying them, and so we cannot say that rhythm is a universal component of music. We can, however, appreciate that rhythm underpins the vast majority of the music we listen to and enjoy.

In a musical composition, rhythm is the backbone and thus

gives the piece its structure. But although rhythm is ubiquitous, what makes a rhythm is not. There are cultural variations in rhythm patterns and beat perception, and we seem to prefer what we already understand. "What we hear in music is conditioned not only by what sound is actually produced," Phillip Ball writes, "but also by what sound one's ear is attuned to and expects."[7]

Similar to our daily lives, music need not have only one rhythm. Polyrhythmic music is common in many musical cultures, most notably African drum music, as Powell explains:

> One of the oldest African musical genres is drums-only music, which often employs polyrhythms. A polyrhythm is produced when two or more drummers follow different but linked agendas at the same time, creating complex and interesting effects from a combination of rhythms.[8]

The broadest generalization which can be made about the rhythmic experience is that it provides for the listener a sense of motion and direction.

—MARGARET MARY BARELA[9]

Our bodies easily find themselves in tune with rhythms. John Powell explains that scientific studies and our everyday experiences show us that "under the right conditions your heart rate can rise or fall toward the beat of the music you are listening to, and this fools your brain into experiencing the emotion that is appropriate to your new heart rate."[10]

Our emotions are easily influenced by rhythm. "The speed of the music gives the clearest indicator of its mood."[11] Generally, fast speeds signify happiness, fear, or anger, while slow speeds indicate tenderness or sadness. We look for other cues in music to figure out the mood the music is trying to convey, but the conventions are far from universal; it's possible, for example, to have very sad music that moves quickly. Rhythm, however, usually forms our largest impression of the mood of the music. David Byrne suggests that the "happiness" of rhythms can override "melancholy" melodies for many listeners of the tragic lyrics of flamenco and salsa songs.[12]

Rhythm is not unique to the musical arts. Like all the models from this section of the book, richer insight on where to apply the model in your life comes from first using it as a lens for other arts.

Rhythm impacts the structure of individual works of poetry, dance, and literature. Virginia Woolf asserted, "All writing is nothing but putting words on the backs of rhythm. If they fall off the rhythm, one's done."[13]

When we come across rhythm, we identify it as the base of what we are experiencing. It provides a structure that we can easily pick out and mimic. Therefore, most humans can share an experience of togetherness when listening to rhythms.

Rhythms also form the backdrop to our days, as many elements of our world follow a beat through time. Using rhythm as a model helps us understand what we can change and accomplish by modifying a rhythm.

It is because it is thus inborn in us that we can never silence music, any more than we can stop our heart from beating; and it is for this reason too that music is so universal and has the strange and illimitable power of a natural force.

—VIRGINIA WOOLF[14]

Daily Rhythms

Rhythm is the backdrop to our day. Look at your life through the lens of rhythms and notice how many you encounter.

> We perform different activities at different frequencies, whether weekly, monthly, or yearly, yet the one with the most impact is arguably the one we repeat most often: the rhythm of our everyday lives.
>
> —SARA ADHITYA[15]

Rhythm is something we experience within our own bodies, as we hear or feel our heartbeats or breath. We identify it in other biological processes, such as our circadian rhythm. We see rhythm in the changing seasons or the pattern of sunrise and sunset—things with which to mark the passage of time. The rhythm of the moon gives us tides. There are rhythms found in the hours of our workday, the flow of transportation, and the activity in a town or city. Margaret Mary Barela argues, "The experience of meter, and rhythm as well, is kinetic. It is organic. We experience flow *if* we allow ourselves to focus on the kinetic aspect of the musical experience."[16] Identifying and feeling the multiple rhythms in our day helps us appreciate the kinetic reality of rhythm.

We are probably all familiar with the idea that there is something in us that functions like a clock. We can also see regularly recurring rhythms in plants and animals, as if they too function on a clock. Living things seem to have times for rest and times for eating, rhythms that seem to occur on a regular, daily basis. Our biological clocks tick along in pretty steady, reliable rhythms, and they are internal to us.

Rhythm is thus a fundamental part of all living creatures. Sunlight may modify, or entrain, our circadian rhythm as the periods of darkness and light vary throughout the year. But light does not tell us when to get up. Our bodies are already beginning the process of waking up and being ready to start the day before our eyes register the sun through our lids. "Much of the behaviour of living organisms is anticipatory of regular and predictable daily environmental changes," write Russell G. Foster and Leon Kreitzman in their book *Rhythms of Life*, "rather than reactive."[17] Foster and Kreitzman cover years of research showing that biological clocks still operate in plants and animals, even if they are separated from external calibration sources.

When you think about it, internal clocks make evolutionary sense. They allow us to prepare for when conditions are optimal.

Humans are the only species that can create our own optimal conditions. If we're more creative at night, that's fine, because we've invented artificial light sources. If our bodies aren't well adapted to living in the desert, no problem; we've got air conditioning. For every other living thing on the planet, being able to anticipate things like when a food source will be most abundant is critical to survival. Russell and Kreitzman explain, "Organisms mold their lives around the natural rhythms of their environment rather than try and work against it. If the animal or plant in the wild has the means for predicting regular environmental changes, then it can behave in such a way as to exploit the conditions."[18]

There is no reason for plants and animals to get away from the rhythms of nature. The rhythms of nature exist and are both strong and consistent: Sunrise. Sunset. The earth will turn and tilt according to schedule, and we will experience both days and years.

But the larger point about biological rhythms means that it may not be so great for humans to completely ignore them. Ultimately, the rhythms of the environment offer some predictability, and "although we may have obscured the natural rhythm that for thousands of years dictated human life, success still comes, just as it did for the ancient Egyptians, from anticipating the future and organizing to meet it."[19]

In order to anticipate the future, we have to contend with more than naturally occurring rhythms. We also hear and process the rhythms we've created. Open your window, and what do you hear? Traffic? Lawnmowers? Construction? Sirens? Navigating through our day means noticing and anticipating the rhythms of traffic or public transportation on our daily commute, the rhythm of people as they walk around buildings or go in and out of stores, when restaurants are open, where entertainment is happening. When it comes to how we live, researcher Sara Adhitya points out in *Musical Cities*, "the simultaneous presence of such a wide spectrum of rhythms at any given point in time renders urban life a complex, polyrhythmic composition."[20]

Big cities, towns, suburbs: wherever humans live, there are the rhythms created as we all go about our days.

When we notice the rhythms around us, when we listen to our environment, one result is that we understand what is happening—where cars are, or people. But paying attention to our environment doesn't only give us a retroactive view. We also use sound information to make inferences about the space we are in, which helps us navigate it better in the immediate future.

There's a clear connection between how our cities are designed and how we flow through them. Thus, there is a relationship between design and rhythm. For example, Adhitya explains, "Urban designer Jan Gehl observed that streets with uniform, inactive facades (i.e., no openings or activities) motivated people to move past as quickly as possible, whereas a street with varied and active facades encouraged them to stop and linger, filling the street with social life."[21] The two visions of a city street described in this quote confer the idea of two very different rhythms.

There is a sense, then, that the rhythms we encounter on a daily basis might have a huge impact on how we feel and how much we enjoy our day. Adhitya argues, "We must first be able to speak to our internal rhythms in order to generate the urban experiences we desire."[22] Given that the rhythm in music can prompt feelings of sadness or excitement, it stands to reason that the daily rhythms we interact with might have a similar effect. Moving quickly around hundreds of people streaming in different directions produces a different emotional state than moving slowly through a park—not that one is better than the other, but the idea is that the rhythm we are following will impact how we feel.

Understanding where and how rhythm is present in our daily lives can offer us insight for how rhythm influences our day. From the innate rhythms of our biology to the external rhythms of our environment, and all the modifications and additions in between, there is no doubt that rhythm is an inescapable part of living.

> Rhythm provokes an expectation, arouses a yearning. If it is interrupted, we feel a shock. Something has been broken. If it continues, we expect something that we cannot identify precisely. Rhythm engenders in us a state of mind that will only be calmed when "something" happens. It puts us in an attitude of waiting. We feel that the rhythm is a moving toward something, even though we may not know what that something is.
>
> —OCTAVIO PAZ[23]

Marching in Time

Using rhythm as a lens shows us how prevalent rhythms are in our daily life. However, rhythm's value as a model also includes providing insight into where we can use rhythm to improve how we work with others. The same rhythm can be experienced by multiple people at the same time. We don't need years of musical training to recognize a rhythm. This accessibility makes rhythm an easy tool to use to develop group cohesion.

Rhythm is used outside of music to provide structure for activity. For example, it can be used to make types of manual labor, such as rowing or even walking, more efficient. One area where rhythm has been used for centuries to create optimal conditions for group success is in military drill.

In many militaries around the world, soldiers at all levels train in a drill. The *Encyclopedia Britannica* defines military drill as "preparation of soldiers for performance of their duties in peace and war through the practice of prescribed movements."[24] Often ceremonial now, drill nonetheless continues to be a valuable component of military training. Moving to a beat helps you anticipate how everyone else in the group is going to move. Knowing how everyone is going to move helps you organize, because you know where everyone is going to be next.

Rhythm offers a way to synchronize people and give them a common bond, no matter how large their individual differences. The Canadian Armed Forces (CAF) *Manual of Drill and Ceremonial* states that "drill is the basis of all teamwork." Moving together to a prescribed beat is part of the foundation that future operations build on. The manual asserts that the military practices drill because it "contributes to the operational effectiveness of the CAF by a) ensuring that the CAF efficiently march and maneuver together as one in duty and routine; and b) promoting discipline, alertness, precision, pride, steadiness and the cohesion necessary for success."[25]—a remarkable set of achievements for an activity that is anchored by rhythm.

The movements in drill happen in time. For example, a standard pause is defined as "the pause between movements of drill. The standard pause for drill at the halt is based on two beats of quick time. The standard pause for drill on the march is the period of time required to take two paces."[26] The CAF manual notes that drill must be conducted to a specific cadence, with cadence being defined as "the number of beats to the minute." To that end, drill leaders can use mechanical training aids such as drums or a metronome. Drums, for example, "may be used to beat the time for troops who are learning to judge correct timings and beat the cadence."[27] The rhythm of drill is very precise. This precision is what allows everyone to synchronize their movements. The American military also uses cadence "to keep soldiers stepping in time while marching or running in formation." Here too cadence is precisely defined, so there is no ambiguity. It is "the beat, time, or measure of rhythmical motion or activity."[28]

The use of drill by militaries goes back millennia and has served critical functions. A US Marine Corps article, "The History of Drill," states, "Drill has enabled commanders to quickly move their forces from one point to another, mass their forces into a battle formation that afforded maximum firepower, and maneuver those forces as the situation developed."[29] Drill allows groups of soldiers to move together and fight together. It increases one's ability to react automatically in challenging and changing circumstances. It improves soldiers' ability to fight together because of the organizational cohesion created through the predictability of movement.

Since "the concept of drill is to train troops over and over until a task is second nature and everyone knows how the whole formation moves at any given time,"[30] it's easy to understand why drill is built on rhythm. Rhythm is easy to follow and usually interpreted in the same way by everyone. It's also fairly easy to understand why cohesion is so valuable in military teams. The ultimate purpose of a military is to defend the national interest, using force if required. Military units often perform their duties in hostile environments, where the only people they can rely on are the members of their own group. In order to rely on people, you need to trust them. In order to trust others, you need to be able to predict them. And one way to help you predict them is to have them act according to the same instincts as you. Drill provides that foundation. Drills "show how troops can move as one in a flawlessly timed effort. These unison movements are still important on the battlefield where mistakes can cost lives."[31]

Moving to a defined rhythm develops instinct. When you know you need to move to a certain beat, there is no choice. You don't have to wonder what to do; the movements become automatic. Developing instinctual responses in certain situations is highly valuable for military units. In situations of conflict, automatic reactions are often needed for survival.

Beyond inculcating automatic, predictable movements, drill serves another function: it connects team members together. "The esprit de corps that tags along with cadence is visible as soldiers block out their worries and move as one."[32] Drill de-emphasizes the individual and promotes the unit. To drill effectively, the soldiers must work together as one. Rhythm is the foundation that shapes this whole. In a military unit, as in any other group, the members are unique. Each has different identities and ways of relating to the world. In order to work together effectively, they must find common ground. That is what rhythm provides: a means of working together to achieve a common goal.

When it comes to looking at teamwork through the lens of rhythm, it's important to remember that the beat is not arbitrary, nor does it continue indefinitely. The rhythm is used for a set amount of time to coordinate a specific set of movements. Eventually, those movements become second nature, and the associated cadence becomes a structure teams can return to over and over, especially in situations where there is little time for analysis.

Rhythm helps us react in a way that allows those around us to anticipate our movements. The more we can anticipate where others are headed, the more we feel confident in working together.

Conclusion

Rhythm is the universe's heartbeat, the pulse animating life. From our steady heartbeats to the sun's rise and fall, from crashing waves to swaying trees, rhythm is the pattern underlying existence. It's the organizing principle bringing order to chaos, the recurring cycle shaping time.

In music, rhythm is the foundation, the backbone supporting melody and harmony. Without rhythm, music would be a formless wash of sound, lacking structure and impact. The steady beat of the drum, the driving strum of the guitar, the pulsing throb of the bass—these rhythms grab us on a visceral level, moving our bodies and stirring our souls.

But rhythm isn't just about regularity, the even spacing of beats. It's also variation, the interplay of different rhythmic patterns. In jazz, the syncopated rhythms, the unexpected accents, are what give the music its improvisational feel. In classical music, the shifting rhythms, from the stately march to the lively dance, are what convey the emotional arc of the piece.

Rhythm is also a fundamental to language. The cadence of a phrase, the meter of a poem, the rise and fall of a great orator's speech—these rhythms communicate meaning beyond the literal content of the words. They create their own music, a pattern resonating in the ear and lingering in the mind.

Even in our daily lives, rhythm plays a crucial role. The routines we establish, the habits we cultivate, the cycles of work and rest, of activity and reflection—these rhythms give structure and meaning to our existence. Without rhythm, life would be a formless blur, a ceaseless stream of unrelated moments. Rhythm allows us to make sense of time, to find our place in life's larger patterns.

Melody

Tones tell tales.

Music is the melody to which the world is the text.

—ARTHUR SCHOPENHAUER[1]

M elody is a useful tool for identifying connections needed to tie various elements together and communicate the whole picture.

A song's melody is often its most memorable and recognizable part—it's what you sing along to or whistle or hum after the fact. It's what lives in your memory long after you think you've forgotten it, quickly resurfacing whenever you're confronted with just a couple of notes. Melody is like the first principles of a piece of music: you can change many other aspects, but if the melody is the same, the music is still recognizable.

Nolan Gasser says melody "may be likened to a . . . human face. Like a face, each melody is unique, with its own character, sharing traits with those related to it and those not."[2]

Melody is a succession of notes arranged into a musical phrase. A phrase in music is similar to a phrase in writing—it's a group of words that make sense together and communicate something but are not a complete sentence. So, a melodic phrase is a group of notes that make sense together and communicate a certain musical idea, but you need multiple phrases to make a melody. Melodies usually contain a small pause between phrases.

Most compositions consist of multiple melodies that repeat. The notes that you hear in a piece of music that form the line through time are the melody: the horizontal presentation of pitch. If notes can be removed, and the song still makes the same sense without them, they are probably not part of the melody but are instead embellishments. What is amazing is that we are good at picking out the melody even in songs we've never heard before, regardless of how much else is going on in a song. John Powell writes, "In a harmonized piece of music there are so many possible tunes going on simultaneously that our ability to spot the one the composer had in mind is astonishing."[3] But most of us do it with ease.

Being able to assume, predict, and anticipate is central to our ability to perceive a string of notes as a melody. We're also good at knowing where a melody won't go, Powell observes: "Even when we can't forecast the exact note, we can be pretty confident certain notes are unlikely."[4] Phillip Ball says, "Everything we value in a melody (and in a soccer match) comes from the relationships between the elements that constitute it, and the context we create for them from the knowledge and expectation we bring to the experience of perceiving it."[5] We like to have a balance between familiarity and surprise.

We process melody the same way we process other types of information: we unconsciously look for patterns. We chunk notes together. We make sense of the notes we are hearing in the context of the notes we've just heard. We build up an expectation of what we think we might hear. We also compare what we are hearing to the memories we have of music we've heard before.

The four main skills used in identifying melody are similarity, proximity, good continuation, and common fate. Whatever instrument is producing the melody has a distinct sound, so we group together all of the sounds made by that instrument, even if it's a voice. We follow the sounds through time as the melody progresses.

Powell explains, "A tune [melody] is always on its way somewhere," and our natural pattern-seeking powers help us follow that journey.[6]

Listening to music is actually a very active process. "So when we listen to a melody unfold," Ball writes, "we hear each note in the light of many remembered things: what the previous note was, whether the melodic contour is going up or down, whether we've heard this phrase (or one like it) before in the piece, whether it seems like a response to the previous phrase or a completely new idea."[7] We keep ahold of what has come before in our minds as we process each note in order to understand the story of that melody.

It is often assumed that musicians composing lyrical music create a melody to match words they have written. But some actually start with the melody, then write lyrics to match. Musician David Byrne says of his process for writing a few of his songs, "I filled page after page with phrases [lyrics] that matched the melodic lines of the verses and choruses, hoping that some of them might complement the feelings the music generated."[8] When a strong connection occurs, the lyrics and the music combine to make the melody memorable— not merely as an intellectual activity, but because of the emotional impact.

We have all experienced the phenomenon of hearing a song and having it instantly remind us of a particular moment of feeling. Experiencing similar feelings too can conjure up that same song. Because melodies are often tied with emotion in our memories, we easily pick songs to set specific moods or relive episodes in our lives upon hearing a line of music.

What we like in terms of melody is often culturally influenced rather than purely a matter of individual taste. Melodies are public, in the sense that large groups of people often have a similar understanding of and attraction to a melody. Music scholar Gino Stefani writes, "Why is a melody truly popular? . . . Because it is better suited than others for appropriation, in more ways, for more purposes."[9] Whether it's because a melody is great for selling a variety of products, or because it can conjure up a variety of emotions and feelings that we enjoy having, there are some melodies that have exhibited exceptional staying power.

Melodies thus are something shared among groups of people who are otherwise different; they transcend many disparate identities. The French philosopher Jean-Jacques Rousseau thought that melodies could be used in political organization, that they were a way of having something in common without everyone needing to be the same.

> Occasionally, when a melody gets too persistent and haunts us to death, one can fight it with its own weapon; that is, with another melody.
>
> —GINO STEFANI[10]

Octaves Everywhere

John Newlands, who worked on the [periodic] table, discovered in 1865 that "at every eighth element a distinct repetition of properties occurs"–a pattern which he called the Law of Octaves. Newlands was ridiculed, and his paper on the subject wasn't accepted. But when his prediction that "missing" elements should therefore exist was later proven to be true, he was recognized as the discoverer of the Periodic Law.

—DAVID BYRNE[11]

How Many Batmans Are There?

We often like something simply because it is familiar. A song may not objectively be that good, but we've heard the melody so many times that we're not challenged when we listen to it. We can easily tap our foot and anticipate what is to come. Recognizable melodies make for easy engagement, which is one reason most unknown bands play at least a few cover songs when they perform on Thursdays at the local bar. Even if we don't recognize the band, and even if the performance has different elements, the familiarity of popular melodies increases the chances we'll stay and listen.

Many comic book characters are iconic and, over the years, become familiar much the way melodies do. Regardless of whether we like them, most of us have heard of Batman, Wonder Woman, and Iron Man. Although they appear in movies and television, as well as on countless products, these characters all got their start in comics. And whether Spider-Man is played by Tobey Maguire, Andrew Garfield, or Tom Holland, you go to each franchise reboot knowing the main storyline. The actors change, MJ gets updated, new villains are fought, but the basic Spider-Man melody is still there.

DC Comics was the first company to dominate the market, with characters like Superman and Batman. These superheroes were the protagonists of comic books, visual stories printed on cheap paper and sold at newsstands. Marvel Comics came along in the 1960s, with characters like Spider-Man and Captain America, and gradually took over the lead in terms of sales of comic books. Yet over time, the demands of the medium have led to an underlying, unchanging refrain in the stories about their iconic characters. Right from the early days, in the 1930s and '40s, there was an expectation from readers of a new comic book every few weeks. The superheroes would have new adventures, and readers, mostly children, would pay a few cents to follow the characters. But the competition that developed between DC and Marvel drove comic book output to incredible heights. In 1962 alone, DC released 343 individual comics.[12]

The pressure to put out new, visually engaging, and fresh material was intense. Editors were always searching their company's archives to see which characters they could revive. For example, DC's the Flash, whose original solo series had been canceled in 1949, came back in 1959 with a new series.[13] In the 1960s, DC also revived its Justice League comic, which was another way to meet output demands. Characters in the Justice League, such as Superman and Wonder Woman, had individual series, and then they would work together in the Justice League series—no new characters required.

Marvel used the same strategy of recycling characters. As journalist Reed Tucker describes in his book *Slugfest*, when an artist fell behind in his work in 1963, "[Stan] Lee was forced to go to plan B. Taking a page from DC's playbook, Lee tossed together members of the company's existing superhero roster into one powerful team, just like the Justice League. Using existing characters saved him and artist Jack Kirby from having to come up with brand-new ones and allowed the issues to be completed more quickly so it made it to the printer in time."[14]

Publishing deadlines meant that creative teams at both Marvel and DC didn't always have the space to think up completely new characters. Instead, tight turnarounds could leave an editor succumbing to the availability bias. Tucker tells this story of one attempt at a brand-new character: "Gerber intended Wundarr as an homage to Superman, but in this case the line between homage and simply borrowing everything about Superman to meet your deadline was blurred."[15]

To compete in the market, comics needed to be released frequently. One possibility was to take the same characters and insert them into major new plotlines. But if you're going to give Wonder Woman a new series of comics, you have to keep the elements that make her Wonder Woman. The melody must be maintained. In the 1970s, both DC and Marvel stepped up production demand by starting yearly comic book "event" issues. Events were based around a "big important story that was perceived to matter more than the now-pedestrian yarns that filled the books month after month." Tucker further explains that "in a few years events would become so frequent that they would begin to lose their cachet. After all, when everything is an event, nothing is."[16]

The events drove the phenomenon of character recycling to new levels. Characters normally appear within a series, and each issue of a series is numbered. So, issue #1 in a series would presumably be the first appearance of that character. There was not, however, time for many brand-new characters. In 1990 Marvel launched a "new Spider-Man title—Marvel's fourth starring the webslinger."[17] There are, by now, quite a few "Spider-Man #1s." Batman, being almost twenty-five years older than Spider-Man, has been revamped so many times that it's hard to imagine how else his story can be told. But at the very least we know that he'll be dressed in black, his real name will be Bruce Wayne, and he'll have a tortured soul that he only reveals to his long-standing servant. Tucker states, "Titles are started so often with a new #1 that the number has basically lost its currency. Wolverine, Marvel's popular mutant hero, has had his title restarted three times since 2010 alone."[18]

Once in a while, one of the comics companies produces completely original characters in a brand-new storyline. For example, DC released *Watchmen* in 1986, and its popularity has continued to this day. Tucker writes of this dark comic for an older audience, "DC was playing a longer game, attempting to elevate the medium and have a shelf life longer than four weeks."[19] However, this is the exception, not the norm. Most comics feature characters that we've seen many times and that have been revamped continually in order to sell books to an increasingly smaller hard-core audience.

Using the model of melody, we can understand how publishing demands impacted the development of comic book characters and storylines. When you are under a time crunch, you are much more likely to stick with what you know.

Common Elements in Uncommon Groups

A melody is the path of a song, a common element that links all the parts of the song together. Using this model more metaphorically helps us see common elements in groups that might appear to have little in common. The model of melody is one lens through which to appreciate the connections made along the early Silk Road.

The term "Silk Road" refers, despite the name, not to a single path but to a network of east–west exchange that eventually linked the Pacific Ocean with the Mediterranean Sea. Trade along the Silk Road in central Asia started between pastoral and agricultural communities as early as 3000 BCE.[20] The routes expanded both westward and eastward; there were offshoots into northern Africa and Europe, as well as north–south spurs at various points. "By the opening of the second millennium BC, a trading route stretched clear across Asia; not a continuous road to be traversed by any one person, but a chain of many trading links, connecting Western Asia and China over a distance of almost 5,000 miles."[21]

Thus, the Silk Roads facilitated an incredible number of connections among different cultures and geographies. "These pathways serve as the world's central nervous system, connecting people and places together," historian Peter Frankopan suggests in *The Silk Roads*, "but lying beneath the skin, invisible to the naked eye. Just as anatomy explains how the body functions, understanding these connections allows us to understand how the world works."[22] The links offered by the Silk Road connected people, customs, ideas, goods, and disease.

The Silk Road is so named because one good it transported for centuries was silk. Originating in China and traveling with merchants across vast distances, "silk became an international currency as well as a luxury product."[23] Silk became common, not in the sense that everyone had it (they didn't, because it was expensive) but in that it was available to anyone with the means to buy it. It became a recognizable commodity from the Pacific to the Mediterranean.

Goods like silk were not the only things that traveled the road. "Ideas, themes and stories coursed through the highways, spread by travelers, merchants and pilgrims."[24] Knowledge of the concept of zero and its relevance to mathematics traveled, as did the religions of Judaism, Christianity, Islam, and Buddhism. Ideas like siege warfare and innovations in transportation and agriculture also made their way along the roads, hand in hand with goods like ceramics and precious metals. Frankopan explains, "There was good reason why the cultures, cities and peoples who lived along the Silk Roads developed and advanced: as they traded and exchanged ideas, they learned and borrowed from each other, stimulating further advances in philosophy, the sciences, language and religion."[25]

Goods and ideas flowed in both directions along this east–west route. The Silk Road did not support the primacy of any one society; the towns and cities along its routes ebbed and flowed with geopolitical changes and disease. Some, like Kandahar, still exist. Others, like Merv, most of us have never heard of. The Silk Road was a progenitor of constant exchange and change. Accordingly, we can generate some interesting insights when we look at the early Silk Road through the model of melody.

The regions, civilizations, and cities along the Silk Road were far from homogenous. Differences in geography, climate, political organizations, and more meant that travelers would pass through very different environments as they journeyed on the roads. But there would also be constants: goods and ideas that were recognizable wherever they were. Silk and some spices could be found at even the most remote outposts. By about 700 CE, spices from India could be found in Mainz, Germany, and silk has been found in Viking graves. These widespread elements served to create a sort of melody, a way for any traveler along the Silk Road to orient themselves to wherever they were. As Frankopan writes:

> For the vast majority of the population in antiquity, horizons were decidedly local—with trade and interaction between people being carried out over short distances. Nevertheless, the webs of communities wove into each other to create a world that was complex, where tastes and ideas were shaped by products, artistic principles and influences thousands of miles apart.[26]

So, even if you never left your village, you were often still exposed to something that had traveled along the Silk Road.

Thinking about the Silk Road in the context of melody also

suggests how interesting it can be to see common elements in disparate settings. Seeing silk in a town thousands of miles from our own can allow us to appreciate the newness around us, because of the anchoring the silk gives us.

In melody, we make sense of the notes we are hearing in the context of the notes we've just heard, and we also compare what we are hearing with the memories we have of music we've heard before. It is possible to imagine the goods and ideas traveling along the Silk Road functioning in a similar way for the people who came across them; namely, they provided context that facilitated understanding. For example, whomever a traveler saw wearing silk was likely to be in a position of power.

To be fair, exchange along the Silk Road was not at a constant volume. It waxed and waned as fortunes changed and centers of power rose and fell. But as late as around 1000 CE, the value of the routes was still recognized. Frankopan notes, "Merchants could be assured of security wherever they went, regardless of their faith, and regardless of whether there was peace or war."[27] Through tax treaties or local punishments, the movement of goods, and consequently ideas, was supported. Although the perceived value of the Silk Road was largely economic, we can appreciate the social value in having goods and ideas flow over thousands of miles. Trade and exchange can happen only if people can work together to some extent.

The vastness of the Silk Road meant that many people interacted with the network in some capacity. These trade routes were "the largest single network of exchanges on earth before the sixteenth century."[28] Yet this system of exchanges, although providing some commonalities, nonetheless did not produce homogeneity. Historian David Christian notes that what did not travel well on the Silk Roads was accurate geographical and cultural knowledge.

One of the reasons for this was that before the end of the Mongol empire in 1368, "very few individuals traveled the length of the Silk Roads."[29] They were too long, and one might never come home. It was the goods and ideas that flowed all the way along the network.

Different cultures and societies flourished and fell. People stayed different. Yet, Christian observes, "Despite its great diversity, the history of Afro-Eurasia has always preserved an underlying unity, which was expressed in common technologies, styles, cultures, and religions, even disease patterns."[30] People can work together more easily if, underneath all the local particularities, there are common, recognizable elements. Whether that element was silk or, later, silver, accounting, or paper, the Silk Road facilitated something analogous to the notes of a melody that was easily recognized by anyone who traveled.

Conclusion

Melody is music's soul, the ethereal thread weaving through sound's tapestry. It's the part of a song that we hum in the shower, the tune that gets stuck in our head and won't let go. Melody is the musical expression of a fundamental human need: the need to tell a story, to convey an emotion, to connect with others on a level beyond words.

At its core, a melody is simply a sequence of notes, a pattern of pitches and rhythms. But melody's magic transcends these basic building blocks. A great melody is more than the sum of its parts. It has a shape, a contour, an arc that carries us from one note to the next. It has a sense of inevitability, as if each note is the only possible choice, even as the melody surprises us with its freshness and novelty.

In this sense, melody is a lot like language. As we arrange words infinitely to express different ideas, we arrange notes to express emotions and experiences. A rising melody might convey a sense of hope and aspiration, while a falling melody might suggest sadness or resignation. A melody with large leaps might feel adventurous and daring, while one with small, stepwise motion might feel intimate and confiding.

But melody isn't just about individual expressions. It's also about communication and connection. When a melody resonates with us, it's as if the composer is speaking directly to our hearts. We feel understood, validated, less alone. And when we sing or play a melody with others, we create a bond, a shared experience that transcends our individual differences.

This is why melody has such power across cultures and throughout history. From the chants of ancient rituals to the latest pop hits, melody has been a constant in human musical expression. It's a universal language, requiring no translation or explanation. A beautiful melody can move us regardless of whether we understand the words or know the cultural context.

Of course, not all melodies are equal. Just as there are great works of literature and forgettable pulp novels, there are melodies that stand the test of time and others that quickly fade from memory. The best melodies balance the familiar and the new. They have a memorable shape, a satisfying resolution, a feeling of completeness.

In a world often fragmented and chaotic, melody is a source of unity and coherence, a way of finding beauty and meaning amid the noise.

Representation

Influence through presentation.

Before human nature can escape from representation in art, it must first escape from the will to represent. That would appear to be no easy matter, either for the caveman or for the Futurist.

—*THE AMERICAN MAGAZINE OF ART*[1]

To better understand something, we often need to look at the purpose behind it. Representation, as a model, has us looking beyond the surface. Using it as a lens prompts us to remember to consider what we might better understand if we dig a little deeper into why things appear the way they do.

Visual art is the representation of things. Because this is a book about mental models, not art criticism or history, we won't get more detailed than that. It may be possible to conceive of a painting that contains no representation of any sort. But even a casual perusal of art across time and cultures reveals a world full of paintings and sculptures that contain representations of ideas and things found in the world. We may admire a piece many centuries later because, to our sensibilities, it is beautiful, but fundamental to art is that it contains representations, and in doing so, it often has a purpose. Why did the artist choose to represent this thing rather than that thing? And why in this way, versus another of a thousand ways that thing could be represented?

Representation involves choice, and considering those choices can tell you a lot about the purpose behind the representation. Cave paintings were possibly created to try to influence the outcomes of upcoming hunts. Tomb art was a way of securing prosperity in the afterlife. Church paintings provided spiritual and moral guidance by telling stories from the Bible. Chinese paintings from a certain period were material for meditation. Portraits were commissioned to capture someone's likeness for posterity. Historical scenes were painted to set down a perspective on a moment in history. Some art is created to express the artist's personality, or to provide a commentary on a specific social situation, or to expand the definition of art.

Representation is not always literal. Some artists have tried to depict, with detailed exactness, the scene before them, but others choose to represent the scene through a different mode. For example, for the Egyptians, "everything had to be represented from its most characteristic angle,"[2] which is why each figure in Egyptian art is depicted simultaneously from different angles (i.e., the head, torso, feet, etc.). For Egyptian artists, art was meant to contain all the forms they considered important. It was not supposed to be a literal representation of what they saw, but rather a representation of what they knew to exist.[3] In addition, most of the time, Egyptian art followed a set of rules[4]—the artists were aiming not to be creative but to create what had already been established as desirable. Thus, it would be a mistake to conclude that ancient Egyptians weren't very good artists. Rather, how they represented their world tells you a lot about what they valued.

This model reminds us that humans use the same types of maps to represent vastly different territories. Art historian Whitney Davis notes there is a likelihood "that commonality of culture is best defined to begin with as the mutually intelligible use of various representational systems."[5] Most cultures engage in visual representation of some sort, so we can see one another's art. Problems arise, though, when we fail to appreciate that there are differences in how and why those visual representations come to be, and judge them as if they are a product of our own system. Representation therefore can be a gateway to understanding not only an individual artist but the sensibilities of that artist's culture.

Consider these examples:

- Chinese artists who were influenced by Buddhism and thus wished to provide material for thought and contemplation had no desire to paint a landscape with all of the details it contains. Instead, their representations of mountains and trees were often constructed of few brush strokes, suggesting of the artist, for example, "the awe he must have felt for these majestic peaks."[6]

- Muslim artists, being in some places and times banned from depicting figures, represented a dream world through shape and color patterns. Later, in places where figures were allowed, the legacy of these patterns still influenced how they represented stories and scenes.

- Impressionists explored the impact of light on outdoor spaces and physical forms in movement to represent scenes not in photographic detail but the way we experience them. We are not able to notice all details at once; instead we focus on a small area and have only an impression of the rest. Of impressionist paintings, Julian Bell says, "The painter was no longer aiming to represent objects as such, but rather to respond to a temporary pattern of stimuli to the retina."[7]

Artists must deal with a certain tension in representation, because there is always a difference between what is there and what you see in the context surrounding it. Julian Bell says of later Egyptian art that it "got itself hooked on the tension between nature and the ideal," and the Greek sculptor Lysippos "spoke of representing men not as they are, but as they appear."[8]

There is also the challenge presented by constraints imposed by representing things visually. For example, visual art must take into consideration how the eyes work. In describing *Night Revels of Han Xizai*, a painting by Gu Hongzhong circa 1070, Bell explains, "If everything in the scroll recedes at 45 degrees, then the sequence will read more smoothly as it runs before the eyes. That's not 'the way things look,'"[9] but it serves the purpose of making the scene easier for the viewer to process and comprehend.

To understand representation in visual art, we need to also consider who was paying for or supporting the creation of the work. Governments, religious institutions, wealthy patrons, gallery owners, the general public—all have impacted what art gets produced and thus what gets represented at various times in history. This explains why, for example, in Western Europe there are a thousand years' worth of paintings of the Virgin Mary and the birth of Christ: for centuries, the Catholic church was one of the only institutions with the money to commission the art and the space to display it.

The famous terra-cotta warriors in Xi'An, China, are another example of the relationship between art and its patron. There are more than six thousand terra-cotta statues in the tomb of the first Qin emperor, who died in 210 BCE. The soldiers were meant to accompany the emperor into the afterlife, and each one was individualized. They are meant to represent, among other things, a real army. As Bell notes, one of the goals here is "representing facts faithfully on an industrial scale."[10] The effort required to produce these individual, lifelike soldiers is reflective of the sensibilities of the society in which they were produced.

Without a doubt, we become used to the representations in art we are most familiar with. When confronted with representations that don't fit, we are inclined to dismiss them as "not art." Art historian E. H. Gombrich suggests, "We are all inclined to judge pictures by what we *know* rather than what we *see.*"[11] It can be hard to put aside everything we've absorbed about visual art in order to look at different representations with curiosity. Sometimes the path to appreciation is through the adage, "Less is more." Julian Bell describes the intentions of painter Mark Rothko, who used very few forms and images, as creating "an art that expanded representation rather than excluded it, giving viewers access to a wider range of emotions."[12]

Representation as a model thus helps us understand that liking (or disliking) something and understanding something are two different activities. Regardless of whether you like a particular work of art, looking not only at what is represented but how it is represented is a way of appreciating a perspective that is likely quite different from yours. Understanding that representation is influenced by the context in which it occurs can also offer insights into the cultures and societies that gave rise to that representation.

The Value of Open-source Intelligence

When people think of espionage and the intelligence products it yields, what often comes to mind are clandestine activities and top-secret reports. In the world of spy craft, intelligence is considered information you have to intercept, steal, or smuggle out of enemy territory. In reality, the majority of intelligence is generated from open-source information. Called OSINT, open-source intelligence is that which is freely and publicly available. It is not classified, and it is accessed by more than just government intelligence programs. Everything from newspaper articles and radio broadcasts to technical manuals and, these days, social media posts counts as open-source information. All OSINT that is gathered is processed and analyzed, and it forms the basis of many intelligence agency reports.

Intelligence can be defined, in the words of scholar H. Akin Ünver, as "the methodical collection of high-value information in a way that yields comparative advantage to decision makers."[13] In the day-to-day world of intelligence, much of that high value comes from the analysis of open-source information. Even in the early days of information collection for intelligence purposes, leaders recognized the value of collecting and analyzing open-source information. In her book *Information Hunters*, Kathy Peiss states, "The early managers of the CIA believed that 80 percent of intelligence came from foreign publications, radio, and people with general knowledge, although they focused especially on monitoring communication and broadcasting."[14]

It seems counterintuitive: Why would publicly available information be so valuable for intelligence purposes? After all, if everyone has it, then how can it give any government an edge? The value of open-source information comes in the analysis, and the analysis involves looking for clues to build an understanding of the context surrounding that information. It is in understanding the larger context of OSINT where the real value lies, because understanding context is what allows agencies to process and evaluate *all* of the information they take in. Akin Ünver argues, "Although an intelligence agency's capacity is primarily measured by how well it can detect and transmit critical information, its ability to understand and contextualize what is important requires the foreknowledge of what is 'out there' and easily available."[15]

Think of it this way: If a war suddenly broke out in Spendu and you had no idea where or what Spendu was (a country? an organization?), how would you be able to undertake the analysis for whether and how to respond? A lot of the information you would need would be publicly available on maps, in news reports, and in academic journals. Similarly, how do you know where to look for potential threats to your country if you don't have a good sense of geopolitical issues? You can learn about those issues in unclassified, open-source products.

When we look at open-source information through the model of representation, we begin to understand how publicly available products can produce unique intelligence reports. What is represented by the information gives clues to the context surrounding that information. Evaluating what an enemy puts out into the world is a great way of understanding them.

Analysis is required to turn open-source information into intelligence. Various sources need to be combined and processed according to organizing principles such as keywords or categories. That way, seemingly disparate content is juxtaposed to reveal trends or themes. During World War II, Peiss writes that

> scientific periodicals, technical manuals, and industrial directories directly from Axis and occupied countries were studied closely for evidence of enemy troop strength and weaponry, and economic production. Even trivial items could prove meaningful. Society pages might reveal the location of a regiment, and gossip columns "provide clues to scandals which a secret agent would exploit."[16]

Open-source information is also useful for assessing foreign policy and devising propaganda campaigns. Essentially, open-source information is a critical means of knowing one's enemy well enough to be able to craft measures and countermeasures to thwart their agenda and advance your own.

Open-source information can also provide insight on how your measures are working and the effect they're having on your adversary. In a fascinating anecdote, Peiss relates how music librarian Richard Hill "surveyed the newspaper *Deutsche Allgemeine Zeitung*, tracing patterns of concert reviews, the presence or absence of certain theaters in the news, last-minute changes in operas, and notices to ticket holders about refunds. From this information, he drew conclusions about the timing, location, and extent of bomb damage in Berlin during the initial phase of Allied air attacks."[17] This is classic open-source analysis. It's not about cancellations of arts performances in and of themselves, but what they represent—in this case, the success of Allied bombing.

Open-source intelligence provides context that other types of intelligence production cannot. Clandestine intelligence gathering is, by definition, more narrow and targeted. Without the broader understanding gained from evaluating open-source information, the value of other types of intelligence—let alone the knowledge of where to find them—would be significantly undermined. Akin Ünver notes that open-source intelligence covers "the spectrum of events, actors and roles that determines strategic relativity (i.e., how to define a country's interests in relation to ongoing events), as well as which assets to deploy to achieve them."[18]

The value of all intelligence is produced through analysis of connections and consideration of nuance. Open-source intelligence analysts do not stop at the representation but go deeper by asking, what does that representation tell me about my adversary? In doing so, they give their country a strategic advantage in hostile operations.

Powerful Women

Most of us are familiar with the game of chess, and most of us probably assume that the way we play it now is the way it's always been played. In that assumption, however, we would be wrong. Looking at the development of the game—particularly at the role of the queen—demonstrates the symbiotic relationship between how things are and how they are represented.

The earliest known chess sets come from India, circa the sixth century. In these sets, there is no queen. The square beside the king is inhabited by a vizier, a chief counselor to the king. Descriptions of early chess also make note that the vizier is not a very powerful figure, able to only move one diagonal square at a time.

Today, the queen is the most powerful piece on a chessboard, able to move many spaces in any direction, and often a critical component of eventually winning the game. If a pawn manages to make it across the board, it is rewarded by being transformed into another all-powerful queen. No player wants to lose their queen, and she is usually sacrificed only to ensure checkmate.

How this evolution from a weak male support figure to a powerful female warrior next to the king came about is not completely known. But there is a strong correlation between the rise of female power in European monarchies and the development of the chess queen. What cannot be doubted is that the power of the chess queen would likely never have come about if it had no corresponding representation of female power in the societies that played the game.

After its origins in India, chess made its way to Persia and the Arab countries bordering the Mediterranean. "It was only after the Arabs invaded Southern Europe in the eighth century and brought chess with them that the queen appeared on the board," writes scholar Marilyn Yalom in *Birth of the Chess Queen*. "Around the year 1000 she began to replace the vizier, and by 1200 she could be found all over Western Europe, from Italy to Norway."[19]

Ultimately, chess is the playing out of a strategic battle among multiple figures who each have a set of powers and roles. It is thus not really surprising that those attributes would reflect elements of the related roles in the social hierarchy in which the game was played. Yalom explains, "When the Arabs carried the game across the Mediterranean into Spain and Sicily, chess began to reflect Western feudal structures and took on a social dimension." In medieval European society, chess was played at multiple levels of social class, and it was one of the few activities men and women could do together. Far from causing upheaval in social dynamics, "the game of chess, adapted to European Christendom, provided the perfect representation of a social order in which everyone was expected to know his or her exact place."[20] It would seem, then, that we can understand a lot about the role of queens in medieval western Europe by reflecting on the development of the chess queen.

The piece's coming into existence is likely reflective of the role royal women had at the side of their kings. Western Europe at that time was predominantly Christian, and Christianity promoted the idea of monogamous unions for life. A king was not complete without a queen by his side. Furthermore, in the region there was both acceptance of and precedent for women inheriting the regency in their own right; women could become queens by right of birth, not because they had married into the role.

The chess queen was understood as a representation of real-life queens—so much so that there long remained a prohibition in chess against having multiple queens on the board. The current rule of turning a pawn that crosses the board into a queen was unacceptable in medieval times, as the king's wife "was his only permissible conjugal mate according to Chrisitan doctrine."[21]

When the queen first appeared on the chessboard, she had the same powers and range of movement as the original vizier: one diagonal square at a time. By the end of the fifteenth century, she had acquired the power she has today. The growth of the queen's power on the board might be reflective of the power exercised by European queens in those five hundred years: there was the reign of Urraca, queen of Leon-Castile, from 1109 to 1126; of Constance of Hauteville, queen of Sicily and Holy Roman Empress from 1154 to 1198; of Eleanor of Aquitaine, queen of France from 1137 to 1152 and of England from 1154 to 1189; and of Margaret of Denmark, who ruled in Denmark, Norway, and Sweden from 1387 to 1412. And this is not an exhaustive list.

Female rulers were common enough, and they commanded significant power during their reigns. The most powerful female monarch during the late medieval period in Europe, and who had the most influence on how the chessboard queen was perceived, was possibly Isabella I of Castile. Reigning from 1451 to 1504, she fought wars, supported exploration, and significantly grew the power of the Spanish throne. Hers is a mixed legacy, as it also includes funding the exploitation of the Americas and the Spanish Inquisition. But we can appreciate that in her time, there was no European queen as powerful.

Yalom writes that it is not surprising that the chess queen achieved the height of her powers during Isabella's reign. "In 1497 when Isabella of Castile reigned over Spain . . . a Spanish book recognized that the chess queen had become the most potent piece on the board."[22] Able to move in any direction over multiple squares, the queen is the strongest piece in the game. Without her, many players feel they have no chance to capture the opponent's king.

Was the chess queen given her powers as an homage to Isabella? We will likely never know. But it's possible. "A militant queen more powerful than her husband had arisen in Castille; why not on the chessboard as well? This may have been the thinking of those players from Valencia who endowed the chess queen with her extended range of motion. Yet it is just as likely that those Valencian players unconsciously redesigned the queen on the model of the all-powerful Isabella."[23] However it happened, one element is certain: the appearance of the chess queen and her growth in power reflected the role of female rulers in European society.

The chess queen's rise was not smooth, and as her powers grew, so did the vitriol hurled against her. For some medieval male writers, criticism of moves of the chess queen was used as an analogy to attack all women. Her power, relative to the king's, the bishop's, and the knight's, was a threat. What she represented made some people uncomfortable, for if her power could both grow and be asserted, what did that say about the real female rulers of the world?

Representation is thus a useful model for considering the development of the chess queen. Games, like art, often represent norms, ideas, and ideals of the society they are a part of. They may reflect who we are or who we want to be. "The reality of female rule," Yalom explains, "was undoubtedly entwined with the emergence and evolution of the chess queen. In time, the chess queen would become the quintessential metaphor for female power in the Western World."[24]

Conclusion

Representation is the mental shorthand we use to navigate the complexities of reality, the symbols and images we use to communicate our thoughts and experiences. Representation is how we construct meaning, how we bridge the gap between the raw data of our senses and the narratives we tell about ourselves and our world.

At its core, representation is about standing in for something else. A word stands in for an object or concept, a map for a territory, a musical note for a sound. We use representations because we can't hold the entirety of reality in our minds at once. We need abstractions, simplifications, models that we can manipulate and reason about.

But representation is not neutral. Every representation is an interpretation, a way of framing reality that highlights some aspects and obscures others. An emoji might represent a feeling, but it doesn't show the lived experience that causes that feeling. In this sense, representation is always a kind of distortion. It's a lens that shapes how we see the world, for better or worse. A good representation can illuminate hidden truths, help us see patterns and connections that we might otherwise miss. But a bad representation can mislead us, reinforce stereotypes and prejudices, limit our ability to imagine alternatives.

Representation is not just about mirroring reality; it's also about shaping it. The representations we create and consume have the power to influence how we think and act, to change the very world they purport to describe. A powerful piece of art can shift cultural attitudes, a persuasive political narrative can sway elections, a compelling scientific model can guide research and policy. In this way, representation is a kind of feedback loop. We create representations based on our understanding of reality, but those representations in turn shape our understanding, which influences the representations we create next. It's a constant dance between map and territory, between symbol and referent.

Balance

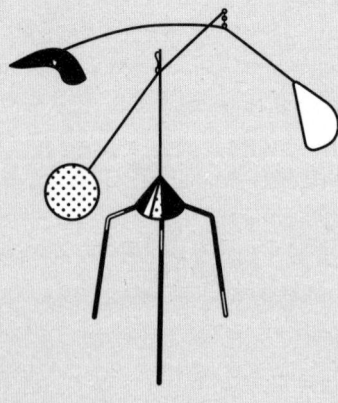

> To set all in equilibrium is well; to put all in harmony is better.
>
> —VICTOR HUGO[25]

WHETHER WE REALIZE IT OR NOT, WE ARE CONSTANTLY IN SEARCH OF and appreciate balance—the arrangement of elements in a way that feels beautiful, stable, and harmonious. Balance is when things come together just right.

Balance in visual art refers to the use of artistic elements such as line, texture, color, space, and form in the creation of artworks in a way that renders visual stability. Balance in visual art can also be conceptualized as harmony. There is no prescription or formula for what makes a work balanced and therefore harmonious. Looking at sketches that artists have done before painting the final "great work" demonstrates the need for ongoing experimentation in order to have the result be "just so." E. H. Gombrich says of one of Raphael's series of sketches before the final painting, "What he tried again and again to get was the right balance between the figures, the right relationship which would make the most harmonious whole."[26]

Balance is not easily definable. In two-dimensional art, balance often involves using the space in a way that renders the entire piece easily observable. In three-dimensional art, balance is more obvious—if an object, such as a sculpture, can't stand up to display as desired, it is not balanced. However, balance is more than just the ability to stand, and thus sculpture too often displays a visual balance.

We use the concept of balance in more areas than art. A balanced diet is one in which less nutritious foods are offset by more nutritious ones. Work-life balance is when someone can even out the time and energy they give to work and nonwork activities, like socializing or exercising. A balanced view of something is one that considers multiple opinions on it. We have an intuitive sense of balance as something important and necessary.

Visual artists need to consider the balance of left to right, of up to down, of foreground to background. They can use elements such as color, shading, or forms to achieve the harmonious effect they are aiming for. Artists sometimes need to compromise among competing goals, such as painting all of what they see, accurate rendering of all the details, or emphasis on a particular motif or story. "The suggestion of space and the faithful imitation of reality must not be allowed to destroy the balance of the composition" was a statement written by Gombrich in reference to one particular piece, but it highlights various challenges an artist may face when trying to create something that feels balanced.[27]

Visual artists can achieve balance using various techniques but must always contend with the human preference for symmetry. As humans, we find something about symmetry inherently attractive and appealing. It is believed that the more symmetrical a person's face is, the more attractive people are likely to find them on average. Biologists believe that, for our ancestors, facial symmetry may have signaled overall health and, consequently, genetic fitness. This meant someone with a symmetrical face was likely to be a good choice as a mate.[28]

Our attraction to symmetry extends far beyond faces. Research indicates that symmetrical text, like the balanced columns of *The New Yorker*, may aid us in paying attention to what we read.[29] We find it easier to cognitively process what is symmetrical.[30]

Many of the objects in nature we find most beautiful, such as flowers or shells, have an element of symmetry. Indeed, symmetry is encoded within our bodies. Most of our organs are bilaterally symmetrical, and there is fossil evidence showing that animals have been built this way for at least the last five hundred million years.[31] There might then be a survival benefit to this kind of balance.

When it comes to art, we don't require perfect and obvious symmetry, such as the same forms repeated on both the left and right sides of a painting. Artists use asymmetry all the time, and thus we can be attracted to a variety of visual arrangements. But the way all of the elements of an artwork are brought together is what creates a feeling of harmony or engagement: the forms may be stacked to one side, but the shading balances them out, or the lines are arranged to offset the clusters of color.

Life is the pursuit of balance.

> Anybody who has ever tried to arrange a bunch of flow-ers, to shuffle and shift the colours, to add a little here and take away there, has experienced this strange sen-sation of balancing forms and colours without being able to tell exactly what kind of harmony it is he is trying to achieve.
>
> —E. H. GOMBRICH[32]

What is perceived as balanced and harmonious in a work of art is not universal. The experience of art is heavily influenced by cultural sensibilities and personal preference. Thus, one way to present art is to more actively engage the viewer in applying themselves to an appreciation of the piece. Julian Bell says of *Tableau I: with Red, Black, Blue and Yellow* that artist Piet Mondrian "was asking the eye to focus on its own capacity to judge relations and balances, and on its own desire for clarity."[33] The art critic Peter Schjeldahl says of another Mondrian piece, "We intuitively gauge weights and tensions that constitute the picture's stability. Epiphany happens when you grasp how finely calibrated the stability is, poised at a breaking point."[34]

There are many ways to create a visually appealing work of art. But the more you learn, the easier it becomes to know when something is as good as it can be. When harmony is achieved, everything feels right.

The power is in the balance: we are our injuries, as much as we are our successes.

—BARBARA KINGSOLVER[35]

Plot

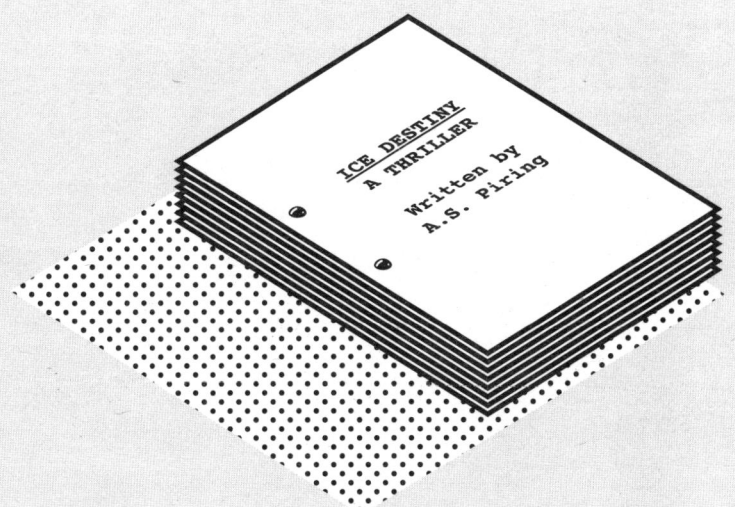

ICE DESTINY
A THRILLER

Written by
A.S. Piring

Sequence shapes story.

Plot is the knowing
of destination.

—ELIZABETH BOWEN[1]

Humans love telling and hearing stories. People who can turn buying milk into an interesting adventure are rewarded with our attention. Plot is a story's road map, guiding you through twists, turns, challenges, and discoveries. A good plot keeps you hooked; a bad one feels like a drag.

Organizing events into a plot helps us make sense of them, but we need to watch out for two red flags: first, being swayed by the better of two plots; and second, letting the stories we tell ourselves blind us to new information.

Plot is the chain of connected events that make up a narrative. According to the playwright and novelist Gustav Freytag, causality in the chain of plot events is what lends a story believability and interests the audience in getting to the end. Most relevant to fiction, plots, scholar Marie-Laure Ryan notes, "are heavily dependent on the circulation of information."[2] Characters learn new things, which prompts them to take certain actions, which move the story through the narrative arc.

Freytag identified five typical elements of a plot:[3]

- "Exposition" (beginning/introduction) brings us into the world of the story, providing a sense of the starting point. It gives the reader context for subsequent events.

- "Rising action" (including conflict, which may be internal, external, or both) begins at the point at which the initial sense of normalcy in the story is disrupted.

- "Climax" tends to be a point of high emotions and lots of action, when you don't want to put a book down or turn off a film.

- "Falling action" is the stage in a story when the pieces begin to fit together, dilemmas begin to resolve, and questions begin to receive answers.

- "Resolution" (end/conclusion) will typically tie up all the loose ends of a story and leave the reader with a satisfying sense of completion.

The novelist E. M. Forster, who also thought of plot as a chain of events linked by causality, says in his 1927 work *Aspects of the Novel*, "'The king died and then the queen died' may be a story, but it is not a plot. However, 'the king died and then the queen died of grief' is a plot. The same two events occur, the difference is that one is the result of the other." The creation of conflict is a key role of a plot, as conflict is the "primary source of narrative interest."[4]

Plots are used most frequently in novels, movies, and plays, but they can also be found in visual art and dance. We can think of a plot like a skeleton: it provides the base for a structure, but on its own it's not enough for a story. Characters, setting, emotions, desires, and details are combined with the skeleton of plot to produce a story. Aristotle, writing in *Poetics*, viewed plot as the core component of drama, more crucial than anything else—even than the characters.

Plots are necessary for any story, including true stories, such as a newspaper article or book-length work of nonfiction. While reality might not map onto the same five-part sequence described above, we can still see the narrative structure in "introduction, background, new information, putting it all together, and conclusion." Even in nonfiction, there is a tendency for writers to create an aha moment, similar to the climax, where the point of their writing becomes clear to the reader. A story can have more than one plot at once, with multiple threads occurring in tandem or intermingling. There may also be subplots, such as a separate sequence of events happening to a supporting character.

Storytellers need to balance placing realistic characters in logical situations in the world they've created alongside the extraordinary events of the story. Thus, plots in literature are not meant to mirror reality exactly. There has to be something special, even in nonfiction, that makes this particular plot worth telling.

Although the resolution of all plotlines by a story's end is not required, some kind of resolution is necessary for the plot to be finished. It may take a couple of novels, or a series of movies, but at some point, the audience likes to get to an ending. Some endings are more satisfying than others. Readers generally like resolutions to be the logical outcome of decisions made throughout the story, versus what is called a "deus ex machina" (something brand-new that is dumped into the story strictly to bring about a resolution because the characters, on account of the parameters that have been set up, cannot bring about the resolution themselves).

Not all plots are perfectly constructed. A flaw or inconsistency in a plot is known as a "plot hole" and can ruin an otherwise sound story. Even if we can't quite articulate how exactly a plot has let us down, plot holes impact our enjoyment of a work of fiction. While plot holes are typically an error, some authors will make a deliberate effort to subvert traditional plot structures; for example, by not supplying a story with a satisfactory ending. As with any deliberate thwarting of artistic principles and conventions, the effect is often jarring for the audience and is more commonly the basis of more modern and rebellious literary movements.

Another way to look at plot is to see that works of literature have two plots. There is the storyline created by the author, in which things happen, but there are also the plots of many of the characters, "who," as Marie-Laure Ryan explains, "set goals, devise plans, schemes and conspiracies, and try to arrange events to their advantage."[5] Thus, authors have to be careful when creating characters, so as to not end up with characters who are ill-suited to advancing their plot as it progresses. Each choice made in story writing closes many doors, and a plot will often develop based on the constraints dictated by earlier choices.

A good plot follows a line of causality: things happen for a reason. Life, however, does not always follow the same clear-cut pattern of cause and effect. For this reason, plot is the most useful lens to help counteract narrative bias. Challenging yourself to look at situations through the lens of plot helps you determine whether you're being led astray by assuming a relationship between events that doesn't exist. Conversely, this model also helps you determine when it is in your interest to craft a better story.

Chekhov's Gun and Red Herrings

> There's an old rule of theater that goes, "If there's a gun on the mantel in Act I, it must go off in Act III." The reverse is also true.
>
> —STEPHEN KING[6]

The principle of Chekhov's gun states that everything that appears in a story must serve some overall purpose in the wider plot. Playwright Anton Chekov advised that a gun hanging on the wall in one scene must go off later in the text. Otherwise, its presence is unnecessary.

Distinct from Chekhov's gun is the importance of foreshadowing, which is when events early in a narrative give clues as to what is going to happen later. What happens early on in a story essentially makes a promise to the audience about what might happen later, so it's important for a writer to fulfill that promise. However, sometimes an author may deliberately mislead the audience with what seems like a future plot device but in fact goes nowhere. Known as a "red herring," when this technique is used deliberately, it can be an effective means of keeping an audience on their toes and of challenging their expectations. To surprise readers in an even stronger way, a writer may incorporate a plot twist. This occurs when a plot changes direction, breaking the previous chain of causality.

One of the challenges of the principle of Chekhov's gun is that in real life, not everything present in one moment is relevant to something that might happen later. In life, there are coincidences and lots of props that don't matter. Life is not a novel.

Who Told the Better Story?

Humans are narrative creatures. We like listening to stories. We like it when a narrative of events has a beginning, a middle, and an end. What would you find more memorable: a presentation on ice density in various locations around the globe, or a story about the chain of events that led from speculation in a university classroom to a massive multinational effort to collect information on ice to a group of scientists finding information about density that will impact forever how we think about ice density? The vast majority of us would find the latter more memorable. What's more, we'd probably learn more about ice density along the way.

Plots are essential components of narratives. They link cause and effect throughout a story and, in so doing, provide a structure that we find familiar and comforting: Something happened, and there's a reason for it. Then it led to these other things, with some twists and tense moments. But eventually we get to The End, where everything makes sense.

One thing we can learn by looking through the lens of plot is that although facts matter, the story you tell with them matters even more. Often, whoever can tell the better story is the one who wins the audience.

Johannes Kepler is on most everyone's list as one of history's great scientists. He is remembered for contributing to the sciences of astronomy and optics, and for promoting the value and beauty of scientific investigation. He was a devout Lutheran, a defender of Copernicus, and devoted to the idea of rational inquiry as the main tool for discovering the wonders of God's universe.

Less well known about Kepler's life is that in 1615, his mother, Katharina, was accused of witchcraft. It was a serious charge that, for many of those accused, resulted in torture and death. Although the experience of a trial and being jailed for more than a year certainly wasn't pleasant for her, Katharina Kepler avoided a much worse fate because her son Johannes told a better story than those accusing her.

For those accusing Katharina of being a witch, the plot was very simple. There were forty-nine accusations against her, all following a simple cause-and-effect storyline. Scenes like, "She hit the girl's arm, and the girl's pain increased by the hour. Now the child was unable to move one finger," and "Katharina had given her a harmful drink four years previously and she had suffered 'inhuman' pains ever since," characterized the prosecution's story.[7] They can all be summed up as some version of "Something bad or weird or unexpected happened, and Katharina was in the vicinity at the time, so she must have caused it."

In the book *The Astronomer and the Witch*, Ulinka Rublack explains that in the Keplers' part of Germany at that time (Leonberg, in the duchy of Württemberg), "witchcraft was used to explain misfortunes and . . . something grave, disorienting, and out of the ordinary in a person's life." Although the Lutheran spiritual and legal leadership cautioned against the idea of witches having any real power and taking accusations at face value, sorcery was considered a legitimate explanation for some occurrences.[8]

Katharina's original accuser was a woman named Ursula Reinbold. In the lead-up to the trial, it was primarily Ursula and her compatriots who encouraged others who had also had run-ins with Katharina to come forward. Each of these witnesses provided a deposition that became part of the public record. "Taken together," Rublack writes, "all of the depositions provided a mish-mash of contradictory evidence. Katharina appeared hospitable and helpful to some, but pushy and dubious to others." Not everyone was convinced Katharina was a witch, and "those who were skeptical deployed a clear set of common sense criteria to make causal connections."[9]

But ultimately, Katharina was not going to be convicted or acquitted by popular vote. It was a group of legal professors in nearby Tübingen who would decide her fate.

Kepler decided he had to take on his mother's defense, and he was uniquely well suited to the task. His background in mathematics gave him an understanding of logic, and the need to secure patronage throughout his career meant that he had experience generating support and sympathy from an audience.[10] Furthermore, his scholarship was based on "using words to resolve rival sets of hypotheses, to analyze motives and causes, and to engage in historical reconstruction."[11] Kepler had already defended the findings of Nicolaus Copernicus against superstition and intellectual inertia. Thus, in many ways, he was the right man for the job of defending Katharina.

First, he questioned his mother in detail "to learn about Leonberg people, their stories and their practices." He also provided a list of detailed questions to each witness, to gather more precise details of their stories.[12] Kepler knew his audience. He knew that the law professors needed to have counterarguments grounded in contemporary legal understanding and logical and verifiable contextual explanation.

And so he began. "To present an effective defense, Kepler now needed to discredit every single witness through legal reasoning. He used particular facts derived from a close investigation of the evidence." He showed that some people were too young to testify. He exposed discrepancies in testimony. He linked accusations to the rumors started by Reinbold.[13]

As he systematically refuted the details of the prosecution's case, he also told the story of the defense. He explained what had come to pass in many of the accusations (sickness, infirmity) within the context of more rational explanations grounded in the scientific knowledge of the day. He replaced the cause and effect attributed to witchcraft with the cause and effect of contemporary science. He offered an alternate, plausible explanation for each of the circumstances that underpinned each of the forty-nine accusations against Katharina. In the end, "every element of seemingly damning testimony was therefore addressed and explained in its wider context—of natural disease, a person's bias, family quarreling, or simple mishaps."[14]

Kepler's thoughtfully written defense was comprised of dozens of pages submitted to the Tübingen legal professors. Their answer required only one page: Katharina was convicted but would not be tortured. After a final round of threatening from the executioner, during which she steadfastly maintained her innocence, Katharina was essentially sentenced to time served and released into the care of her family.

In the end, Kepler saved his mother's life because he was able to tell a better story, with a more convincing plot, to the audience that controlled her fate.

Stories We Tell Ourselves

There are a lot of things now that we likely can't imagine doing without: electricity, antibiotics, indoor plumbing, anesthetic. When the power goes off for an hour, it's a nuisance; when it goes off for a week, you're unable to meet all your commitments and responsibilities. Strep throat isn't all that terrifying anymore, and neither is surgery to have your appendix removed. Certain technologies and inventions we have completely accepted. They've become part of the story of our lives.

History teaches us that technological change is often accompanied by narrative change. Many new inventions mean new ways of doing things, and new ways of doing things can be scary. What if the new way leads to something worse than we've got now? Often, before a new invention is fully integrated into society, there is a change in the stories we tell ourselves about what we need and what is good for us.

Nowadays, if you go to the doctor for any even mildly painful procedure, it's pretty much a given that you'll be offered some sort of painkiller. Whether it's something low level, like acetaminophen or acupuncture, or more heavy-duty, like the hugely problematic opiates that are nonetheless a godsend for many, you don't expect to be left to suffer. Most of us are also not averse to self-medicating with over-the-counter painkillers either. Even if we choose to avoid taking them whenever possible, we have the comfort of knowing we can switch off or lessen most forms of pain, should we wish to.

It's easy to forget that for most of human history, it wasn't like this. Up until roughly the mid-nineteenth century, your only option for dealing with pain would have been learning to grit your teeth and bear it. Maybe you could have gotten drunk, to numb yourself a bit, or used simple remedies like chewing willow bark for a headache. But for the most part, pain was something people had to bear throughout their lives. People had to endure many painful conditions we don't have to think about anymore, from polio and smallpox in young children to amputations on battlefields and rotten teeth for almost everyone.

Given that physical pain was pretty much inevitable, and considering how much we avoid pain now, you might imagine that discovering effective painkillers was a big priority for medical practitioners and researchers. You might also imagine that anyone who discovered a substance capable of dulling the senses to pain would have been instantly lauded as a hero, and their invention swiftly dispatched to people all over the world. In fact, the opposite is true. Early painkillers were usually met with a blasé reaction and essentially remained recreational for decades before anyone thought to introduce them into a medical setting.

Take the case of nitrous oxide, also known as laughing gas. It was first discovered by chemist and polymath Joseph Priestley in 1772, and chemist Humphry Davy noticed its pain-killing properties in 1800. Davy wrote, "As nitrous oxide appears capable of destroying physical pain, it may probably be used with advantage during surgical operations in which no great effusion of blood takes place."[15] Yet Davy's comment on the potential benefit of pain relief was a throwaway; he barely saw it as worth including in his notes.

As Joanna Bourke explains in *The Story of Pain*, there was a significant gap after Davy's discovery before medical practitioners started to use nitrous oxide during operations;[16] the gas remained a recreational drug until the mid- to late nineteenth century.[17] It wasn't until about one hundred years later that it began to be used during medical procedures. The same is true for other painkilling substances, like ether and opiates; they were used recreationally for a long time before the medical establishment took notice.

Once nitrous oxide did come into medical use, it took many more years to become widespread, because many patients initially declined to use it. Why didn't people race to start using nitrous oxide in surgery and the like? Why were patients and doctors so averse to implementing it once its pain-relieving properties were discovered? And why didn't anyone try to invent anything similar earlier?

One way of understanding the use of painkillers is to look at this story through the lens of plot. Pain historically was part of a social narrative that is very different from the one we have today. Western culture in the nineteenth century and before didn't have the same societal expectation that everyone was entitled to happiness and a life free from suffering.[18]

First, as Bourke writes, our attitudes to pain have always been closely connected to our perception of the value of different groups. If pain is integral to what it means to be human, denying that certain people could feel pain was an effective way of dehumanizing them. Doctors believed that a whole laundry list of groups either didn't feel pain or only felt it in a mild way: soldiers, women, children, the elderly, immigrants, the working classes, slaves, and so on. Even as late as 1939, one medical author was adamant that children could undergo minor surgical procedures without feeling any pain.[19] For many doctors, their attitude toward pain medication was wrapped up in their beliefs about certain types of people. If someone couldn't feel pain because they were somehow less than human, then there was no need to give medication for it.

Second, the way people do things over a period of time often comes to feel normal. As when we analyze a plot, in life, we have expectations of what is going to happen on the way to our anticipated ending. For both doctors and patients, the new story of pain medication felt like it didn't have the same cause-and-effect elements that had previously defined their genre. Some surgeons, for example, said they disliked operating on silent, unmoving patients; it wasn't like the good old days of surgery (which included, presumably, the need to be quick and to hold the patient down).

Patients too weren't immediately sold on the idea of pain-free surgery. The idea of being unconscious disturbed many. People wanted to be aware and in control during procedures, even major ones. They weren't sure how things like nitrous oxide worked, so they were naturally suspicious of them. The side effects painkillers cause in most patients added fuel to that fire. People felt that it was unnatural not to feel pain. They were used to it and worried that taking it away would have worse consequences.[20]

Finally, and perhaps the most important factor of all, was the fact that many people saw pain as something positive. The ability to bear it with grace was the ultimate hallmark of self-control and bravery. Those who underwent painful procedures without complaint were lauded for their courage. Religious beliefs at the time presented the ability to endure extreme pain as a virtue that would help secure a sufferer's place in heaven. If someone were on their deathbed, coping with agonizing pain was a final chance to earn some extra brownie points and up their chances of getting into heaven.

Pain played a large role in many of the social narratives about bravery, courage, and virtue. Take it away, and now the possible cause-and-effect plot changes: If I don't experience pain stoically anymore, am I still a good person?

Today, you're likely to receive nitrous oxide for dental work and some other procedures. You're not likely to think much of it or even consider refusing it. This shows us that we do, over time, changes our narratives. The story of pain has continued. What's interesting, though, are the consequences of the new narrative. In our current world, pain is not a plot point we seem to want in our stories. The proverbial pendulum has swung too far.

There seems to be a widespread feeling now that humans should be able to go through life without feeling any pain at all. Our ability to finally manage pain seems to have triggered a set of beliefs that associate pain with negative outcomes. Therefore, if we can get rid of pain, we figure we should. Yet pain serves as a biological signal telling us when something is not right. The consequences of trying to eliminate all physical pain can end up leading to far greater negative and unintended consequences.

An example of the manifestation of the new narrative that pain is bad is the development of the opioid crisis in the United States. As a result of the belief that no one should have to feel any pain, access to pain medication seemingly became a right.

In the 1980s, the World Health Organization "began advocating more aggressive use of opioids for pain control for anyone who had 'pain.'"[21] Governing agencies in the U.S. began to evaluate doctors and hospitals regarding their control of patients' pain, and reimbursement of costs became tied to patients' perception of pain control (not the outcomes of their treatment). The outcome has been an epidemic of addiction, leading many people to turn to illegal opioid drugs once their doctor cuts off their supply, resulting in overdoses, rising crime, and entire communities being torn apart.

There were other factors in the widespread uptake of opioids in the U.S. Major policy decisions were based on flimsy anecdotal evidence of the lack of addictive properties in opioids, and certain pharmaceutical companies lied about the addictiveness of the opioids they sold. These factors, however, played out against the social backdrop of the new belief that allowing patients to experience pain was inhumane.

Most concerningly, there is no real evidence for opioids producing long-term benefit for those with chronic pain. Indeed, more recent research indicates that opioid painkillers can slow the healing of wounds and that their overuse can make it difficult for doctors to assess the severity of a patient's injuries. The type of pain a patient experiences can offer useful clues to their condition. For instance, it would be expected that the pain someone experiences after surgery would decrease over time. If it doesn't, that's a sign that something is going wrong and they should return to their medical practitioner for follow-up care. But if a patient is unable to feel anything at any point, they may not receive this sign.[22]

There is no doubt that strong painkillers are useful in some situations, but we have yet to determine with complete precision what those situations are. Bad science, overprescribing, undereducation, and a lack of clarity about some medicines' addictive qualities have also led to untold misery. With the current narrative that pain is always bad, it is likely to take us a long time to reach a more nuanced perspective, where we respect both the positives and negatives of physical pain and can manage it in appropriate ways.

The history of pain medication shows us that change in how we do something quite often requires a narrative change. The stories we tell ourselves, the cause-and-effect-based series of understandings that we use to make sense of our world, have a huge impact on the choices we make and how we live our lives.

Conclusion

Plot is the engine of story, the mechanism propelling characters and events through time. It's the sequence of causally connected events that leads from the beginning of a narrative to its resolution. Without plot, a story is just disconnected moments, unrelated incidents. With plot, a story becomes a journey, a transformative experience for characters and readers.

At its most basic level, a plot is a series of events connected by cause and effect. Event A leads to Event B, which in turn leads to Event C, and so on until the story reaches its resolution. But a good plot is more than just a linear chain of events. It's a complex web of actions and reactions, of conflicts and resolutions, of setups and payoffs.

Conflict is the heart of any plot. Without conflict, there is no story, no reason for characters to act or change. Conflict can take many forms—person versus person, person versus nature, person versus society, person versus self. But all conflicts share a fundamental structure: a character wants something but faces obstacles in getting it. The plot is the sequence of events that arise from the character's attempts to overcome these obstacles and achieve their goal.

But plot is not just about external conflicts and goals. It's also about the internal journey of the characters, the way they grow and change because of the events they experience. A good plot presents a character with external challenges and forces them to confront their own flaws, beliefs, and desires.

In this sense, plot is a crucible for character. It's the fire that tests and transforms the protagonist, revealling their true nature and potential. A character who ends a story unchanged, unaffected by the events of the plot, is a character in a story that hasn't really gone anywhere. The best plots leave characters fundamentally altered, through triumph or tragedy.

Plot is also personal. The most powerful story in the world is the one you tell yourself about the obstacles and challenges in front of you. A positive story doesn't always ensure success, but a negative one almost guarantees failure.

Once a story takes root, no matter how false, it can be hard to change. This applies to both humanity in general and to each of us individually. Change the story to change the results.

Character

Heroes and villains.

Watergate is an immensely complicated scandal with a cast of characters as varied as a Tolstoy novel.

—BOB WOODWARD[1]

haracters are who we identify with in a story, influencing our perception of events. The mental model of character helps us identify who is telling the story.

Information does not come to us impartially but rather is crafted and shaped by those who provide it. Understanding how those people relate to the larger story being told is invaluable for determining how they have interpreted and packaged the information they are sharing. This model also reminds us that we can become very connected to characters, giving unreal things immense power in the process.

A character is a person, animal, being, creature, or thing with agency in a story. Each has personality, values, quirks, and a story. Just as getting to know someone reveals their hopes, fears, and dreams, understanding a character deeply lets you see the world through their eyes.

Writers use characters to perform actions and speak dialogue that moves the story along a plotline. Compelling characters are usually crucial to a successful novel; it's much harder for a story to be interesting or a plot to be compelling with boring, flat, inauthentic characters. We normally use the word "character" to refer to fictional beings, but it can also apply to narratives that include real people. Here, we will focus for the most part on the way characters are used in literature, theater, television, and film.

In works of fiction, the reader is usually set up to identify with the protagonist, the character that we follow through the plot. Protagonists do not need to always be good, and readers can easily be made to sympathize with or cheer for characters whom in other circumstances they might consider bad. Protagonists stand in contrast to antagonists, the characters who are in the way of the protagonist reaching their goals. Protagonists require obstacles. These may come in the form of a specific character (a villain), a group of characters who aren't actively working to oppose the character but enforce social norms that are in the character's way, or perceived limitations within the protagonist themselves. Often, we can only understand characters by considering them as part of a web woven of their relationships with other characters.

Characters work within plots, but they have their own goals and desires. The gap between what characters want and what is happening in the story drives a lot of the conflict. As audience members, we develop expectations of the characters we encounter. As literature scholar Marie-Laure Ryan explains, "We want the characters to [appear to] be autonomous agents who exercise some degree of control over their own lives, rather than puppets of authorial whimsy."[2] Authors achieve this autonomy by putting characters in a world and then having them react logically based on their personalities. Kurt Vonnegut wrote that one of the eight basic principles of creative writing is to always make every character want something, even if all they want is a glass of water.[3] It is that motivation to get what they want that will drive the plot.

Characters can be dynamic or static: they may develop and change throughout the work, or they may remain the same. In general, the protagonist of a work will be dynamic, but the antagonist and supporting characters may be either dynamic or consistent. Events throughout the plot further character development, often as a result of moments of conflict and crisis.[4]

There are three types of conflict a character may experience, which may be physical, psychological, spiritual, or some combination thereof:

- Character vs. another character (or society)

- Characters vs. themselves

- Character vs. nature

Static characters may sometimes exist not truly as fully formed beings but as representations of particular ideas or qualities. Characters who have absolutely no depth and rely on generalizations about types of people are known as "stock characters." An artist can insert stock characters into their work as a plot device, comfortable in the knowledge that their audience will find them easy to envision, even if they're not realistic. Stock characters essentially exist as props, perhaps to lend believability to a setting. Their internal world is not of much significance, and their motivations are taken for granted.

An artist may develop a character directly or indirectly: they may directly describe their qualities, personality, appearance, and other details, or they may indirectly give hints as to what the character is like, which the audience can then interpret, such as by describing their actions or how they treat other characters. For instance, a writer could say that a character is rude and entitled, or they could describe the character shouting at waitstaff in a restaurant for getting their order wrong, thereby showing those qualities through the character's behavior.

Aristotle believed that plot was the most important part of drama, and that an artist could tell a story without characters, but not without a plot. However, for audiences, characters can often seem like the most important part. They are what we tend to remember in the most vivid way. We don't experience the components of a narrative as separate parts. Without engaging characters, even the most well-crafted plot can become dull. With them, even a weak plot can hold an audience's attention.

Characters are what engage our emotions. Indeed, characters who show the negative sides of people can have greater resonance than the positive ones. They may not be likable, but they are what we find memorable.

Archetypes

In works of literature, an archetype is something that recurs again and again in stories throughout history and across cultures. The psychologist Carl Jung believed that archetypes emerge from the collective unconscious of the human race, hence the reason they are almost universal. In addition, Jung believed they show up in our dreams, religion, and art.

The word "archetype" means "original pattern," using root words from ancient Greek. While writers may use archetypes in new and creative ways, the underlying symbolism remains. Writers continue to use them for a reason: they resonate in powerful ways, and their centrality to our psyches makes them hard to avoid. Each archetype has its own distinctive qualities, features, values, and motivations. However, books with archetypical characters who never really evolve are not stories. Rather, they are usually polemics or morality lessons disguised as stories.

Cults of Personality

In any art that has characters, including novels and films, not all characters will be developed to the same extent. There is often a main character, or small group of main characters, who is the focus of audience attention. They are easy to identify because they are the ones we follow through the course of the story. Main characters are those we become invested in, and by the end of the piece, we hope to see them experience some resolution to whatever conflict we were following them through.

After main characters, there are secondary characters. These characters are necessary to the story in some way; they can do things like further the plot or help develop the main characters. But we know they are secondary because we don't see much of their inner life. They don't develop over the course of the action very much, and they don't get their own story arc. We don't spend much, if any, time looking at things from their perspective. Secondary characters, however, are important. Without them, the events of the plot could not unfold. The contrast they provide gives us a much richer sense of who our main characters are.

There have been many examples in the twentieth century of political regimes that consolidated and maintained power through storytelling. Not at all focused on truth, these regimes reimagined the past and invented a narrative to justify their actions. Hitler's Nazi Germany and Stalin's Communist Russia are two classic examples. Stories need characters, and so the leader of a political regime will cast themselves as the main character, the protagonist, the one trying to save the day by combating the opposition to make everything great for the people. To strengthen the narrative, leaders will add secondary characters to their story—people the leader can use to highlight their own actions in a positive way.

The need for a secondary-character role is one way to understand some instances of cults of personality. According to scholars Thomas A. Wright and Tyler L. Lauer, "The cult of personality phenomenon refers to the idealized, even god-like, public image of an individual consciously shaped and molded through constant propaganda and media exposure."[5] In history, some leaders have created the cult around themselves, as Hitler did. But there are also many examples of cults being created around historical figures to reinforce the legitimacy of the current leadership. Using the model of character, we will explore one such example here.

Sun Yat-sen was a political activist who agitated for regime change in China. Born in 1866, during the reign of the last emperor, Sun worked in various capacities to end the empire and bring in a new political system. He was well known in China as someone who wanted change. Over the years, he aligned with many different people and groups, including Soviet Communists, in his quest to lead China into a new era.[6]

The Ming empire collapsed in 1911, and there is no doubt Sun contributed to the changing political scene. He did not, however, lead China in any capacity as it transitioned away from being an empire. There were some tumultuous years when China seemed on the path to democracy, but there were also those who wanted to take power for themselves via one-party systems. In 1928, the Nationalist Party took over and led China until Mao Zedong and the Communists replaced them in 1949.

Sun Yat-sen was human. Like all humans, he was complex. He did some good things, like raise awareness of the political alternatives to rule by emperor.[7] He also did some awful things, like having political opponents killed. And he had a host of all-too-common foibles. According to Jung Chang, who wrote a book about Sun's wife Ching-ling and her sisters, Sun was a womanizer who treated his family poorly. He raised money to support a revolution and tried to codify his ideas into a political philosophy. He also used his wife as bait to escape adversaries.[8]

When Sun died, in 1925, the Nationalist Party was in an ongoing fight to rule China. They were led by Chiang Kai-shek, Sun's brother-in-law by marriage, who sought to align himself with Sun's legacy. But first that legacy had to be definitively established. So "the Nationalists began a Lenin-style cult right away. The title of 'the Father of China' was used for the first time."[9] The nationalists erected statues of Sun all over the country. They produced propaganda describing Sun as "the liberator of the Chinese nation" and "the greatest man in the 5,000-year history of China."[10] All over the country, "in organizations like schools and offices, people were made to gather once a week to commemorate Sun," and they built a mausoleum covering 30 million square meters (compared with the 1.7 million-square-meter mausoleum for the last emperor).[11]

Why did they do all this? Creating a cult of personality around Sun was instrumental to establishing support for the authority of Chiang Kai-shek and the Nationalist Party. As Jung Chang summarizes, "In the ensuing years, especially when the Nationalists conquered China in 1928 and needed Sun's name to claim legitimacy, the Cult of Sun reached fantastic dimensions."[12]

Thomas Wright and Tyler Laurer explain that "the cult of personality perspective focuses on the often shallow, external images that many public figures cultivate to create an idealized and heroic image."[13] Heroes are great. They inspire us. We trust them. They are the people in stories who save the day or die trying. When the nationalists turned Sun into a hero, they stripped him of his complexity and created a character more like a superhero. When Chiang associated himself with this idealized image, he was sharing in the heroics.

Eventually, the nationalists lost leadership of China via revolution to Mao and the Communist Party of China (CCP). The cult of personality around Sun Yat-sen quieted for a while as the Communists settled in, but they too found a need to give Sun a prominent role in their narrative. Even though Sun had had a very uneasy relationship with the Soviets and was never exactly aligned with them, he had worked with them on many occasions.[14] Probably because he'd already been branded and memorialized as "the Father of China," the Communists updated his backstory and brought him in as the kind of supporting character who lends credibility to the actions of the protagonist. In 1956, for the ninetieth anniversary of Sun Yat-sen's birth, his widow, Ching-ling, "wrote articles about Sun for the *People's Daily*, the Party's mouthpiece. She portrayed Sun as China's Lenin, saying that the CCP 'took over his mission' after he died."[15] The nationalists, then, were just an aberration, a detour on the path from Sun to Chinese Communism.

More than thirty years later, after the death of Mao, the CCP was still placing the cult of Sun in its narrative. Pulling out such a prominent character from the past continued to be a technique to achieve legitimacy in the present. Writing in 1988, Key Ray Chong and Fang-fu-Luan concluded, "In short, [the CCP] has used and will continue to use Sun Yat-sen as a means to ends, particularly when the country runs into a political or economic crisis."[16]

In the end, it's almost as if Sun Yat-sen became a stock character— someone who no longer has any depth, just a bunch of easily recognizable, simple characteristics, someone whom the audience can easily identify and immediately know what role they are playing.

Emotional Engagement with Nonliving Things

Many of us have had the experience of being devastated by the death of a fictional character. There we are, going along with the story, following the plot, and before we know it, we are so caught up in what is happening to the characters involved that we begin to feel for them. We are happy when they find resolution and happiness. We are empathetic when they go through struggles that mirror our own. We understand their fears. And we can feel genuine loss when a character we've followed and supported and built a connection with dies during the course of a story.

It's no secret that we can grow emotionally attached to characters. We are capable of caring about what happens to people who aren't real. For example, authors have been viciously attacked for killing off fan favorites, and an ill-timed character death can cause sales of a series to plummet. It makes sense: caring is part of what keeps us coming back.

Although engaging characters are just one part of a successful story, they are usually the part that has the most powerful effect on us. Understanding that we can engage so deeply with something that isn't real helps explain the attachments we form. Using the lens of the character model, we can understand how engaging emotionally with nonliving things can impact choices we make. To explore this concept, let's take a look at the story of the Barbie doll.

Barbie is very well known in North American culture. Many of us have had a Barbie or know someone who has had one, and we would be hard-pressed to find someone who hasn't at least heard of the toy.

Since her creation in 1959, Barbie has grown into an icon of cultural representation who inspires countless articles and books that cover a spectrum of analysis. For some, she is a valuable playmate who helps children act out their dreams, creating detailed visions of what they want to achieve. For others, she presents a negative, unattainable vision of womanhood that is detrimental to girls' self-esteem. Although she is technically a toy doll, using the mental model of character helps us understand the wide-ranging and emotionally charged reactions to Barbie.

From the beginning, Barbie was presented to consumers as a character. She wasn't a generic doll, she was Barbara Millicent Roberts. She was immediately marketed with a backstory: She grew up in Willows, Wisconsin, as the daughter of George and Margaret. Her high-end and unerring fashion sense was no doubt developed when she attended Manhattan International High School. As Tanya Lee Stone argues in her book *The Good, the Bad, and the Barbie*, "Mattel reinforced the desire in us to make Barbie real by creating a life story for her."[17] As the brand developed, Barbie received a boyfriend—Ken—and numerous friends and family members who all came with stories that integrated into hers.

To augment the realness of Barbie, she is not just a generic doll sold in one way. She has changed with the times and has been portrayed in more than 120 careers. "Encouraging people to think of Barbie as 'real' was also paramount to Mattel's success—cleverly and consciously set up," Stone says. "One of the reasons people still talk about Barbie by name, instead of calling her a doll, is that she was marketed as a real person from the beginning."[18] This realness helps explain a lot of the attitudes toward Barbie.

For some, Barbie became a friend. She was able to help children act out their dreams and desires. If someone wanted to become a vet, well, their Barbie could take care of her many pets and open a veterinary clinic. Barbie and friends could help budding novelists figure out plot points and character development. Using Barbie to explain schoolwork to younger siblings developed skills for those who wanted to teach in the future. There is thus one view of Barbie that she "almost becomes an empty container to be filled at will by the player or commentator."[19] Playing with Barbie becomes an exercise in experimentation, allowing for things like creativity and social exploration.

On the other end of the spectrum, Barbie has been attacked for being a terrible role model. Some people argue that her inhuman body proportions give girls unhealthy ideals to try to live up to. Author Germaine Greer wrote of Barbie, "With her non-functional body, . . . and feet so tiny she cannot stand on them, Barbie is unlikely to have been very effective in her career roles as astronaut, vet, or stewardess."[20] And that is true—except Barbie was never a human. She was never an astronaut. She never actually had to walk on those feet. Part of the reason we would even explore Barbie's limitations as an actual human is because we see her as a character.

Another frequent criticism of Barbie is that no matter what ethnicity she takes on, many feel they can't see themselves in her. There are many different Barbies: there is Puerto Rican Barbie and Canadian Barbie, Nigerian Barbie and Japanese Barbie. Although some changes are sometimes made to reflect broad physical traits, these different ethnic Barbies still have her standard plastic-toy form. To many, Barbie continues to represent an unattainable physical standard. But as Stone argues, "There is no more one typical representation of an African American, Hispanic, Middle Eastern, Native American, or Asian girl than there is one of a Caucasian girl. . . . There is no one way for a doll to represent women as a whole. It would be an insurmountable task for any company to do that."[21] It's our ability to connect with characters that would even have us considering a doll as a role model, as needing to represent a certain lifestyle or set of values.

Ultimately, Barbie is a toy. Not even her backstory and marketing can change that, if we really think about it. As Ann Treneman writes, "Every year the company creates yet more cousins and siblings for Barbie, not to mention outfits, pets, nationalities, and careers. If Barbie were real she would have a nervous breakdown about it all, renounce pink for life, and tell her ineffectual boyfriend Ken that it's all over."[22] What has been created in the Barbie group of products is more than one person could ever have and be.

The idea of Barbie's realness persists, however. Barbie may not be someone you know, but she is a character that you recognize. And like all good characters, she has engaged us. We care what happens to her. We can be angry with her or sympathetic to her. We can have opinions on who she is. We can be affected by how her life unfolds.

Near the end of her book, Stone asks, "Why does she irritate—even enrage—so many people and attract so many others to leap to her defense? She is just a doll, after all. But she is *not* just a doll. . . . It started at the moment of her inception. That very first television commercial, with Barbie as an active companion, plated the illusion in our minds that she was 'real.'"[23] The answer to Stone's question may be found through the lens of the mental model of character. When we turn something into a character—a very natural human tendency—we imbue it with a realness that engages our emotions. That kind of investment, once created, doesn't go away easily.

Conclusion

At their core, characters are bundles of traits and motivations, of habits and histories, of strengths and flaws. They are the total of their choices and actions, the product of genetics, choices, and circumstances. But a great character is more than just a list of attributes. A great character is a paradox, a contradiction, a mystery who unfolds over the course of a story.

In many ways, character is destiny. The choices a character makes, the actions they take, flow inevitably from who they are. A cautious, thoughtful character will approach a problem differently than an impulsive, emotional one. A character with a strong moral compass will make different decisions than one with a flexible relationship to the truth. Obstacles reveal character.

But character is not static, not a fixed point but a journey. The best characters are the ones who grow and change over the course of a story, who are transformed by the events of the plot and the interactions with other characters. Think of Ebenezer Scrooge, the miserly old man who learns the true meaning of generosity. Easy choices in the moment almost always makes the future harder. Harder choices in the moment often makes the future easier.

Understanding a person's character allows you to see someone for who they are at their core and step into their shoes. This helps you understand why they make the choices they do, predict their behavior, and empathize with their story. But remember, character is not set in stone. What happened yesterday is over. Today's obstacles and challenges are nothing more than an opportunity to take a step toward or away from the person you want to be. No single choice satisfies the pursuit, only repeated steps in the right direction.

Setting

Where the action happens.

Places are never just places in a piece of writing. If they are, the author has failed. Setting is not inert. It is activated by point of view.

—CARMEN MARIA MACHADO[1]

Where something happens influences what happens. Your environment changes your behavior as much as your behavior changes your environment. Too often, we think we can move action to a new location and expect the same result.

Setting is the place and time in which a story happens, giving context to the events that are happening and the decisions the characters make. A dark, stormy setting gives a sense of danger or mystery, just as a sunny setting with a cloudless sky gives a sense of beauty and peace. Not only does setting offer hints about what is to come, it influences how we feel.

Novels, plays, and movies all have a setting, even if it can only be described as a vague "on some other planet, sometime in the future." Nonfiction too has a setting: the time and place in which the events described came to pass. Even in nonfiction that is a collection of facts about a certain subject—say, physics—one would do well to consider the time and place from which the information communicated came. In this latter case, considering the setting can help us avoid assuming the information applies everywhere and forever.

Books, plays, and other works usually contain settings nested within settings. For example, the broad or high-level setting encompasses all subsequent settings: a book set in Berlin in 1975 will contain scenes or chapters that usually have more specific settings, like a guardhouse at Checkpoint Charlie or a one-bedroom apartment overlooking the Tiergarten. These unique settings fit within the broad setting by being consistent with it: if Berlin in 1975 didn't have horse-drawn carriages, then you can't have one driving through the Tiergarten while two characters are talking.

Of course, stories can take place in multiple time periods and locations, but each of these will have a logical consistency within the story in terms of the characters they contain and the specific settings they encompass.

How a story develops is closely intertwined with setting. The choice of setting will determine many of the elements that can be included in the plot and some of the aspects of the characters. For example, setting a story in 1975 will mean the characters can't use cell phones and the plot can't be furthered by a character researching something on the internet.

Settings usually have subjective qualities. In the context of a novel, the description of the setting comes from the narrator or characters, and thus tells us a lot about who they are. Often in stories we are shown "the way in which a single physical setting prompts vastly different reactions from different inhabitants," thereby giving indications of the characters' personalities and how they might impact the plot. Three characters might describe the local countryside in three different ways, and the depiction of the French Riviera could easily change from book to book.

Setting, far from being a detailed, objective component, is fluid. Setting interacts with character and plot to communicate a story. For example, whether we find a graveyard creepy or sad or something else is heavily influenced by both the characters' perceptions of it and the action taking place in it.

As with characters, settings too have archetypes. Even if an author sets their story in a city without identifying which specific one, we as readers will associate certain characteristics with the setting. When we imagine cities, we think of them as full of people and the latest technology, fast-paced and demanding. Certain settings thus have what we might call stock elements. A Western can be set in the American West in 1920 or on Tatooine,[2] but probably not in modern downtown Beijing.

Setting places valuable constraints on story development, narrowing the range of choices a storyteller can make. It's also a factor in the performance of art, whether it be theater, music, or visual arts. You are always constrained by the space you are in. David Byrne says of himself and his fellow musicians, "In a sense, we work backward, either consciously or unconsciously, creating work that fits the venue available to us."[3] He gives historical examples to explain:

- On African drum music: "Percussive music carries well outdoors, where people might be both dancing and milling about. The extremely intricate and layered rhythms that are typical of this music don't get sonically mashed together as they would in, say, a school gymnasium . . . or a cathedral." Thus, "the music perfectly fits the place where it is heard, sonically and structurally."[4]

- On the development of classical music: "As time passed, symphonic music came to be performed in larger and larger halls. That musical format, originally conceived for rooms in palaces and the more modest-sized opera halls, was now somewhat unfairly being asked to accommodate more reverberant spaces. Subsequent classical composers therefore wrote music for these new halls, with their new sound, and it was music that emphasized texture, and sometimes employed audio shock and awe in order to reach the back that was now farther away."[5]

Around 1900, there was a shift in how audiences were expected to behave during a live performance, whether it was a theatrical or musical performance. In short, they were now expected to just sit and watch. Byrne writes, "This exclusionary policy affected the music being written too—since no one was talking, eating, or dancing anymore, the music could have extreme dynamics. Composers knew that every detail would be heard, so very quiet passages could now be written."[6]

Finally, "In the sixties the most successful pop music began to be performed in basketball arenas and stadiums, which tend to have terrible acoustics—only a narrow range of music works at all in such environments. . . . The music those bands ended up writing in response—arena rock."[7]

As a mental model, setting teaches us that where you do something influences what you can do. It also teaches us to think about what's around us, because our choices and options are always confined by where we are.

> I would direct a play very differently if the space is different, if the space is deeper, if the space is taller: something begins to happen that is different.
>
> —MARIA IRENE FORNÉS[8]

Work with What You've Got

Settings provide constraints that influence how things develop. We must work with what we have, the materials on hand, and the tools available. Not everything is available everywhere, and the use of setting in the arts teaches us that the place in which our art exists will shape the content of the art.

Cuisines are shaped by the constraints introduced by their settings. For many thousands of years, people ate only what they could grow locally. Plants were chosen as foodstuffs in part as a response to differing amounts of water or daylight. Certain foods grow better in certain soils. The decision about which animals to raise or domesticate was influenced not only by the animals in the territory but also by the ability to grow enough food for the people there to eat.

What we cooked with depended on the materials around us. Clay pots were not found all over the globe, and neither were copper pots. How we prepared foods too was dependent on our settings. What suited our homes best (knowing those homes were also a reaction to setting)—open pits? Ash ovens? And our cuisines, even our modern ones, can trace some of their particulars back to the amount and type of fuel locally available hundreds of years ago.

In the sixteenth century, should you have taken a trip around the wealthy homes in England, you would have invariably eaten roasted meat of some sort. Meat arranged and set close to a blazingly hot open fire, turned continuously for hours (often by young male servants), then brought to the table and carved with special knives, was standard fare for the upper classes. A carver would give you a chunk of meat, which you would then eat with the aid of your personal knife.[9]

England had an abundant fuel source in easily harvestable wood and areas for grazing animals in large pasturelands. In *Consider the Fork*, Bee Wilson explains, "English cooks chose to roast great carcasses by the heat of great fires in part because . . . the English were abundantly well-endowed with firewood." English cuisine and cooking culture grew around fuel availability. The abundance of firewood led to the development and refinement of the roasting technique. "The roast beef of England reflected a densely wooded landscape, and the fact that there was plenty of grass for grazing animals. The English could afford to cook entire beasts beside the heat of a fierce fire, throwing on as many logs as it took, until the meat was done to perfection."[10]

The open roasting of big English game had a knock-on effect in terms of table utensils and etiquette. For the English, because the cutting of meat came after the cooking, carving meat was part of the dining experience. "The knives at the carver's disposal were many: large, heavy knives for carving big roast such as stag and oxen; tiny knives for game birds; broad spatula-like serving knives for lifting the meat onto the trencher; and thin, blunt-bladed credence knives for clearing all the crumbs from the tablecloth."[11] Not all cultures developed the use of knives at the table. For some, knifework is mostly done in the kitchen. It was elements in the setting—namely, resource availability in terms of food and fuel—that gave rise to many elements of the dining experience.

The English needed knives at multiple stages, from preparation to consumption, and because various meats maintained their differences up to the moment they were served, with venison having a different texture than mutton, the final meal lent itself to the development of an even wider variety of knives. The English gave knives a place at the table, so that the final step in meat consumption was people doing their own carving.[12] English meals are still prepared with the expectation that knives will be on the table as well as in the kitchen. And even though few people in England are roasting whole animals over an open fire, going over to someone's house for Sunday roast is still a quintessentially English activity.

We don't have to go very far to find numerous examples of the interplay between setting and cuisine. Every culture has started with what's on hand, then developed technologies and dishes to adjust what they have to what they want: preserving fruits and vegetables for consumption in the months they don't grow, salting meat to have it available on a more regular basis instead of only after a hunt.

The story of sherbet in the Ottoman Empire follows the classic pattern of adjusting to constraints based on the weather and seasonal food availability. "After water, the principal beverage was sherbet,"[13] writes Priscilla Mary Isin in her book *Bountiful Empire*. Sherbert, however, was not a single drink. Similar, maybe, to tea in North America today, sherbet was a type of drink that was adjusted based on the weather, where it was served, and who was drinking it.

Sherbet could be served either cold or hot, depending on the season. "Sherbet was chilled with ice in the summer, and in the winter hot spiced sherbets were sold in the streets,"[14] explains Isin. It could warm you up or cool you down. In the age before personal electric icemakers, you might think iced sherbet would have been only for the upper classes. But the transience of the medium actually led to its accessibility. "In hot weather sherbet was chilled using snow collected during the winter," says Isin. "Shops selling snow were 'as numerous as butchers,' and since it melted quickly in hot weather it was sold at a price affordable even by the poor."[15] Because most everyone could afford some type of sherbet, it became part of many cultural traditions. It was given out at religious feasts and celebrations like weddings. It became part of the ritual of new motherhood. Sherbet was how travelers were traditionally welcomed home.

The only limits on sherbet flavors were what was available and what could be preserved somewhere in the empire. Flavorings included pomegranate, lemon, violet, tamarind, plum, myrtle, fig, lily, mint, honey, rose, bitter orange, winter cherry, apple, quince, and mulberry[16]—and this is not an exhaustive list. If you were poor, you may have only drunk chilled water with a little honey. If you were the sultan or in his entourage, your sherbet might have "luxury ingredients such as coconut, rosewater, musk, and ambergris."[17]

Part of the reason sherbet was served year-round is that the ingredients used to make it were preserved when they were fresh. Isin explains that "sherbet mixes in the form of syrups, pastes, or tablets were prepared by Ottoman housewives and confectioners when each fruit or flower was in season."[18] That way, they were available whenever anyone had a craving for quince or mint.

Sherbet spread from the Ottoman Empire all over Europe. In each place, it was adapted to the setting. In Italy, flavors included pistachio, strawberry, and fennel and may have evolved from there into the modern sorbetto. By the time sherbet got to England in the mid-seventeenth century, sugar had replaced the honey, and baking soda was added to give it fizz, to reflect local tastes and easier-to-obtain ingredients.

The lesson here is that our setting impacts us far more than we realize. The conditions it presents and the constraints it contains define the range of choices we can make. Not everything is possible everywhere. As food is shared, it adapts to local constraints and often evolves into new delicacies.

The First Zero

Setting influences how art is developed and interpreted. Within the context of a piece of art itself, such as a novel or film, it makes no sense to talk of a story without setting. All stories must take place somewhere. Where and when that place is located impacts the story told. As we have seen, settings introduce constraints and parameters that must be respected. Within a story, everything the characters do, every event that carries the plot, must respect the construct of the setting. A setting can be completely made up, but it will still have rules.

Art is also constructed and consumed in a setting. In the arts, setting matters for more than stories. Where people will hear your music can change what you write or how you play. The dialogue you write for the stage is unlikely to be the same dialogue you write for a film, even if both depict the same story. Where people will interact with your art guides choices about the art itself.

Some stories are just not possible in some settings. If there are logical inconsistencies between the plot of a story and where it occurs, your art isn't going to go very far. People will tune out if it doesn't make sense. A chase scene set in, say, present-day Tokyo can't disobey the laws of physics. Art also struggles if the setting it's consumed in is not the one the artist intended. Trying to look at a painting in dim light or experience a symphony by reading sheet music isn't going to pan out very well.

Setting is thus very important in art. No art can be separated from its setting. As a mental model, setting reveals how much location matters. Where we do something has great impact on both what we do and how we do it.

The concept of zero is now a ubiquitous component of our understanding. It's taught in the very first grades, and no math is done without it. Yet despite now being present in all settings, it grew out of a very specific one. The zero is a relative newcomer to the number set, because what it represents is not intuitive to most people. We can easily understand the idea of three deer in a field, but it's much harder to get our head around the idea that no deer in a field can be represented by a symbol describing the number of deer.

Very few cultures have ever invented the zero. The Mayans had a numerical representation for nothing, but it didn't develop as part of the number system and was never shared further. It is the ancient Eastern cultures around present-day Cambodia and Indonesia from which our zero came.

A lot of ancient math was done without the zero. Pythagoras's famous conclusion—that in a right-angled triangle, the square of the hypotenuse is equal to the sum of the squares of the other two sides—was achieved without a zero, as was Euclid's entire *Elements*. In *Number: The Language of Science*, Tobias Dantzig offers as a possible explanation: "The concrete mind of the ancient Greeks could not conceive the void as a number, let alone endow the void with a symbol."[19] This explanation hints that you must first understand the concept of the void before you can name it.

As mathematician Amir Aczel explains, the key function of a zero is that it grants "the ability of the numbers to cycle so that the same signs could be used over and over again to mean different things."[20] It was thought that the number zero was invented in the pursuit of ancient commerce. Something was needed as a placeholder; otherwise, 65 would be indistinguishable from 605 or 6,050. The zero represents "no units" of the particular place that it holds. So, for that last number, we have six thousands, no hundreds, five tens, and no singles. However, the zero predates its use in commerce.

The oldest known zero arose in an Indian-influenced culture in what is now Cambodia. "In the ruins of the temple of Trapang Pei at Sambor on Mekong, in 1891 [a French archaeologist] found two stone inscriptions written in Old Khmer." These were eventually translated by French scholar George Coedès. The zero "was clearly discernible and only slightly different in form from Indian zeros: instead of a circle, it was a dot" on an old stone table Coedès labeled K-127.[21]

In his book *Finding Zero*, Aczel describes his journey to Cambodia to find K-127 and understand its origins. What he learns propels him to argue for the invention of zero being dependent on the characteristics of the place in which it was invented. He claims that the people who discovered the zero must have had an appreciation of the emptiness that it represented. They were labeling a concept with which they were already familiar.

On his quest to find this zero, Aczel realized that it was far more natural for the zero to first appear in the Far East, rather than in Western or Arab cultures, due to the philosophical and religious understandings prevalent in the region. Western society was, and still is in many ways, a binary culture: Good and evil. Mind and body. You're either with us or against us, a patriot or a terrorist. Many of us naturally try to fit our world into these binary understandings. If something is "A," then it cannot be "not A." The very definition of "A" is that it is not "not A." A thing cannot be both.

Aczel writes that this duality is not universal. He describes the *catuskoti*, found in early Buddhist logic, that presents four possibilities, instead of two, for any state: that something is, is not, is both, or is neither.[22] It may seem hard to grasp, but actually, our world and words are full of events and expressions that defy binary categorization. A dinner at a fancy restaurant may just be average, which is a way of saying it is neither good nor bad. Your child leaving home may be something you consider both great and devastating.

Aczel quotes Buddhist writer Thich Nhat Hanh, writing, "Emptiness is the Middle Way between existent and nonexistent." Reflecting on this statement, Aczel explains, "I came to believe that I could even read the quoted verses as saying: existence = 1, nonexistence = -1, and emptiness = 0. Emptiness was the door from nonexistence to existence, in the same way that zero was the conduit from positive to negative numbers."[23] Innovations are extensions of the world in which they originate. They use pieces of what already exists to build something new. Finding the oldest known zero in present-day Cambodia makes sense if we consider that zero is an innovation on concepts that already existed, like emptiness and the void.

The idea of nothing being something is harder to process in binary thinking. A thing is something and is not nothing. Nothing is, by definition, not something. No thing can be both.

In conversations with a Buddhist monk, Aczel is told, "When we meditate, we count. We close our eyes and are aware only of where we are at the moment and of nothing else. We count breathing in, 1; and we count breathing out, 2; and we go on this way. When we stop counting, that is the void, the number zero, the emptiness." Aczel concludes, "Here was the intellectual source of the number zero. It came from Buddhist meditation."[24]

The zero itself defies binary categorization. It is something and nothing simultaneously. Cambodia circa the sixth century CE had the intellectual elements needed for a zero. It was a setting that produced thinkers who were comfortable with the idea that nothingness was a thing that could be represented.

Since Aczel found the zero in Cambodia, zeros predating that one by a few years have been found in Indonesia. They are artifacts of the Srivijaya empire.[25] Srivijaya too was Buddhist and therefore familiar with exploring the concept of the void. When it comes to history, the oldest thing found is only the oldest until the next oldest one is found. We'll never know if we've found the very first zero. But we can be confident that the ideas of the culture of the first zero will include the concept of nothing being something.

Conclusion

Setting is the stage upon which the drama of story unfolds, the physical and temporal context that shapes and reflects the actions of characters. An active participant in the narrative, setting is a force that can enable or hinder, reveal or conceal, enlighten or deceive. Setting is not just where the story happens, but in a very real sense, it's why the story happens.

Setting anchors a story in time and place, providing sensory details that make it real. But setting is more than just physical description. It's also the social, cultural, and historical context that defines the parameters of what is possible and what is permissible for the characters.

A story set in medieval Europe will have different constraints and opportunities than one set in modern-day Tokyo. A character in a small, gossipy village will face different challenges than one in a large, anonymous city. Setting shapes the choices characters make, the conflicts they face, the resolutions they find.

But setting is not just a one-way street, not just the environment acting upon the characters. Characters also act upon and interact with their setting. They navigate its challenges, exploit its opportunities, and leave their mark on its landscape. Every story is a symbiotic relationship between character and setting, a reciprocal exchange of influence and transformation.

Setting is the silent force that influences our fate. What we think and do is greatly impacted by our environment. This leads to a powerful and profound point: to change your behavior, change your environment. If you don't, it will change you.

Subtext

IN ANY WORK OF ART, THERE ARE TWO LEVELS OF MEANING. THERE IS the meaning the artist is directly giving to the audience, known as the text. Then there is the meaning the artist conveys without outright stating it–the subtext.

Subtext is what we find ourselves intuitively picking up on and understanding, sometimes without quite knowing how.[26] We're good at noticing subtext because it's often there in speech when we talk to people. We constantly hear people saying things that have a different meaning than the literal one, and we learn to detect it. "What time does this meeting end?" might mean "Is it rude for me to leave now?"

Subtext gives us a much richer experience of a piece of art.

By adding more layers, an artist enables their audience to enjoy their work on multiple levels and to revel in the satisfaction of seeing the subtext. It's usually a deliberate act, but sometimes a subtext may emerge that the artist did not notice during the creative process, or audiences may pick up on what appears to be subtext but is merely the result of their own interpretation. Subtext may be something that the characters within a work are aware of or something only revealed to the audience.

We can appreciate the use of subtext as the sign of a masterful, skilled artist. It takes great ability to follow Alfred Hitchcock's maxim "Show, don't tell." For instance, the artist Paul Nash served as the official war artist for Britain during part of World War I. During his time on the front and afterward, he produced numerous paintings and drawings inspired by the landscape he had seen. His dark, often surreal works showed little of the typical iconography of war and instead depicted trees, bushes, streams, fields, and the countryside above all else. When people, planes, and weapons appeared, they seemed integrated into their surroundings, usually overshadowed. The subtext was clear: Nash's devastated landscapes represented his assessment of the impact of war on people.[27] He didn't directly reveal his opinions, but they were unmistakable. To convey something in a subtle fashion can have far more impact than stating it outright.

When an audience must work a little harder to understand a piece of art, it builds engagement. It makes characters more believable—real people rarely say exactly what they mean all the time. It can turn what looks to be a simple tale on the surface, such as George Orwell's *Animal Farm*, into a profound and moving work with lasting impact.

During times of oppression, artists may turn to subtext as a means of conveying messages that would otherwise be censored or cause them to incur personal risks. The subtext of a work of art may be critical of the current regime, and that may be obvious to the audience, but as there is no actual critique present in the work, the creator may not face penalties.

Religious or political subtext is common. For example, Arthur Miller's play *The Crucible* is ostensibly about the Salem witch trials of the seventeenth century. But Miller is holding a mirror to America at the time he was writing: in the 1950s, when Senator Joseph McCarthy was aggressively hunting down suspected communists. The subtext of *The Crucible* is that McCarthyism featured the same paranoia and hysteria as the Salem witch trials. Miller didn't need to make a direct comparison; he knew the impact his play would have on the audience. Indeed, we can assume that much of *The Crucible*'s success was a result of the statement it made about current affairs at the time. If Miller had outright criticized McCarthyism, the probable outcome would have been the senator labeling him as a communist and communist sympathizer and attempting to ruin his career. Because subtext is implied and subjective, an oppressive regime may not be able to take it as proof of dissent.

Performance

Break a leg.

The essence of performance is that the audience and the performer make the piece together.

—MARINA ABRAMOVIĆ[1]

In live performance, the interaction between performers and environment is unique, ensuring that no two performances are alike. As a model, performance teaches us to factor in how engaging with the world can subtly yet profoundly influence our actions.

In theater, performance involves using physical things to tell a story, whether it's simply human bodies expressing words, or props, or staging. It is making something that exists only in words or imagination come alive. Performance in theater can have a wide variety of components, but it requires at least three elements: actor, space, and audience.

Often, theater consists of the performance of a play with dialogue and sometimes music. But a story is not a requirement of performance. Ancient Greek tragedy was the mainstay of performance for centuries in Western Europe, and the plots of plays such as *Oedipus Rex* or *Antigone* carried just as much instruction on human virtues and flaws as they did plot. Noh drama, from Japan, had actors and singers, but "often little or no plot; conflict—the element crucial to Western drama—is absent, and there is no concession to realism."[2] Antonin Artaud described his Theater of Cruelty in the 1940s, wherein "the audience is, by intention anyway, encompassed in a hallucinatory world, where the rules of time and motion do not exist. Words are less important than action, rhythm, sound and gesture, and behaviour is immune to conventional morality."[3]

Performance has always had space for improvisation. Sometimes the improv is built right in, such as with commedia dell'arte, which originated in Italy in the sixteenth century. These performances had dialogue, but no script—just "an agreed framework of scenario, and even some memorized speeches that could be adapted according to the way the performance developed."[4] In places such as seventeenth-century England and Spain, people who paid lower admission stood directly in front of the stage, in an area called the "pit." If a performance wasn't captivating, they expressed their displeasure by talking to one another, mocking the story, or "launching missiles at the performers."[5] We can easily imagine an actor improvising some immediate changes in their performance in order to respond to such feedback.

Actors have individual perspectives on a text, which means a performance will be influenced by who is performing. Space too influences how a piece can be performed, simultaneously imposing limits and offering opportunities. The space doesn't have to be conventional, and not all of the spectators need to be aware that they are watching a piece of theater. For example, theater has been staged in restaurants where there are regular patrons having a meal.

In the long history of theater, there have been many ways the audience engages with the performance. We are now accustomed to a dark, hushed space, where the audience sits in silence as the play unfolds before them. But, given the dynamic nature of performance, it's easy to understand that this current experience has not always been the case.

In sixteenth-century China, for example, certain forms of theater could go on for many hours, even days, and so watching was combined with eating and drinking. Sixteenth-century Kabuki theater in Japan could also last all day, and thus "the audience would tend to concentrate its attention on the big set-pieces, reserving its eating, drinking, and gossip for the less enthralling parts."[6] It wasn't until the eighteenth century in France that audience members were officially banished from getting on the stage. Bertolt Brecht, staging his plays from the 1920s into the 1940s, consciously tried to distance the audience from the performance. He called it alienation and used it to create a "new objectivity" in the audience.

Performance thus has a history of being more than entertainment.

> **The play on its opening night is very different from the play that closes.**
>
> —DECLAN DONNELLAN[7]

In live performance, the audience changes for every show. So, in more subtle ways, does the space. Actors responding to each new environment change how they perform and thus change the total experience. So, there is built into performance a dynamic component, as there is continual change in the realization of a piece of theater. Live performance is what makes theater very different from movies. The live element is part of the reason people go to the theater—there is always the possibility of the unexpected for both the audience and the actors.

> If a mistake happens on the stage you live with it. If a line has gone or you've invented a new move, it's part of the performance.
>
> —JATINDER VERMA[8]

"The peculiar chemistry engendered by live performance lends it a power . . . explaining why theater in the past has often fallen foul of authority."[9] In fourteenth-century England, so-called "Robin Hood" plays, a form of folk theater, were "suppressed as dangerously subversive," perhaps due to their widespread popularity.[10] The greater the reach, the greater the influence, the larger the potential threat.

Performance is not confined to the theater. Music is regularly performed live and usually sounds very different from a recording of the same piece performed by the same musicians. David Byrne explains, "Many musicians make music influenced by this social aspect of performance; what we write is, in part, based on what the live experience of it may be. And the performing experience for the folks on stage is absolutely as moving as it is for the audience, so we're writing in the anxious hope of generating a moment for ourselves as much as for the listener."[11]

Byrne also argues that the live aspect of music is often a critical component of why people love it. More than notes, live music is a full sensory experience. "Hearing a recording of a live performance one has witnessed and enjoyed can prove disappointing. An experience that was auditory, visual, and social has now been reduced to something coming out of stereo speakers or headphones. In performance, sound comes from an infinite number of points—

even if the performer is in front of you, the sound is bouncing off walls and ceilings, and that's part of the experience."[12]

Performance art contains many of the elements of more traditional visual arts but combines them with audience interaction to produce something unique in each performance. When describing the development of her pieces, performance artist Marina Abramović explains that as the artist, she puts the elements together, but embedded into her art is the unknown, as it is impossible to predict how an audience will interact with a particular piece.[13]

We tend to think of the creation of something as its end: we write the speech or craft the presentation, and that's the finish line. The model of performance reminds us that things continue to develop when they interact with the world.

> The writing starts when you perform.
>
> —ROBERT LEPAGE[14]

Performance for Social Change

> How could you possibly allow the election of a citizen of a socialist country as pope?
>
> —SOVIET CHAIRMAN OF THE KGB YURI ANDROPOV TO COMMUNIST LEADER OF POLAND WOJCIECH JARUZELSKI[15]

In 1979, Karol Wojtyla was elected pope of the Roman Catholic Church. Taking the name John Paul II, he was the first non-Italian pope in 455 years, and the first Polish man to hold the title. That year was also the height of an uneasy stalemate in the Cold War; democracy and communism continued to exist uneasily side by side. Nuclear weapons that could obliterate humankind had been developed by both the Americans and the Soviets. Neither side wanted war; neither did they want to relinquish power. Much of the world was caught in the orbit of one side or the other. The general feeling was that both sides would continue to exist, and so the Cold War had become less about winning and more about maintaining the status quo.

The new pope was not on board with maintaining communist power, because it interfered negatively with people's spiritual lives and purpose. Soviet communism included atheism, ostensibly because people were meant to get everything they needed from the communist state, not a god. There is a clear power dynamic at stake here, because allegiance to any religious community would disperse power away from communist leadership. However, communist regimes were never able to actually eliminate religion from their states, especially in Poland.

Into this power struggle stepped the new pope. John Lewis Gaddis explains in *The Cold War*, "Wojtyla had been working quietly for years—as priest, archbishop, and cardinal—to preserve, strengthen, and expand the ties between the individual morality of Poles and the universal morality of the Roman Catholic Church."[16]

The new pope decided his first foreign trip would be to his native Poland. It was the first time a pope would set foot in a communist country. The nine-day visit was a carefully planned set of events in thoughtfully chosen settings that utilized the range of talents of the main performer. Gaddis writes:

> The Pope had been an actor before he became a priest, and
> his triumphant return to Poland in 1979 revealed that he

had lost none of his theatrical skills. Few leaders of his era could match him in his ability to use words, gestures, exhortations, rebukes—even jokes—to move the hearts and minds of the millions who saw and heard him. All at once a single individual, through a series of dramatic performances, was changing the course of history.[17]

The performance began when the pope walked off the plane. He kissed the ground, demonstrating his love for his country and, by extension, the people in it. He performed his opening mass in Warsaw's Victory Square, which scholar Paul Kengor calls "a symbol of withstanding World War II totalitarianism that was now, with Pope John Paul II's presence, a symbol of withstanding Cold War totalitarianism."[18] Throughout the trip, the new pope chose his settings deliberately, speaking at shrines and monuments that had memories many Poles associated with the value of both their Catholic religious heritage and religious freedom in general. "He made," John Cornwell notes, "forty public, highly theatrical appearances in nine days."[19]

The trip was a success for John Paul II. It is estimated that more than one-third of the Polish population saw him live at some point. His last mass, on the Krakow Commons, was the largest outdoor gathering in the nation's history, attracting between two and three million people.[20]

His next visit to Poland, in 1983, was another series of thoughtfully designed performances. First, there was the content of his masses. This time, he spoke more explicitly about freedom and independence, saying, "The sovereignty of the state is deeply linked to its ability to promote freedom of the nation."[21] Second, he adjusted his words to his settings. Concurrent with the pope's involvement with Polish political development was a massive labor movement led by Lech Walesa under the title of Solidarity. The group rejected communism and demanded to be able to organize labor unions. Its leaders spent many years in jail as the Polish government tried to brutally suppress the group.

So the pope went to Poznan, the site of communist suppression three decades earlier that had resulted in the deaths of many workers. "Here, he explicitly mentioned the forbidden word Solidarity for the first time on the trip."[22] In the setting of a previous labor uprising, the pope shone a light on the current labor challenges to communism. Setting influences performance. The pope's words had more impact because of the location in which he spoke them.

He also insisted on meeting with the imprisoned Lech Walesa. In doing so, he gave Walesa an opportunity to join him on stage—to share the audience. As a local Polish priest observed at the time, "By meeting with Walesa, the pope showed the whole world, starting with the Communist bosses, that the movement was alive and that the story was by no means over."[23]

John Paul II went to Poland again in 1987, his last trip before the implosion of the communist system there. It was another spectacular example of a performance designed to respond to both the setting and the audience. For example, "he addressed a congregation of more than a million faithful near Gdansk, scene of the shipyard strike that had launched the Solidarity movement back in 1980. He declared that 'as work contributed to the common good, workers had the right to make decisions regarding the problems of the whole society.'"[24] He spoke to his audience in a language they could easily understand, using symbols and allusions that carried common cultural meanings. He chose settings that reinforced the points he was trying to make. His performances, while ultimately having the same message and goal (religious freedom), were never identical. He adjusted and responded to the particulars of each circumstance to powerful effect. Cornwell describes one gathering outside the Jasna Góra monastery: "The magic he performed was to turn the brooding, potentially violent insurgency into a peaceful but no less determined transformation of consciousness."[25]

Reflecting on the legacy of the pope, John Lewis Gaddis writes, "When John Paul II kissed the ground at the Warsaw airport on June 2, 1979, he began the process by which Communism in Poland—and ultimately everywhere else in Europe—would come to an end."[26] He had this incredible impact because of his exceptional ability to communicate, over the three visits, through a series of performances that demonstrated the power of harnessing the dynamic interaction of actor, space, and audience.

Performance as Tool

Willie Sutton was a performer. He studied his audiences and noted all the details of each setting he was going to perform in. Once he figured out what the audience expected to see and what was the most appropriate role for the setting, he'd decide what part he should play. Each time he performed a role, he robbed a bank.

One of the most successful bank robbers of all time, Willie Sutton stole millions of dollars and never killed anyone. His method was not one of aggression or destruction; he didn't blow up safes or take hostages. He took on roles and played the parts so well that no one could tell he didn't really belong on the stage.

In Sutton's case, the dynamics of the setting and the expectations of the audience dictated his performance. Working from the 1920s to the 1950s, in between various prison terms and corresponding escapes, Sutton successfully robbed more than one hundred banks, primarily in New York. Describing his modus operandi in a biography written by Quentin Reynolds, Sutton explained, "I studied a bank carefully before I robbed it; I studied the habits of the employees and the guards and the cops on the beat. . . . I rehearsed my men thoroughly in their parts."[27] All of the study was dedicated to figuring out what part Sutton needed to act to pull off the crime.

Each setting and audience demanded a specific role. Sutton recounts, "By turns I was a Western Union messenger, postman, policeman, and on one job, I was a window cleaner, complete with ladder, belt, and what men in this profession call a squeegee, and varied my facial make-up to suit."[28] In his performance, Sutton would be whatever the audience was expecting.

How did he do it? First, he learned makeup techniques from dating an actress. He learned how to alter his appearance to make himself look older, or tired, and very different from the wanted posters with his image. Second, he rented uniforms, because "the right uniform was an open sesame that would unlock any door."[29] He found that most guards saw the uniform and not the face. Finally, he fully committed to the performance. When he put on a policeman's uniform, he would lecture people about obeying laws. In the uniform of a mailman, writes Andreas Schroeder, "he *became* a dedicated member of the US Postal Service."[30] One time, Sutton turned up disguised as the bank manager.

Referring to when he started with his technique, Sutton said, "I was beginning to think of this as a drama, with myself as director and main actor."[31] And like all good actors, he adjusted as the performance went on, making changes according to the setting and audience. He engaged with his audience to figure out what would motivate them, either to keep quiet or to open the safe. He improvised his script, if direct threats didn't work, simply by appealing to a bank manager's sense of responsibility to their staff.

It was because Willie Sutton "considered casing a bank as important as actually robbing it"[32] that he could execute his performances flawlessly. His study of the performance space meant that he was often in and out of a bank within minutes, and he was never caught during a robbery.

Sutton was quite famous during his years as a bank robber. The fact that there was no violence in his crimes made it easy for the public to be enthralled with him. Law enforcement was also grudgingly impressed, admitting that "when it came to planning and executing a bank robbery, the police say that Sutton's equal never lived."[33]

Great performances often appear effortless. They come together in a way that captivates the audience, who marvel at the seamlessness of what they have just witnessed. But great performances are supported by great effort. One must understand the limits and opportunities of the space in which the performance will take place. And in order to captivate an audience, one must have a sense of who that audience is. What do they want? And how can the actors interact with the space to get them to buy into the illusion?

Considering the story of Willie Sutton through the lens of performance teaches us how much preparation is needed for things to go off without a hitch. Performers must immerse themselves in the details in order to execute flawlessly. But good performers also know that given the dynamic nature of performance, not everything can be controlled. Thus, preparation is necessary to make sure that if improvisation is needed, the overall illusion is still maintained.

Despite his success, Willie Sutton himself was the first to admit that his life of crime was far from the best life he could have lived. At one point he said, "I'm fifty-one, I've spent most of my adult life in prison or in hiding, and I haven't a penny."[34] Eventually, through studying law in prison, he was able to argue his way out based on time served. His final years were lived modestly, and Willie the Actor died in 1980.

Conclusion

Performance is the art of the ephemeral, the fleeting moment of creative expression existing only in the here and now. It's where the boundaries between art and life blur, the artist's body and actions become the medium, and the audience's presence and participation become integral.

At its core, performance is about presence, about the immediacy and intimacy of live action. In a world increasingly mediated by screens, live performance asserts the primacy of embodied experience, of the direct encounter between performer and spectator. It's a reminder that art is not just a thing to be consumed but an event to be lived.

But performance is also about absence, the gaps and spaces between action and interpretation, intention and reception. Unlike a painting or a sculpture, a performance can never be fully captured or contained. It exists only in the memories and testimonies of those who were there, in the ripples and reverberations it sends through the culture. Performance embraces the contingency and open-endedness of the live event, the sense that anything could happen, that meaning is always in the making.

This contingency is both the power and the challenge of performance. It allows for spontaneity and responsiveness, adapting to and incorporating the unpredictable elements of the moment. Yet, it makes performance resistant to the control and perfection other art forms aspire to. A performance is always a collaboration with chance, a dance with the unknown.

As audience members, we are not just passive observers but active participants in the performance. Our presence, our reactions, our energy all become part of the work. Think of fans transmitting energy to a team to rally them from behind with a few minutes left in the game. Performance invites us to be cocreators, to complete the work through our own interpretations and responses. In so doing, we become part of something larger than ourselves.

When we are fully present in any performance where someone is making themselves vulnerable in the moment, we may just catch a glimpse of the raw, unedited, unpolished essence of what it means to be human.

Afterthoughts

You've read the last book in *The Great Mental Models* series. Hopefully, you found it insightful. But now what? How do you turn these ideas into real improvements in your life?

Reading is just the first step. To gain wisdom, you have to test what you've learned. Mental models aren't something you can just read about and expect to change your life. You have to use them. Pick a model each week and look at your life through that lens. What's different? Write down what you notice. Reflect on your experiences using the model, because that's how you build valuable knowledge. Notice when you make different choices based on the model's insights. Pay attention to what works and what doesn't. Learn from your mistakes. Over time, you'll figure out where each model is most useful.

As you use more models, you'll start to build a latticework. You'll see connections and notice that some models work best when paired with others. Eventually, your latticework will be comprehensive enough to use in any situation, reducing your blind spots and preventing problems before they happen. Using mental models is a lifelong journey, and while this may be the last book in the series, the journey has just begun.

To improve our lives, we need to see the world as it is and learn to work with the principles that govern it. Having a diverse set of mental models that reflect how the world works is crucial for making better decisions and living a more meaningful life. Soon, using mental models will be an integral part of your thought process, and you'll see every situation through the valuable lenses they provide. As *The Great Mental Models* expands into the world, we will continue to create and update resources on fs.blog/tgmm to help you integrate these models into your thinking.

Acknowledgments

I'm forever indebted to Charlie Munger, Peter D. Kaufman, Warren Buffett, and Peter Bevelin, who, to varying degrees, started me down the path of multidisciplinary thinking. I owe them a huge debt of gratitude.

Thank you to my coauthor, Rhiannon Beaubien, for making this series possible. It's impossible to overstate her contributions to this volume and the entire series. Without her, you would not be holding this book in your hands. And thank you to Rosie Leizrowice for your support in getting this book started and your willingness to discuss and share ideas.

This series would be lost without our talented illustrator, Marcia Mihotich. Thank you for seeing these words and ideas and bringing them to life in simple and exceptional ways.

While this is a revised volume 4, I wanted to give a special mention to Garvin Hirt and Morgwn Rimel for shaping the creativity of the original version. Working with you both has encouraged me to make things beautiful and timeless. And thank you to Néna Rawdah and our OG editor, Kristen Hall-Geisler, for their willingness to dive in and ensure the material flows and comes together in the end.

The original version of this series would not have been possible without our partnership with Automattic and their incredible CEO, Matt Mullenweg. Thank you to Niki Papadopoulos and the entire team at Portfolio for re-releasing this series and supporting my efforts to make it as beautiful and as timeless as we can.

Thank you to Simon Hørup Eskildsen, Zachary Smith, Paul Ciampa, Devon Anderson, Alex Duncan, Vicky Cosenzo, Laurence Endersen, David Epstein, Ozan Gurcan, Will Bowers, Ran Klein, Sanjay Bakshi, Jeff Annello, Tara Small, Tina Cantrill, Nathan Taggart, Tim Bragassa, Yves Colomb, Rick Jones, Ran Klein, Maria Petrova, and Dr. Gregory P. Moore for taking the time to review books in this series. Your comments and contributions have helped make everything better.

Thank you to my sons, Will and Mack, for reminding me to continue to learn and grow along with you. This series was largely written for you and future generations.

Thank you to the entire *Farnam Street* team for your hard work and dedication over the years to bring this series to life.

And finally, thanks to you, the reader. I continue to be amazed by how many of you want to take this mental-models journey with me. I hope this book is one you can reference time and again as you seek to better understand the world.

Shane

Notes

Introduction

1. Ben Graham, as quoted in Warren Buffett, "Letter to Shareholders, 2013," dated February 28, 2014, BerkshireHathaway.com, accessed March 4, 2024, berkshirehathaway.com/letters/2013ltr.pdf.
2. Ha-Joon Chang, *23 Things They Don't Tell You About Capitalism* (Doha: Bloomsbury Qatar Foundation, 2013).
3. Dore Ashton, ed., *Picasso on Art: A Selection of Views* (New York: Da Capo Press, 1988).
4. Marina Abramović, *Walk Through Walls: A Memoir* (New York: Crown Archetype, 2016).

ECONOMICS

1. Charles T. Munger, *Poor Charlie's Almanack: The Wit and Wisdom of Charles T. Munger* (Virginia Beach, VA: Donning Company Publishers, 2005).

Scarcity

1. Matt Haig, *Notes on a Nervous Planet* (London: Penguin Life, 2019).
2. Sendhil Mullainathan and Eldar Shafir, *Scarcity: Why Having Too Little Means So Much* (New York: Henry Holt and Company, 2013).
3. Ibid.
4. Christopher de Hamel, *Making Medieval Manuscripts* (Oxford, UK: Bodleian Library, 2018).
5. Elizabeth Eisenstein, *The Printing Press as an Agent of Change*, vols. 1 and 2 (Cambridge, UK: Cambridge University Press, 1979).
6. Ibid.
7. Ibid.

8. Ibid.
9. Ibid.
10. Ibid.
11. Ibid.
12. Ibid.
13. Ibid.
14. Herbert A. Simon as quoted in Hal R. Varian, "The Information Economy," *Scientific American*, September 1995, 200–201. Retrieved from Berkeley School of Information, accessed March 5, 2024, people.ischool.berkeley .edu/~hal/pages/sciam.html.

Supply and Demand

1. David Graeber, *Debt: The First 5,000 Years* (New York: Melville House, 2011).
2. Eric D. Beinhocker, *The Origin of Wealth: The Radical Remaking of Economics and What It Means for Business and Society* (Cambridge, MA: Harvard Business School Press, 2006).
3. Josh Kaufman, *The Personal MBA: Master the Art of Business* (New York: Portfolio, 2010).
4. Joel Mokyr, *The Lever of Riches: Technological Creativity and Economic Progress* (New York: Oxford University Press, 1992).
5. Kate Lister, *Harlots, Whores and Hackabouts: A History of Sex for Sale* (London: Thames and Hudson, 2021).
6. Ibid.
7. Ibid.
8. Ibid.
9. Ibid.
10. Ibid.
11. Ibid.
12. Thorstein Veblen, The *Instinct of Workmanship and the State of the Industrial Arts* (Abingdon, UK: Routledge, 2017).
13. Tom Standage, *A Brief History of Motion: From the Wheel, to the Car, to What Comes Next* (New York: Bloomsbury Publishing, 2021).
14. William Knoedelseder, *Fins: Harley Earl, the Rise of General Motors, and the Glory Days of Detroit* (New York: HarperCollins, 2018).
15. Ibid.
16. Standage, *A Brief History of Motion.*
17. David Gartman, *Auto Opium: A Social History of American Automobile Design* (London: Routledge, 1994).
18. Knoedelseder, *Fins.*
19. Ibid.
20. Ibid.
21. Ibid.

Optimization

1. Jon Bentley, *Writing Efficient Programs* (Englewood Cliffs, NJ: Prentice Hall, 1982).
2. Niall Kishtainy, *A Little History of Economics*, Little Histories (New Haven, CT: Yale University Press, 2017).
3. See the publications of the Santa Fe Institute on complexity economics (santafe.edu), and *The Origin of Wealth* by Eric. D. Beinhocker.
4. Beinhocker, *The Origin of Wealth*.
5. Beinhocker, *The Origin of Wealth*.
6. Nancy Folbre, "Cooperation & Conflict in the Patriarchal Labyrinth," *Daedalus* 149, no. 1, Women and Equality (Winter 2020): 198–212, doi.org/10.1162/daed_a_01782.
7. Beinhocker, *The Origin of Wealth*.
8. Matthew F. Bonnan, *The Bare Bones: An Unconventional Evolutionary History of the Skeleton* (Bloomington: Indiana University Press, 2016).
9. Ibid.
10. Ibid.
11. Jeff Ryan, *Super Mario: How Nintendo Conquered America* (New York: Portfolio, 2011).
12. Ibid.
13. Ibid.
14. Ibid.
15. Zhuangzi, as quoted in John Bartlett, *Bartlett's Words to Live By: Advice and Inspiration for Everyday Life* (New York: Little, Brown, 2009).
16. Beinhocker, *The Origin of Wealth*.
17. Karl Marx, *Capital, Volume One: A Critique of Political Economy,* trans. Samuel Moore and Edward B. Aveling, Friedrich Engels, ed. (Mineola, NY: Dover Pubications, 2019).
18. Beinhocker, *The Origin of Wealth*.
19. Julie A. Nelson, *Economics for Humans* (Chicago: University of Chicago Press, 2006).
20. Chris Mabey, "Optimizing vs Satisficing: Tips for Product Design and Designing Your Life," *BYU Design Review* (blog), accessed March 11, 2024, designreview.byu.edu/collections/optimizing-vs-satisficing-tips-for-product-design-and-designing-your-life.
21. David Rooney, *About Time: A History of Civilization in Twelve Clocks* (New York: W. W. Norton and Company, 2021).
22. Ibid.
23. Ibid.
24. Ibid.

Trade-offs

1. Russell D. Roberts, *How Adam Smith Can Change Your Life: An Unexpected Guide to Human Nature and Happiness* (New York: Portfolio, 2014).
2. Ha-Joon Chang, *23 Things They Don't Tell You About Capitalism* (Doha: Bloomsbury Qatar Foundation, 2013).
3. Paul Dolan, *Happiness by Design: Finding Pleasure and Purpose in Everyday Life* (London: Penguin Books, 2015).
4. Sendhil Mullainathan and Eldar Shafir, *Scarcity: Why Having Too Little Means So Much* (New York: Henry Holt and Company, 2013).
5. J. E. Gordon, *Structures: Or Why Things Don't Fall Down* (New York: Da Capo Press, 2003).
6. A. Oliver et al., "Design, Decision-making and Trade-offs in the Centre for Sustainable Development (La Maison du Développement Durable) in Canada," IOP Conference Series: Earth and Environmental Science 294 (August 2019), doi.org/10.1088/1755-1315/294/1/012055.
7. Ibid.
8. Mullainathan and Shafir, *Scarcity*, 86.
9. Theodore Garland Jr., Cynthia J. Downs, and Anthony R. Ives, "Trade-offs (and Constraints) in Organismal Biology," *Physiological and Biochemical Zoology* 95, no. 1 (2022): 82–112.
10. Hisla Bates, "My Heart's Journey Home," in *Alien Nation: 36 True Tales of Immigration,* ed. Sofija Stefanovic (New York: HarperVia, 2021).
11. Stephen Castles, Hein de Haas, and Mark J. Miller, *The Age of Migration: International Population Movements in the Modern World*, 5th ed. (New York: The Guilford Press, 2014).
12. Ibid.
13. Ibid.
14. Mazin Sidahmed, "My Family WhatsApp Group," in *Alien Nation*, ed. Sofija Stefanovic (New York: HarperVia, 2021).
15. Kay Iguh, "Mortar, Porcelain, Brick," in *Alien Nation*, ed. Sofija Stefanovic (New York: HarperVia, 2021).

Specialization

1. As quoted in "Charlie Munger," *25iq* (blog), accessed March 11, 2024, 25iq.com/quotations/charlie-munger.
2. Adam Smith, *An Inquiry into the Nature and Causes of the Wealth of Nations* (Chicago: University of Chicago Press, 1977).
3. Eric D. Beinhocker, The Origin of Wealth: *The Radical Remaking of Economics and What It Means for Business and Society* (Cambridge, MA: Harvard Business School Press, 2006).
4. Gary S. Becker, *Human Capital: A Theoretical and Empirical Analysis with Special Reference to Education*, 3rd ed. (Chicago: University of Chicago Press, 1993).

5. Friedrich A. Hayek, "The Use of Knowledge in Society," *The American Economic Review* 35, no. 4 (September 1945): 524.
6. Claire L. Evans, *Broad Band: The Untold Story of the Women Who Made the Internet* (New York: Portfolio, 2018).
7. Ibid.
8. Ibid.
9. Ibid.
10. Ibid.
11. Ibid.
12. Ibid.
13. Beinhocker, *The Origin of Wealth*, 354.
14. Niall Kishtainy, *A Little History of Economics*, Little Histories (New Haven, CT: Yale University Press, 2017).
15. Nancy Folbre, *Greed, Lust and Gender: A History of Economic Ideas* (Oxford: Oxford University Press, 2009).
16. Becker, *Human Capital*, 308.
17. Wayne Gretzky with Kirstie McLellan Day, *99: Stories of the Game* (Toronto: Viking Canada, 2016).
18. Ibid.
19. Ibid.
20. Ibid.
21. Ibid.
22. Hayley Wickenheiser, *Over the Boards: Lessons from the Ice* (Toronto: Viking Canada, 2021).
23. Ibid.
24. Gretzky with McLellan Day, *99*.

Interdependence

1. *Field Theory in Social Science: Selected Theoretical Papers*, Dorwin Cartwright, ed. (New York: Harper & Row, 1951), 165.
2. Leonard E. Read, "I, Pencil," Foundation for Economic Education, accessed March 12, 2024, fee.org/resources/i-pencil.
3. Kenneth J. Arrow and Gérard Debreu, "Existence of an Equilibrium for a Competitive Economy," *Econometrica* 22, no. 3 (July 1954): 265–90, doi.org/10.2307/1907353.
4. Elizabeth Marshall Thomas, *The Old Way: A Story of the First People* (New York: Farrar, Straus and Giroux, 2006).
5. Ibid.
6. Ibid.
7. Ibid.
8. Ibid.
9. Ibid.
10. Ibid.

Efficiency

1. Ha-Joon Chang, *23 Things They Don't Tell You About Capitalism* (Doha: Bloomsbury Qatar Foundation, 2013).
2. Niall Kishtainy, *A Little History of Economics*, Little Histories (New Haven, CT: Yale University Press, 2017).
3. Milton Friedman, as quoted in Lanny Ebenstein, *Milton Friedman: A Biography* (New York: Palgrave Macmillan, 2007), 246.
4. Kishtainy, *A Little History of Economics*.
5. Walter Block and Gabriel Philbois, "The Z Curve: Supply and Demand for Giffen Goods," *MISES: Interdisciplinary Journal of Philosophy, Law and Economics* 6, no. 3 (September–December 2018), doi.org/10.30800/mises .2018.v6.311.
6. Anne Rubenstein, *Bad Language, Naked Ladies, and Other Threats to the Nation* (Durham, NC: Duke University Press, 1998).
7. Ibid.
8. Amy S. Bruckman, *Should You Believe Wikipedia? Online Communities and the Construction of Knowledge* (Cambridge, UK: Cambridge University Press, 2022).
9. Quoted in Steven Johnson, *Wonderland: How Play Made the Modern World* (New York: Riverhead, 2016).
10. David W. Conroy, *In Public Houses: Drink and the Revolution of Authority in Colonial Massachusetts* (Chapel Hill: University of North Carolina Press, 1995).
11. Johnson, *Wonderland*.
12. Ibid.
13. Ibid.

Debt

1. Kent Nerburn, *Simple Truths: Clear & Gentle Guidance on the Big Issues in Life* (New World Library. Kindle Edition), 25.
2. Promothesh Chatterjee and Randall L. Rose, "Do Payment Mechanisms Change the Way Consumers Perceive Products?" *Journal of Consumer Research* 38, no. 6 (April 2012): 1129–39, doi.org/10.1086/661730.
3. Robert Howse, "The Concept of Odious Debt in Public International Law," United Nations Conference on Trade and Development, Discussion Papers, no. 185, July 2007, unctad.org/system/files/official-document/osgdp20074 _en.pdf.
4. Michael Hudson, . . . *And Forgive Them Their Debts: Lending, Foreclosure and Redemption from Bronze Age Finance to the Jubilee Year* (Dresden, Germany: Islet-Verlag, 2018).
5. Barry Eichengreen, Asmaa El-Ganainy, Rui Esteves, and Kris James Mitchener, *In Defense of Public Debt* (Oxford: Oxford University Press, 2021).

6. Yuval Noah Harari, *Money* (New York: Vintage Classics, 2018).

7. Jody Williams, *My Name Is Jody Williams: A Vermont Girl's Winding Path to the Nobel Peace Prize* (Berkeley: University of California Press, 2013).

8. Ibid.

9. Ibid.

10. "Landmines," United Nations Office for Disarmament Affairs, accessed November 28, 2022, un.org/disarmament/convarms/landmines.

11. Ibid.

12. "Why Are Landmines Still Killing People?" BBC News, October 25, 2018, video, 2:55, youtube.com/watch?v=NWh5j3Y_dkU.

13. Hudson, . . . *And Forgive Them Their Debts.*

14. Ibid.

15. Ibid.

16. Ibid.

17. Ibid.

18. Ibid.

19. Ibid.

Monopoly and Competition

1. Ralph Waldo Emerson, *Nature* (Kaysville, UT: Gibbs Smith, 2019).

2. Niall Kishtainy, *A Little History of Economics* (New Haven, CT: Yale University Press, 2017).

3. Ibid.

4. Paul Grootendorst et al., "New Approaches to Rewarding Pharmaceutical Innovation," *Canadian Medical Association Journal* 183, no. 6 (April 5, 2011): 681–85, doi.org/10.1503/cmaj.1003750.

5. Robert H. Frank, *Success and Luck: Good Fortune and the Myth of Meritocracy* (Princeton, NJ: Princeton University Press, 2016).

6. Stephen J. Lee, *European Dictatorships 1918–1945*, 2nd ed. (London: Routledge, 2000).

7. Robert Nisbet, "Arendt on Totalitarianism," review of *The Origins of Totalitarianism*, by Hannah Arendt, *The National Interest*, no. 27 (Spring 1992): 85–91.

8. Quoted in Lee, *European Dictatorships 1918–1945.*

9. Hannah Arendt, *The Origins of Totalitarianism* (Orlando, FL: Harcourt Publishing, 1976).

10. *Merriam-Webster*, s.v. "atomize (*v.*)," accessed June 2, 2023, merriam-webster.com/dictionary/atomize.

11. Arendt, *The Origins of Totalitarianism.*

12. Ibid.

13. Ibid.

Creative Destruction

1. Joel Mokyr, *The Lever of Riches: Technological Creativity and Economic Progress* (New York: Oxford University Press, 1992).
2. Joseph Schumpeter, *Capitalism, Socialism, and Democracy* (Abingdon-on-Thames, UK: Routledge, 1994).
3. Niall Kishtainy, *A Little History of Economics*, Little Histories (New Haven, CT: Yale University Press, 2017).
4. David M. Beatty, *Faith, Force, and Reason: An Armchair History of the Rule of Law* (Toronto: University of Toronto Press, 2022).
5. Ibid.
6. Ibid.
7. Ibid.
8. Schumpeter, *Capitalism, Socialism, and Democracy*.
9. Esben Sloth Andersen, *Schumpeter's Evolutionary Economics: A Theoretical, Historical and Statistical Analysis of the Engine of Capitalism* (London: Anthem Press, 2009), 4.
10. Thomas Kuhn, *The Structure of Scientific Revolutions: 50th Anniversary Edition,* 4th ed. (Chicago: University of Chicago Press, 2012).
11. Parts of this explanation of *The Structure of Scientific Revolutions* previously appeared on *Farnam Street*: "Thomas Kuhn: The Structure of Scientific Revolutions," *Farnam Street* (blog), accessed March 17, 2024, fs.blog/how-scientific-advancement-happens.
12. Charles C. Mann, *1491: New Revelations of the Americas Before Columbus* (New York: Vintage Books, 2011).
13. Paulette F. C. Steeves, *The Indigenous Paleolithic of the Western Hemisphere* (Lincoln: University of Nebraska Press, 2021).
14. Ibid.
15. Ibid.
16. Ibid.
17. Mann, *1491*.
18. Ibid.
19. Steeves, *The Indigenous Paleolithic*.
20. Ibid.

Gresham's Law

1. Abdul Azim Islah, *Economic Concepts of Ibn Taimiyah* (London: The Islamic Foundation, 1988).
2. George A. Akerlof, "The Market for 'Lemons': Quality Uncertainty and the Market Mechanism," *Quarterly Journal of Economics* 84, no. 3 (August 1970): 488–500.
3. Catherine Fogarty, *Murder on the Inside: The True Story of the Deadly Riot at Kingston Penitentiary* (Windsor, ON: Biblioasis, 2021).
4. Ibid.

5. Ibid.
6. Ibid.
7. Ibid.
8. Ibid.
9. Ibid.
10. Ibid.
11. Ibid.
12. Tyler Hamilton and Daniel Coyle, *The Secret Race: Inside the Hidden World of the Tour de France* (New York: Bantam Books, 2013).
13. Ibid.
14. Juliet Macur, "2nd Failed Test Puts Heat on Contador," *New York Times*, October 4, 2010, nytimes.com/2010/10/05/sports/cycling/05cycling.html.
15. Hamilton and Coyle, *The Secret Race.*
16. Ibid.
17. Ibid.
18. Ibid.
19. Ibid.

Bubbles

1. John Kenneth Galbraith, *A Short History of Financial Euphoria* (New York: Whittle Books in association with Penguin Books, 1994).
2. Robert J. Shiller, "Infectious Exuberance," *The Atlantic*, July/August 2008.
3. Morgan Housel, *The Psychology of Money: Timeless Lessons on Wealth, Greed, and Happiness* (Petersfield, UK: Harriman House, 2020).
4. Shiller, "Infectious Exuberance."
5. Ibid.
6. Clifford Geertz, *The Interpretation of Cultures: Selected Essays* (New York: Basic Books, 1973).
7. John Maynard Keynes, *The General Theory of Employment, Interest, and Money* (Buffalo, NY: Prometheus Books, 1997).
8. Roger D. Launius, *Project Apollo: A Retrospective Analysis*, Monographs in Aerospace History no. 3, reprinted July 2004, available at history.nasa.gov /Apollomon/Apollo.html.
9. Harry W. Jones, "Success Factors in Human Space Programs—Why Did Apollo Succeed Better Than Later Programs?" (paper presented at the International Conference on Environmental Systems, Bellevue Hilton Hotel, Bellevue, WA, July 12, 2015), ntrs.nasa.gov/citations/20160001259.
10. Monika Gisler and Didier Sornette, "Exuberant Innovations: The Apollo Program," *Social Science and Public Policy* 46, (2009): 55–68, doi.org/10 .1007/s12115-008-9163-8.
11. Neil M. Maher, "Introduction: Launching the Sixties," in *Apollo in the Age of Aquarius*, by Neil M. Maher (Cambridge, MA: Harvard University Press, 2017), 1–10.
12. Gisler and Sornette, "Exuberant Innovations."

13. Alexis C. Madrigal, "Gil Scott-Heron's Poem, 'Whitey on the Moon,'" *The Atlantic*, May 28, 2011, theatlantic.com/technology/archive/2011/05/gil-scott-herons-poem-whitey-on-the-moon/239622.
14. Gisler and Sornette, "Exuberant Innovations."
15. Ibid.

ART

1. Monica Parker, *The Power of Wonder: The Extraordinary Emotion That Will Change the Way You Live, Learn, and Lead* (New York: TarcherPerigee, 2023).

Audience

1. Emily Temple, "Kurt Vonnegut's Greatest Writing Advice," *Literary Hub*, April 11, 2017, lithub.com/kurt-vonneguts-greatest-writing-advice.
2. Iris Murdoch, "Art Is the Imitation of Nature," in Iris Murdoch, *Existentialism and Mystics: Writings on Philosophy and Literature*, ed. Peter Conradi (New York: Penguin, 1997).
3. Matthew Hemley, "Jatinder Verma: Colonial Attitude Persists in Major British Theatres," The Stage, January 15, 2020, https://www.thestage.co.uk/big-interviews/jatinder-verma.
4. Daniel W. Graham, "Heraclitus," *The Stanford Encyclopedia of Philosophy* (Summer 2021 Edition), ed. Edward N. Zalta, plato.stanford.edu/archives/sum2021/entries/heraclitus.
5. Peter Schjeldahl, *Hot, Cold, Heavy, Light: 100 Art Writings, 1988–2018* (New York: Abrams, 2019), 54.
6. Philip Ball, *The Music Instinct: How Music Works and Why We Can't Do without It* (London: Vintage Books, 2010).
7. Murdoch, *"Art Is the Imitation of Nature."*
8. Ball, *The Music Instinct.*
9. Alberto Rios, "Submitting Individual Works for Literary Publication," Arizona State University, last modified May 24, 2002, public.asu.edu/~aarios/resourcebank/01submittingindividual/page16.html.
10. Neil Grant, *History of Theatre* (London: Hamlyn/Octopus Publishing Group, 2002).
11. "When There's an Audience, People's Performance Improves," press release, Johns Hopkins Medicine Newsroom, Johns Hopkins University, April 20, 2018, hopkinsmedicine.org/news/newsroom/news-releases/2018/04/when-theres-an-audience-peoples-performance-improves.
12. Sara Maitland, *Gossip from the Forest: The Tangled Roots of Our Forests and Fairy Tales* (London: Granta Books, 2012).
13. John A. Farrell, *Clarence Darrow: Attorney for the Damned* (New York: Vintage Books, 2011).
14. Ibid.
15. Ibid.

16. Ibid.
17. Ibid.
18. Ibid.
19. Ibid.
20. Ibid.
21. Ibid.
22. Ibid.

Genre

1. Quoted in Adam Thirlwell, "How Italo Calvino Arrived at a New Ideal for Fiction," *New Republic*, July 26, 2013, newrepublic.com/article/113817/italo -calvinos-letters-reviewed-adam-thirlwell.
2. Oxford English Dictionary, s.v. "genre (*n.*)," accessed May 23, 2023, oed .com/search/dictionary/?scope=Entries&q=genre.
3. Catharine Abell, "Genre, Interpretation and Evaluation," *Proceedings of the Aristotelian Society* 115 (2015): 25–40, jstor.org/stable/44122584.
4. Ibid.
5. Tzvetan Todorov and Richard M. Berrong, "The Origin of Genres," *New Literary History* 8, no. 1 (1976): 159–70, doi.org/10.2307/468619.
6. Wendy Bishop and David Starkey, *Keywords in Creative Writing* (Logan: Utah State University Press, 2006).
7. Todorov and Berrong, "The Origin of Genres."
8. Nolan Gasser, *Why You Like It: The Science and Culture of Musical Taste* (New York: Flatiron Books, 2019).
9. Abell, "Genre, Interpretation and Evaluation."
10. Trudier Harris, "Genre," *Journal of American Folklore* 108, no. 430 (1995): 509–27, doi.org/10.2307/541658.
11. Gasser, *Why You Like It*.
12. Theodor Adorno, *Aesthetic Theory*, trans. Christian Lenhardt, (Oxford: Routledge, 1984).
13. Neil Gaiman, "The Pornography of Genre, or the Genre of Pornography," *Journal of the Fantastic in the Arts* 24, no. 3 (2013): 401–407, jstor.org/stable /24352964.
14. Ibid.
15. Jacques Derrida, "The Law of Genre," trans. Avital Ronell, *Critical Inquiry* 7, no. 1 (1980): 55–81, jstor.org/stable/1343176.
16. Todorov and Berrong, "The Origin of Genres."
17. Gaiman, "The Pornography of Genre."
18. Bishop and Starkey, *Keywords in Creative Writing*.
19. Rob Dunn, *Every Living Thing: Man's Obsessive Quest to Catalog Life, from Nanobacteria to New Monkeys* (New York: HarperCollins, 2009).
20. Ibid.
21. Safi Bahcall, *Loonshots: How to Nurture the Crazy Ideas That Win Wars, Cure Diseases, and Transform Industries* (New York: St. Martin's Press, 2019).

22. Ibid.
23. Ibid.
24. Ibid.
25. "A Selected History of DARPA Innovation," Defense Advanced Research Projects Agency, accessed June 13, 2023, darpa.mil/Timeline/index.

Contrast

1. Frank Auerbach as quoted in Simon Grant, ed., *In My View: Personal Reflections on Art by Today's Leading Artists* (London: Thames and Hudson, 2012).
2. Peter Schjeldahl, *Hot, Cold, Heavy, Light: 100 Art Writings, 1988–2018* (New York: Abrams, 2019).
3. Julian Bell, *Mirror of the World: A New History of Art* (New York: W. W. Norton and Company, 2010).
4. Ibid.
5. Ibid.
6. Margaret Mary Barela, "Motion in Musical Time and Rhythm," *College Music Symposium* 19, no. 1 (1979): 78–92, jstor.org/stable/40351755.
7. Neil Grant, *History of Theatre* (London: Hamlyn/Octopus Publishing Group, 2002).
8. Edward Tufte, *Beautiful Evidence* (Cheshire, CT: Graphics Press, 2006).
9. Edward Tufte, *The Visual Display of Quantitative Information*. Self-published by author, 1983.
10. Ibid.
11. Tufte, *Beautiful Evidence*.
12. Tufte, *Visual Display*.
13. Tim Riffe, Nikola Sander, and Sebastian Klüsener, "Editorial to the Special Issue on Demographic Data Visualization: Getting the Point Across—Reaching the Potential of Demographic Data Visualization," *Demographic Research* 44 (2021): 865–78, jstor.org/stable/27032938.
14. Tufte, *Beautiful Evidence*.
15. Peter Atkins, *The Laws of Thermodynamics: A Very Short Introduction* (New York: Oxford University Press, 2010).
16. Ibid.

Framing

1. Chris George, "Ansel Adams in His Own Words—Memorable Quotes from the World's Most Famous Landscape Photographer," *Digital Camera World*, October 16, 2023, digitalcameraworld.com/features/ansel-adams-in-his-own-words-memorable-quotes-from-the-worlds-most-famous-landscape-photographer.
2. Susanne K. Langer, *Feeling and Form* (New York: Charles Scribner's Sons, 1953).
3. Camille Paglia, *Glittering Images: A Journey through Art from Egypt to Star Wars* (New York: Pantheon Books, 2012).

4. Erving Goffman, *Frame Analysis* (Boston: Northeastern University Press, 1974).
5. Ibid.
6. Paglia, *Glittering Images*.
7. Ruby Lal, *Empress: The Astonishing Reign of Nur Jahan* (New York: W. W. Norton and Company, 2018).
8. Ibid.
9. Ibid.
10. Ibid.
11. Ibid.
12. Ibid.
13. Ibid.
14. Paglia, *Glittering Images*.
15. Ibid.
16. Douglas Brinkley, *Cronkite* (New York: HarperCollins e-books, 2012).
17. Ibid.
18. Karl Marlantes, "Vietnam: The War That Killed Trust," *New York Times*, January 7, 2017, nytimes.com/2017/01/07/opinion/sunday/vietnam-the-war-that-killed-trust.html.
19. Brinkley, *Cronkite*.
20. Ibid.
21. Mark Bowden, *Hué 1968* (New York: Atlantic Monthly Press, 2017).
22. Brinkley, *Cronkite*.
23. Bowden, *Hué 1968*.
24. Walter Cronkite as quoted in Bowden, *Hué 1968*.
25. Bowden, *Hué 1968*.
26. Ibid.
27. Brinkley, *Cronkite*.
28. Lydia Saad, "Gallup Vault: The Urge to Demonstrate," Gallup.com, April 20, 2016, news.gallup.com/vault/190886/gallup-vault-urge-demonstrate.aspx.

Rhythm

1. Nina Kraus, "The Extraordinary Ways Rhythm Shapes Our Lives," *MIT Press Reader*, April 3, 2023, thereader.mitpress.mit.edu/the-extraordinary-ways-rhythm-shapes-our-lives.
2. Margaret Mary Barela, "Motion in Musical Time and Rhythm," *College Music Symposium* 19, no. 1 (1979): 78–92, jstor.org/stable/40351755.
3. Sara Adhitya, *Musical Cities: Listening to Urban Design and Planning* (London: UCL Press, 2017).
4. Barela, "Motion in Musical Time."
5. Philip Ball, *The Music Instinct: How Music Works and Why We Can't Do without It* (London: Vintage Books, 2010).
6. John Powell, *Why You Love Music: From Mozart to Metallica—The Emotional Power of Beautiful Sounds* (New York: Little, Brown and Company, 2016).

7. Ball, *The Music Instinct.*

8. Powell, *Why You Love Music.*

9. Barela, "Motion in Musical Time."

10. Powell, *Why You Love Music.*

11. Ibid.

12. David Byrne, *How Music Works* (San Francisco: McSweeney's, 2012).

13. Virginia Woolf to Ethel Smyth, letter, April 7, 1933, in *The Letters of Virginia Woolf: Vol. 5: 1932–1935*, ed. Nigel Nicolson and Joanne Trautmann (San Diego, CA: Harvest, 1982), 303.

14. Virginia Woolf, "Street Music," in *The National Review* 205 (March 1905): 144.

15. Adhitya, *Musical Cities.*

16. Barela, "Motion in Musical Time."

17. Russell G. Foster and Leon Kreitzman, *Rhythms of Life: The Biological Clocks That Control the Daily Lives of Every Living Thing* (New Haven, CT: Yale University Press, 2004).

18. Ibid.

19. Ibid.

20. Adhitya, *Musical Cities.*

21. Ibid.

22. Ibid.

23. Octavio Paz, *The Bow and the Lyre: The Poem, the Poetic Revelation, Poetry and History,* trans. Ruth L. C. Simms (Austin: University of Texas Press, 1973).

24. Encyclopedia Britannica Online, s.v. "drill (military)," accessed March 21, 2024, britannica.com/topic/drill-military.

25. "Chapter 1: Introduction" in *Canadian Forces Manual of Drill and Ceremonial,* Government of Canada, issued June 15, 2014, canada.ca/en/services/defence/caf/military-identity-system/drill-manual.html.

26. Ibid.

27. Ibid.

28. Marie Berberea, "There's More to Cadences than Just Left-Right-Left," US Army, July 21, 2011, army.mil/article/62043/theres_more_to_cadences_than_just_left_right_left.

29. "The History of Drill," US Marine Corps Junior Reserve Officer Training Corps publication, Category 5—General Military Subjects, Skill 2—Drill and Ceremonies, accessed March 21, 2024, core-docs.s3.amazonaws.com/documents/asset/uploaded_file/3309/RHS/2462615/The_History_of_Drill.pdf.

30. Ibid.

31. Ibid.

32. Berberea, "There's More to Cadences."

Melody

1. David E. Cartwright, *Schopenhauer: A Biography* (Cambridge: Cambridge University Press, 2010), 479.

2. Nolan Gasser, *Why You Like It: The Science and Culture of Musical Taste* (New York: Flatiron Books, 2019).

3. John Powell, *Why You Love Music: From Mozart to Metallica—The Emotional Power of Beautiful Sounds* (New York: Little, Brown and Company, 2016).

4. Ibid.

5. Ball, *The Music Instinct*.

6. Powell, *Why You Love Music*.

7. Ball, *The Music Instinct*.

8. David Byrne, *How Music Works* (San Francisco: McSweeney's, 2012).

9. Gino Stefani, "Melody: A Popular Perspective," *Popular Music* 6, no. 1 (January 1987): 21–35, jstor.org/stable/853163.

10. Ibid.

11. Byrne, *How Music Works*.

12. Reed Tucker, *Slugfest: Inside the Epic, 50-Year Battle between Marvel and DC* (New York: Da Capo Press, 2017).

13. Ibid.

14. Ibid.

15. Ibid.

16. Ibid.

17. Ibid.

18. Ibid.

19. Ibid.

20. David Christian, "Silk Roads or Steppe Roads? The Silk Roads in World History," *Journal of World History* 11, no. 1 (2000): 1–26, jstor.org/stable /20078816.

21. Ibid.

22. Peter Frankopan, *The Silk Roads: A New History of the World* (New York: Alfred A. Knopf, 2016).

23. Ibid.

24. Ibid.

25. Ibid.

26. Ibid.

27. Ibid.

28. Christian, "Silk Roads or Steppe Roads?"

29. Ibid.

30. Ibid.

Representation

1. "Representation in Art," *American Magazine of Art* 7, no. 12 (1916): 506, jstor .org/stable/20559545.

2. E. H. Gombrich, *The Story of Art*, 16th ed. (London: Phaidon Press, 1995).

3. Ibid.

4. Julian Bell. *Mirror of the World: A New History of Art* (New York: W. W. Norton and Company, 2010).

5. Whitney Davis, "Representation and Depiction in Paleolithic Art," *Representations* 19 (July 1987): 111–47, doi.org/10.2307/2928533.
6. Gombrich, *The Story of Art*.
7. Bell, *Mirror of the World*.
8. Ibid.
9. Ibid.
10. Ibid.
11. Gombrich, *The Story of Art*.
12. Bell, *Mirror of the World*.
13. H. Akin Ünver, "Digital Open Source Intelligence and International Security: A Primer," Centre for Economics and Foreign Policy Studies, Cyber Governance and Digital Democracy 2018/8 (July 2018), jstor.org/stable/resrep21048.
14. Kathy Peiss, *Information Hunters: When Librarians, Soldiers, and Spies Banded Together in World War II Europe* (New York: Oxford University Press, 2020).
15. Ünver, "Digital Open Source Intelligence."
16. Peiss, *Information Hunters*.
17. Ibid.
18. Ünver, "Digital Open Source Intelligence."
19. Marilyn Yalom, *Birth of the Chess Queen* (New York: Perennial, 2004).
20. Ibid.
21. Ibid.
22. Ibid.
23. Ibid.
24. Ibid.
25. Victor Hugo, *Ninety-Three*, trans. Frank Lee Benedict (New York: Harper & Brothers, 1874), 344.
26. Gombrich, *The Story of Art*.
27. Ibid.
28. Gillian Rhodes et al., "Facial Symmetry and the Perception of Beauty," *Psychonomic Bulletin & Review* 5, no. 4 (1998): 659–69, doi.org/10.3758/BF03208842.
29. Eric Jaffe, "Science Explains the Enduring Appeal of Bland, Symmetrical Layouts," *Fast Company*, June 9, 2014, fastcompany.com/3031428/science-explains-the-enduring-appeal-of-boring-layouts.
30. Rolf Rebe, "Reasons for the Preference for Symmetry," *Behavioral and Brain Sciences* 25, no. 3 (2002): 415–16, doi.org/10.1017/S0140525X02350076.
31. Ker Than, "Symmetry in Nature: Fundamental Fact or Human Bias?" *LiveScience*, December 21, 2005, livescience.com/4002-symmetry-nature-fundamental-fact-human-bias.html.
32. Gombrich, *The Story of Art*.
33. Bell, *Mirror of the World*.
34. Peter Schjeldahl, *Hot, Cold, Heavy, Light: 100 Art Writings, 1988–2018* (New York: Abrams, 2019).
35. Barbara Kingsolver, *The Poisonwood Bible* (London: Faber and Faber, 2017).

Plot

1. Elizabeth Bowen, *Collected Impressions* (New York: Alfred A. Knopf, 1950).
2. Marie-Laure Ryan, "Cheap Plot Tricks, Plot Holes, and Narrative Design," *Narrative* 17, no. 1 (2009): 56–75, jstor.org/stable/30219290.
3. Gustav Freytag, *Technique of the Drama: An Exposition of Dramatic Composition and Art*, 3rd ed., trans. Elias J. MacEwan (Chicago: Scott, Foresman and Company, 1900).
4. Ryan, "Cheap Plot Tricks."
5. Ibid.
6. Stephen King, *On Writing: A Memoir of the Craft* (New York: Scribner, 2000).
7. Ulinka Rublack, *The Astronomer and the Witch: Johannes Kepler's Fight for His Mother* (Oxford, UK: Oxford University Press, 2015).
8. Ibid.
9. Ibid.
10. James A. Connor, *Kepler's Witch: An Astronomer's Discovery of Cosmic Order Amid Religious War, Political Intrigue, and the Heresy Trial of His Mother* (San Francisco: HarperSanFrancisco, 2004).
11. Rublack, *The Astronomer and the Witch*.
12. Ibid.
13. Ibid.
14. Ibid.
15. David Zuck, "Nitrous Oxide: Are You Having a Laugh?" *Education in Chemistry*, February 29, 2012, edu.rsc.org/feature/nitrous-oxide-are-you-having-a-laugh/2020202.article.
16. Joanna Bourke, *The Story of Pain: From Prayer to Painkillers* (Oxford, UK: Oxford University Press, 2017).
17. I. O'Sullivan and J. Benger, "Nitrous Oxide in Emergency Medicine," *Emergency Medicine Journal* 20, no. 3 (2003): 214–17, doi.org/10.1136/emj.20.3.214.
18. Bourke, *The Story of Pain*.
19. Ibid.
20. Ibid.
21. Teresa A. Rummans, M. Caroline Burton, and Nancy L. Dawson, "How Good Intentions Contributed to Bad Outcomes: The Opioid Crisis," *Mayo Clinic Proceedings* 93, no. 3 (2018): 344–50, doi.org/10.1016/j.mayocp.2017.12.020.
22. Joseph E. Grey, Stuart Enoch, and Keith G. Harding, "Wound Assessment," *British Medical Journal*, February 2, 2006, doi.org/10.1136/bmj.332.7536.285.

Character

1. Bob Woodward, "Watergate: 25 Years Later," *Washington Post*, June 17, 1997, washingtonpost.com/wp-dyn/content/discussion/2006/10/18/DI2006101801349.html.

2. Marie-Laure Ryan, "Cheap Plot Tricks, Plot Holes, and Narrative Design," *Narrative* 17, no. 1 (2009): 56–75, jstor.org/stable/30219290.

3. "Kurt Vonnegut: 8 Basics of Creative Writing," Tips from the Masters, Gotham Writers, accessed September 9, 2019, writingclasses.com/toolbox/tips-masters/kurt-vonnegut-8-basics-of-creative-writing.

4. "Types of Characters in Fiction," *Lexiconic*, accessed May 26, 2023, learn.lexiconic.net/characters.htm.

5. Thomas A. Wright and Tyler L. Lauer, "What Is Character and Why It Really Does Matter," *Business Faculty Publications* 2 (2013), fordham.bepress.com/gsb_facultypubs/2.

6. Jung Chang, *Big Sister, Little Sister, Red Sister: Three Women at the Heart of Twentieth-Century China* (New York: Alfred A. Knopf, 2019).

7. Yu-long Ling, "Dr. Sun Yat-Sen's Doctrine and Impact on the Modern World," *American Journal of Chinese Studies* 19, no. 1 (2012): 1–11, jstor.org/stable/44288973.

8. Chang, *Big Sister, Little Sister*.

9. Ibid.

10. Ibid.

11. Ibid.

12. Ibid.

13. Wright and Laurer, "What Is Character."

14. Chang, *Big Sister, Little Sister*.

15. Ibid.

16. Key Ray Chong and Fang-fu-Ruan, "The Resurrection of Sun Yat-Sen for China's Modernization," *Journal of Third World Studies* 5, no. 1, Roles of Third World Militaries (Spring 1988): 130–45, jstor.org/stable/45192997.

17. Tanya Lee Stone, *The Good, the Bad, and the Barbie: A Doll's History and Her Impact on Us* (New York: Penguin, 2010).

18. Ibid.

19. Claudia Mitchell and Jacqueline Reid-Walsh, "Theorizing Tween Culture within Girlhood Studies," *Counterpoints* 245 (2005): 1–21, jstor.org/stable/42978689.

20. Germaine Greer as quoted in Ann Treneman, "Time to Stop Hating Barbie," *The Independent* (London), March 8, 1999, independent.co.uk/arts-entertainment/time-to-stop-hating-barbie-1079146.html.

21. Stone, *The Good, the Bad, and the Barbie*.

22. Treneman, "Time to Stop Hating Barbie."

23. Stone, *The Good, the Bad, and the Barbie*.

Setting

1. Carmen Maria Machado, *In the Dream House: A Memoir* (Minneapolis: Graywolf Press, 2019).

2. Lane Roth, "'Vraisemblance' and the Western Setting in Contemporary

Science Fiction Film," *Literature/Film Quarterly* 13, no. 3 (1985): 180–86, jstor.org/stable/43797444.

3. David Byrne, *How Music Works* (San Francisco: McSweeney's, 2012).
4. Ibid.
5. Ibid.
6. Ibid.
7. Ibid.
8. Maria M. Delgado and Paul Heritage, eds., *In Contact with the Gods: Directors Talk Theatre* (Manchester, UK: Manchester University Press, 1996).
9. Bee Wilson, *Consider the Fork: A History of How We Cook and Eat* (New York: Basic Books, 2012).
10. Ibid.
11. Ibid.
12. Ibid.
13. Priscilla Mary Isin, *Bountiful Empire: A History of Ottoman Cuisine* (London: Reaktion Books, 2018).
14. Ibid.
15. Ibid.
16. Ibid.
17. Ibid.
18. Ibid.
19. Tobias Dantzig, *Number: The Language of Science* (New York: Plume, 2005).
20. Amir D. Aczel, *Finding Zero: A Mathematician's Odyssey to Uncover the Origins of Numbers* (New York: St. Martin's Press, 2015).
21. Ibid.
22. Ibid.
23. Ibid.
24. Ibid.
25. Frank Swetz and Shaharir bin Mohamad Zain, "The Elusive Origin of Zero," *Scientific American*, July 28, 2022, scientificamerican.com/article/the-elusive-origin-of-zero1.
26. Cris Freese, "How to Create Subtext in Setting in Your Writing," *Writer's Digest*, May 24, 2016, writersdigest.com/editor-blogs/there-are-no-rules/creating-setting-and-subtext-in-your-fiction.
27. Simon Grant, "A Landscape of Mortality: Paul Nash—Essay," Tate Museum, accessed September 7, 2019, tate.org.uk/art/artists/paul-nash-1690/landscape-mortality.

Performance

1. Marina Abramović, *Walk Through Walls: A Memoir* (New York: Crown Archetype, 2016).
2. Neil Grant, *History of Theatre* (London: Hamlyn/Octopus Publishing Group, 2002).

3. Antonin Artaud, *Selected Writings* (Berkeley: University of California Press, 1988).
4. Grant, *History of Theatre.*
5. Ibid.
6. Ibid.
7. Maria M. Delgado and Paul Heritage, eds., *In Contact with the Gods: Directors Talk Theatre* (Manchester, UK: Manchester University Press, 1996).
8. Ibid.
9. Grant, *History of Theatre.*
10. Ibid.
11. David Byrne, *How Music Works* (San Francisco: McSweeney's, 2012).
12. Ibid.
13. Abramović, *Walk Through Walls.*
14. Delgado and Heritage, eds., *In Contact with the Gods.*
15. George Weigel, *Witness to Hope: The Biography of Pope John Paul II* (New York: HarperCollins, 1999), 279. It is worth noting that, while Andropov's exasperated question seems to be quite serious, the KGB was most likely not strong enough to be able to affect the election of a pope.
16. John Lewis Gaddis, *The Cold War: A New History* (New York: Penguin, 2005).
17. Ibid.
18. Paul Kengor, *A Pope and a President: John Paul II, Ronald Reagan, and the Extraordinary Untold Story of the 20th Century* (Washington, DC: ISI Books, 2017).
19. John Cornwell, *The Pontiff in Winter: Triumph and Conflict in the Reign of John Paul II* (New York: Image, 2007).
20. Kengor, *A Pope and a President.*
21. Pope John Paul II as quoted in Kengor, *A Pope and a President.*
22. Kengor, *A Pope and a President.*
23. Quoted in Kengor, *A Pope and a President.*
24. Cornwell, *The Pontiff in Winter.*
25. Ibid.
26. Gaddis, *The Cold War.*
27. Quentin Reynolds, *I, Willie Sutton* (New York: Farrar, Straus and Giroux, 1953).
28. Ibid.
29. Ibid.
30. Andreas Schroeder, *Thieves!* (Toronto: Annick Press, 2005).
31. Reynolds, *I, Willie Sutton.*
32. Schroeder, *Thieves!.*
33. Reynolds, *I, Willie Sutton*
34. Ibid.

Feed your brain in 5 minutes every week, for free.

The Brain Food newsletter delivers actionable ideas and timeless insights every Sunday.

fs.blog/newsletter

'A masterwork'
Ryan Holiday

'Indispensable'
James Clear

Clear Thinking

The Art and Science of
Making Better Decisions

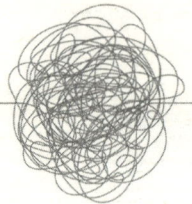 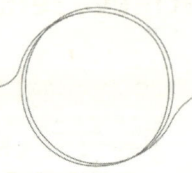

Shane Parrish

The *New York Times* Bestseller

'A must-read' Mark Manson

The Knowledge Project Podcast is one of the most popular podcasts in the world.

Join host Shane Parrish as he uncovers the strategies, mindsets, and hard-earned secrets the very best use to achieve remarkable results.

Listen at

fs.blog/podcast

or search for "the knowledge project" wherever you listen to podcasts.